EVERYDAY THINGS
IN AMERICAN LIFE
1607-1776

EVERYDAY THINGS
IN
AMERICAN LIFE

1607-1776

By

William Chauncy Langdon

CHARLES SCRIBNER'S SONS · NEW YORK
CHARLES SCRIBNER'S SONS · LTD · LONDON

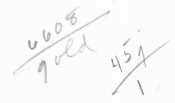

COPYRIGHT, 1937, BY
CHARLES SCRIBNER'S SONS

K–10.58[V]

Printed in the United States of America

Preface

EVERYDAY things take the impress of human character more truly and more permanently than special or extraordinary things. The portrait that shows a man in his everyday working clothes tells more about him than one that shows him dressed up in white shirt and evening clothes. That is the significance of this book.

Again, everyday things have an individual interest, each of its own, every one of them. Every hand-made nail, every tool, every spinning wheel was a distinct and separate article, not merely one of a lot. Extreme standardization, such as we have now, and mass production were in the colonial period far in the future. A rifle was a rifle, but not just a rifle. Daniel Boone's own rifle was somehow different from any other rifle that even he had, and no one could use that particular rifle with the unfailing accuracy that Daniel Boone did. There was a particular fit, made or acquired, between every sharpshooter and his weapon. The everyday and the individual elements enter largely into the make-up of actual historical interest.

One of the delightful things that familiarity with the everyday articles of the colonial period brings to us is the realization that the people of that time were essentially like ourselves, and that we are akin to them. Some of us may have the mistaken idea that because they come early in the story of America they were crude. Not at all. No more than we are crude when we go camping. The conditions in which they lived were simpler; the knowledge they had, of whatever kind, was less extensive. But the nearer we get to the essentials of life the more alike we find the people of then and of now; the more closely akin we see we are; the more we feel justified in the thrill of our national identity with them; and the more confident that as by honesty and ability and reasonableness and co-operation they solved the problem of their times, so we by the exercise of similar qualities may solve ours.

It will be good if this book draws some of its readers into research for themselves along the line of their own families. Much that is of historical interest to be sure has been lost irrevocably. But much that has been lost can still be recovered if keen human attention is given without delay. There is opportunity for all, and especially for those who have the honest prejudice of a member of the family concerned.

Some may question whether what they find, what they may contribute will merit the designation of history. History is not limited to what is of political or of economic importance. The test of what is history is that it enables us to understand the people of other days,—or of our days, for that matter. If it does not do this, it may be or sometime may become historical material, but it is not history, not until it is transformed by the understanding that enables us to understand.

PREFACE

This volume limits itself to the Colonial Period in America, let us say from 1607 to 1776, the period when the Colonies were getting in touch with each other, when they were making it possible to unite. It is expected that this volume will be followed by two other volumes, one covering the hundred years from 1776 to the Centennial at Philadelphia in 1876, the period during which the unity of the country was firmly established; and the other from 1876 to the present, the period during which the federated character of the democracy is being established in all phases and conditions of life. In these periods also we shall find that the everyday things,—the houses, the furniture, the clothes, all the means and instrumentalities,—will unerringly express the character of the times and help interpret to us the mission of the American people.

There are innumerable sources to which I am indebted in the preparation of this book, but I wish specially to take this first opportunity in the book to express grateful appreciation for cordial interest and assistance to certain friends who are authorities in their lines. To *Charles Penrose* of Philadelphia, Vice President for North America of the Newcomen Society of England, and particularly for his permission to reproduce the painting of the "Diligence," built in 1707 by his ancestor, Bartholomew Penrose. To *Stanley M. Arthurs,* the painter of the "Diligence" and of other paintings reproduced as illustrations in this book. To *Charles Rufus Harte* of New Haven, for insight he gave me into the early mining of iron and co-operation in securing illustrations of that work. To *Charles Lyon Chandler* of the Corn Exchange Bank of Philadelphia, for material on the early shipbuilding at Philadelphia. To *Farran Zerbe* of the Chase National Bank, New York, for information and illustrations on the early Massachusetts coinage. To *William Davis Miller* of Kingston, Rhode Island, authority on silverware. To *Julian P. Boyd* of the Historical Society of Pennsylvania; to the *Rev. Dr. Paul de Schweinitz* and *Dr. Albert G. Rau* of the Moravian Historical Society at Bethlehem, and to *Horace M. Mann* of the Bucks County Historical Society at Doylestown, Pennsylvania; to the *Pennsylvania-German Society;* and to *Daniel M. Hopping* of Bronxville, New York, for material from his well-selected architectural library. These and others have made the work on this book richer in interest and truly delightful.

W. C. L.

Contents

CHAPTER   PAGE

I SHELTERS AND FIRST HOUSES   I
Significance of Architecture—Types of Houses—Emphasis of
Various Colonies—Indian and English Wigwams—Begin-
nings at Jamestown at Plymouth and at Salem—Lumber the
First Export—The Salt-Box House—Fastening of Building
Materials—Fire Danger—Stone and Brick Buildings—On the
Delaware.

II THE FIREPLACE CENTER OF THE HOME   18
The Large Fireplace—Open Fire Cooking—Cooking Utensils
—Early Lighting—Increase of "Firerooms"—Tables and
Chests—Official Chairs—The Plymouth Chairs—Beds for Old
and Young—Dress Characteristic—Clothes—Hats.

III IN DUTCH NEW YORK   38
Dutch Settlements Trading Posts—Taken over by England
—As the People Saw It—The Dutch Houses—Signs of Dutch
Descent.

IV PENN'S QUAKER CITY   48
Great Colonial Founders—Prospectus for Penn's Colony—
The Quaker People of Philadelphia—William Penn and His
Houses—The First City Planning—Wide Range of Stand-
ards—Quaker Character and Dress.

V PENNSYLVANIA GERMAN FARMS   63
Whence the Pennsylvania Germans Came—Where They
Settled—Official Caution Regarding Early Immigrants—Log
and Stone Cabins—Fort Zeller—The De Tirck House—
Decorative Home Craft—Tile Roofs and Floors.

ix

CONTENTS

CHAPTER   PAGE

VI   HANDWORK AT EPHRATA   74

Conrad Beissel and His Followers—Community Life and Characteristic Buildings—Literal Symbolism—Dress of the Monastics—Pen Work or Fractur—The Printing Craft—Industries and Industrial Policies—Vocal Music.

VII   AT MORAVIAN BETHLEHEM   87

Normal Rather than Extreme—Count Zinzendorf—The Naming of Bethlehem—Monumental Buildings—The Bell House—The Trombone Choir—Spinet and Organ—Symphony Orchestra—Organizing Farming and Industry—Inns and Taverns—A Town Hotel—Roads and Ferries—Medical and Hospital Service—The Pennsylvania Rifle—In the Revolution —The Bethlehem Water Works.

VIII   SCOTCH-IRISH IN THE MOUNTAINS   110

Racial Character—Route of Migration—The Official Standpoint—Attitude Toward the Indians—Their Leaders—Joseph Doddridge—Taking up Land—Building the Mountain Cabin —Safety in the Fort—The Crossroads at Fort Bedford—General Forbes' Campaign—Dress and Food of the Frontiersmen —Trade and the Packer's Trails.

IX   GEORGIAN MANSIONS   125

Exports of Colonial Commerce—Increasing Wealth—The New Architecture—Architectural Books—Home Architects— Building Materials—From Stoop to Piazza—The Palladian Portico—The Vertical Tendency in Pennsylvania—The Widespread Plan in the South—Detached Buildings—Forms of Roof Structure—Stairways—Wainscoting and Paneling—The Character of Stairs.

X   EIGHTEENTH-CENTURY FURNITURE   147

The Trade in Furniture—Furniture Books—Thomas Chippendale—George and Andrew Hepplewhite—Thomas Sheraton —Modifications of Styles—Chests—Tables—Chairs—The Intimacy of Chairs.

x

CONTENTS

CHAPTER   PAGE

XI IRON MINED AND WROUGHT   158

Introduction of Industry with Iron—The Earliest Furnaces
—Spread of the Industry—The Salisbury Mines—The Blacksmith's Art—The Making of a Nail.

XII PEWTER IN THE COLONIAL HOME   169

Woodenware—Pewter Dishes—Composition of Pewter—
Standards of the Craft and Touches—Sad Ware and Hollow
Ware—The Period of Pewter.

XIII SILVERSMITHS AND SILVERWARE   176

Style in Silverware—Scant Supply of Silver—The Massa-
chusetts Mint—Boston Silversmiths—Commercial Practices—
Oceanic Warfare—Piracy, Privateering and Silver—New York
Silversmiths—Philadelphia Silversmiths—Apprenticeship in
Handwork—Tableware—The Standing Salt—The Depletion
of Colonial Silver.

XIV MEASURES OF VALUE   192

Silver and Hard Money—Barter and Commodity Money—
Wampum—The Pine Tree Coinage—Paper Money—British
Navigation Laws.

XV COLONIAL GLASS   199

Early Glass Works at Nieuw Amsterdam and Boston—The
Wistar Glass Works on the Delaware—Heinrich Wilhelm
Stiegel—Stiegel the Ironmaster—Stiegel Glass—The Tragedy
of Baron Stiegel—The Festival of the Roses.

XVI NEW ENGLAND SHIPS   211

The Fishing Industry—*The Blessing of the Bay*—Co-opera-
tive Shipbuilding—Shipping Records—The Slave Trade—
The Whale Fisheries—War Status of Merchantmen—Salem
Sea Captains—Sir William Phips—Captain William Kidd—
American Privateers—The Derby Family—The Gloucester
Memorial.

xi

CONTENTS

CHAPTER   PAGE

XVII   SHIPBUILDING AT PHILADELPHIA   229

William West the First Shipbuilder—Penn's Marine Policy—
Bartholomew Penrose—The Penrose Yards—The *Diligence*—
Four Generations—Books on Shipbuilding—Commercial
Conditions—Height of Colonial Shipbuilding—Tench Coxe's
Resumé.

XVIII   TRAILS AND ROADS   241

Water Roads and Land Roads—Indian Trails—Roads in
Connecticut—Public and Private Roads—Town Streets and
Country Roads—Madame Knight—Other Travelers' Experi-
ences—Wheeled Vehicles—Roadside Inns—Rev. Peter Powers
—Madame Knight on Taverns—Fraunce's Tavern—The
Raleigh Tavern.

XIX   THE PROVINCIAL POST   255

Communication Essential to Unity—Public Service—Begin-
nings of Postal Regulation—Governor Lovelace's Plan—The
End of the Plan—Boston's First Mail Carrier—Local Postal
Developments—The Postal Monopoly—The Spread of the
System—Political Troubles—Spotswood's Improvements—Ben-
jamin Franklin Postmaster General—Newspapers—Collateral
Interests—Franklin's Dismissal—The Committees of Corre-
spondence.

XX   AGRICULTURE IN THE COLONIES   273

Town and Country—The Early Farming—Maize and Other
Grain Crops—Potatoes and Other Vegetables—Fruit Orchards
—Live Stock and Forage—The Commons—The Opening of
the Meadows—Oxen and Horses as Farm Animals—The
Narragansett Pacer—The Conestoga Horse—Stables and
Barns—Grist Mills and Wind Mills—Dyeing—Fulling Mills—
Agricultural Implements.

xii

CONTENTS

CHAPTER   PAGE

XXI THE COLONIAL TOWN   299

Early American Newspapers—The Freedom of the Press—
The First Twelve—The Town as the Public Center—Wil-
liamsburg in 1759—Philadelphia in 1760—All Country Towns
—Shipping Tobacco—Tobacco as Money—The Financial
Problem—Before Banking—Education—The First Public
Schools—Early School Books—The First Colleges—A Classical
Education—The Beginnings of Science—Domestic Medicine
—Strange Remedies—Quinine and Other Drugs—Specializing
the Medical Profession—Epidemics and Inoculation—The
Hospitable Table—Social Life—Dances and Horse Races—
Singing on the Front Steps—The Living Picture.

Bibliography   335

Index   341

xiii

The greater number of uncredited line

drawings in this work are by E. G. Lutz,

the others are by N. C. Wyeth,

and W. M. Berger

Illustrations

DRAWINGS IN THE TEXT

	PAGE
Little shelters in Pennsylvania served as temporary quarters for people while farms were being laid out	4
A community dwelling of the Iroquois Indians	6
Early brick work	16
"The latch-string is out"	17
Some of the cooking utensils used with an open fireplace	21
Colonial furniture: chairs, chest, and table	29
A New England chest of drawers	31
A flax-wheel	31
A wool-wheel	31
A quilling-wheel	31
A colonial loom	33
A four-post bed with trundle bed	35
A warming pan and foot-stove	37
The *Half Moon*	39
The Stadt Huys	40
Nieuw Amsterdam	41
Indian and Dutch traders bargaining over furs	42
The Beaver Street side of Fort Amsterdam. Pieter Stuyvesant leading the evacuation after the surrender to the English	45
English New York waterfront in 1760	46
William Penn document, 1681	49

ILLUSTRATIONS

PAGE

The Letitia Street house, Pennsylvania 53

The Slate house, Pennsylvania 55

Moravian Seminary buildings, Bethlehem, Pennsylvania 66

Hood and Lintel inscription over second-floor door, John De Turk
house, 1767 70

Hand-made roof tiles 72

Ephrata script alphabet 79

Ephrata pen work 80

Display type from the Kloster font made at Ephrata prior to 1748 83

Seven part Ephrata Chorale 85

The staircase in the great hall—Millbach 88

The first house in Bethlehem, 1741 89

The Bell house, Bethlehem 92

The weather-vane on Bell Tower 93

Count Zinzendorf 94

A Lebanon County decorated dower chest, and German pottery
of the late eighteenth century 98

Apothecary's utensils, 1752 99

The Crown Inn near Bethlehem, Pennsylvania, 1757 100

The Sun Inn, Bethlehem, 1763 101

Order of Safeguard 103

Henry Young's gun factory 105

Early Pennsylvania flint-lock rifle, hunting bag and powder-horn.
Pennsylvania Indian powder-horn. 107

The water works at Bethlehem 108

On horseback with his few belongings on pack-saddles the settler
invaded the western slope of the Alleghenies 115

Study on the frontier by light from the open fireplace 121

ILLUSTRATIONS

PAGE

The one horse shay   126

First floor plan, Westover, Virginia   128

Title page of William and John Halfpenny's *The Modern Build-er's Assistant*   131

Cliveden, Germantown, Pennsylvania   134

John Vassall (Longfellow) house, Cambridge, Massachusetts   135

Graeme Park, Horsham, Pennsylvania   137

The John Hancock House, Boston, Massachusetts   139

The stairway at Westover, Virginia   141

The stairway at Graeme Park, Horsham, Pennsylvania   143

Detail of stairs in the Jeremiah Lee House, Marblehead, Massachusetts   145

Dutch, Queen Anne, Chippendale, Hepplewhite, and Sheraton chairs   150

Early devices for illumination   153

Ruins of the furnace at Roxbury, Connecticut   159

Iron mining at Salisbury, Connecticut   161

Running pig-iron from an early type of furnace   162

Lime rock furnace in 1935   163

Wrought iron gates at Westover, Virginia   165

Wrought iron gate at Westover, Virginia   167

Wooden mugs and trenchers   170

Early American pewter   173

Typical examples of Stiegel glass   204

Glass-blowing   208

The *Mayflower*   214

Whaling   218

Pirates cruised up and down the Atlantic coast both for trade and plunder   222

ILLUSTRATIONS

PAGE

William Penn's plan for the city of Philadelphia 231

River plantation 244

A post rider 257

An early Pennsylvania plow 274

One of the first forms of a plow with mould-board 274

An old farm-yard, Long Island 276

An old farm-house on Newport Island 278

Pitching off a load of hay 281

One of several types of old hay-wagon 282

Threshing grain on the barn floor with flails 285

Every farm had its dairy 287

Tenants of the old barn on a small farm 289

The Conestoga wagon of early Pennsylvania days 293

The New-York Weekly Journal 303

College of William and Mary, and the Botetourt Statue, Williamsburg, Virginia 307

The Raleigh Tavern 308

A Virginia tobacco wharf 311

Tobacco ships in the James River 312

The horn-book 316

The New England primer 317

The barber-surgeon 327

PHOTOGRAPHS

following 58

The arrival of the first woman in Jamestown, Virginia

A section of Captain John Smith's map of New England

Plymouth in 1622

xviii

ILLUSTRATIONS

English Wigwams

1630 Colonial Village erected in Salem, Massachusetts in 1930

The Boardman house, Saugus, Massachusetts, 1651

The birthplaces of John and John Quincy Adams

The John Howard Payne Memorial

Kitchen in Washington's Headquarters, at Morristown, New Jersey

Costumes of the early settlers

An attempt to enforce morality in the Puritan settlement

Wynnestay, Lower Merion

Colonial school days in Pennsylvania

Lower Merion Friends' Meeting House

A Quaker meeting in Philadelphia

St. David's Episcopal Church, Radnor, Pennsylvania

Barn on the Kauffman Farm, Berks County, Pennsylvania

Log house at Lititz, Pennsylvania

The spring-room door, Fort Zeller

Log House, Berks County, Pennsylvania

Saal and Sister's home, Ephrata Cloisters, Ephrata, Pennsylvania

The Ephrata printing press

The house and mill of the miller at Millbach, Pennsylvania

Old spinet of 1754

Indented bill used in lieu of money in the province of Pennsylvania

A settler listens to the warning of a friendly Indian

Colonial forces recruited from the people of the mountain regions

following 186

Westover, Virginia

ILLUSTRATIONS

Van Cortlandt Manor House, New York

Mt. Vernon

The Roger Morris or Jumel Mansion, New York

The State House, Philadelphia, now Independence Hall

Old Philadelphia Court House

The College of Philadelphia

The Zabriskie or von Steuben house, Hackensack, New Jersey

Ackerman (Brinckerhoff) house, 1704

Washington's Headquarters at Valley Forge

Two New England rooms prior to 1750

Interior at Almodington, Somerset County, Maryland

A yellow brocade costume imported from France about 1775

Colonial silver

Coins of the Massachusetts mint and Spanish milled dollar

New England early took the lead in shipbuilding

"A view of a part of the town of Boston"

Philadelphia from the Great tree at Kensington under which
 Penn made his treaty with the Indians

Arch Street Ferry, Philadelphia

The highlands on the Hudson River

Road near Peekskill running down to a river landing on the
 Hudson

Benjamin Franklin in his printing establishment

In the Seventeen Seventies post riders went in all directions

EVERYDAY THINGS
IN AMERICAN LIFE
1607-1776

CHAPTER I

Shelters and First Houses

THE history of American life is the unfolding story of how we Americans have supplied our needs and of how we have learned to do it better and better until the whole system of methods and habits and customs may reasonably be called American civilization.

The way men build houses for their families, and public buildings for their association with each other as communities, is the most lasting of the ways they supply their needs, and the central one. This grows into the art of architecture and into the building trades. Architecture is distinctively the art of human association. People will work to obtain food for themselves individually, and delight in it, each one alone by himself. People will work to make or to get clothes for themselves individually, and delight in wearing them, each one by himself alone—men no less than women. But what man ever built a house for himself to live in alone? It is not until a man thinks of associating himself with a woman as a partner for life that normally he thinks of building or otherwise providing himself with a house. And then it is *for them;* and they call it a home.

Of course the instinct of association enters somewhat into

the supplying of food and of clothes. A dinner party is a great deal more fun than a lone bite, no matter how choice the isolated viand. There is more enjoyment in wearing fine clothes when others, especially of the opposite sex, will see and admire than when only a mirror will reflect comment, and that your own. But it is into the supplying of shelter for the home, whether the more intimate family home or the more public community home, that the instinct of association enters fully and inseparably, to dominate. Due to this fact, so many occupations, interests, and even recreations stem from the home and from the housing structures men build to shelter it.

There is also the association of children and parents as well as of husbands and wives, that is of one generation with another. In buildings this finds expression in durability. The better built a shelter or a house the longer it will last. As ordinary people have not the means to build or to hire as well-built houses as wealthier people, their houses are not so durable, do not last so long, and as the years pass and the generations, there is a steady disappearance of their houses, whereas the finer houses remain to tell a little longer of the people and of their homes and their ways at the time they were built. Furthermore, as a man prospers or the son does better than his father, he is likely to tear down an earlier house and build a finer in its place.

It is not surprising therefore that of the first shelters and houses built for homes in America, whether in Virginia or in Massachusetts, none remains. We do not know what they looked like. A few lines of description or a passing reference is all we have. The earliest house in the English Colonies still standing of which we know the date from authentic documents was built in 1651, twenty years after the settlement of the Massachusetts Bay Colony and thirty years after the Pilgrims landed at Plymouth. It is the so-called Scotch or Boardman House at Saugus, Massachusetts, built to receive Scotch prisoners captured by Cromwell the previous year in the Battle of Dunbar. They worked in the iron works there.

In various parts of the country, however, distinct types of house developed, types suited to the climate and to the occupation and social life of the people in that region. Of these types there are buildings still remaining. While it is true that of all the buildings of the pre-Revolutionary period most are of elaborate character, are the mansions of men of wealth, nonetheless from the typical houses referred to we can form a fairly definite idea of the appearance of the homes of the ordinary people, the main backbone of America in the days before independence.

In this book three sections will be emphasized out of the long stretch of the British Colonies. In the order of their settlement these are the regions centering in 1. Virginia, 2. Massachusetts, and 3. Pennsylvania. For the present purpose a more convenient order will be to go from the region of the simpler type of buildings to the more elaborate, 1. Massachusetts, 2. Pennsylvania, and 3. Virginia. Be it remembered however that there were differences and particular characteristics all through—between Virginia and South Carolina or Maryland; between Pennsylvania and Delaware; between Massachusetts and Connecticut; while New York will be found to assert a very distinctive individuality not only in its earlier Dutch period but later when its

Little shelters in Pennsylvania half sunk in the hillsides served as temporary quarters for people while farms were being laid out

commercial supremacy began to be prominent. So will similarity of regional type gradually melt away until we reach the detail differences characterizing neighboring towns, the differences between houses built by father and son, or alterations in the same house—which differences, it should not be forgotten, constitute the ever-increasing fascination of the study. A rich field awaits every one who wants to investigate for himself, not only in these selected regions but all through the entire extent of the Colonies from Maine to Georgia.

It is easy to think of the first settlers of America as making a fresh start in everything from the beginning. This they did not do. They were good, virile Englishmen of sound common sense, who did not propose to incur more hardship than was necessary, though they were ready to rough it and to rely on their personal resources as much and as long as was really necessary. They knew how to put up a tent or a shack and did so at once, both at Jamestown in 1607 and at Plymouth in 1620, and at Salem in 1628. These shacks were just like the crudest kind of shelter with which they were familiar at home in England. They consisted of a sort of little cellar dug into the side of a hill, over which was put up a frame of saplings and branches, covered with wattles and thatch or daubed with mud. They were not architectural; they were not durable. They supplied their need, which was for a temporary shelter, quick and easy to erect.

These first shelters were somewhat like the shelters of the Indians. The Indian name of wigwam was soon transferred to them and they were called English wigwams,—but they were similar not because the Englishmen copied from the native Americans but because both Indians and Englishmen alike were availing themselves of the simplest way of building with what material was at hand. The account of these beginnings at Jamestown and Plymouth is interesting.

In the first shiploads of settlers, 105 in all, that Captain

Newport brought to Virginia, arriving on the 22d of May, 1607, there were 4 carpenters, 1 mason, 1 blacksmith, and 1 sailer (or sail-maker), so that under strong, able leadership, it was quite practicable to direct the many "gentlemen" in fairly efficient work, even if their rank did not then any more than now necessarily imply ability or inclination

A community dwelling of the Iroquois Indians called a long-house.
It was covered with bark

for manual labor. Captain John Smith said of the very start:

Now falleth every man to work, the council contrive the fort, the rest cut down trees to make place to pitch their tents, some provide clapboard to relade the ships, some make gardens, some nets, &c.

Such crude shelters, whether tents put up under direction of the "sailer," or English wigwams, were of course intended to last only long enough for them to build one or more real though still very simple houses to accommodate them all while they built more permanent structures. Thomas Studley, one of the settlers, wrote of a little later time:

The new President (Ratcliffe) and Martin . . . committed the managing of all things abroad to captaine Smith, who by his owne example, good woords and faire promises set some to mow, others to bind thatch, some to build houses and others to thatch them, himselfe always bearing the greatest taske for his own share, so that in short time he provided most of them lodgings, neglecting any for himselfe.

Captain John Smith took part in this instruction very effectively, as is delightfully told by one of the soldiers, Anas Todkill:

Thirty of us ("gentlemen") President Smith conducted 5 myles from the fort, to learn to . . . cut down trees and make clapboard. . . . Strange were these pleasures to their conditions; yet lodging, eating and drinking, working or playing, they were but doing as the President did himselfe. All these things were carried on so pleasantly as within a week they became masters; making it their delight to heare the trees thunder as they fell; but the axes so oft blistered their tender fingers that many times every third blow had a loud othe to drown the eccho; for remedie of which sinne, the President devised how to have every man's othes numbered, and at night for every othe to have a canne of water powred downe his sleeve, with which every offender was so washed (himselfe and all) that a man should scarce hear an othe in a weeke. [This in cold weather!]

At Plymouth in 1620 a similar procedure was followed—first a temporary shelter or camp, then a common house, and then better houses for families. As told by one of the Pilgrims,

> After our landing and viewing of the places, so well as we could, we came to a conclusion, by most voices, to set on the main land, on the first place, on an high ground. . . . So there we made our randevous, and a place for some of our people, about twenty, resolving in the morning to come ashore and to build houses.

A storm however prevented their going to work the next morning or for several days. It was impossible even for those who were left at the "randevous" on shore to go aboard the *Mayflower*. They worked whenever the weather permitted, about three days out of every week, cutting and preparing lumber.

> Tuesday, the 9 January, (January 19, N.S. 1621) was a reasonable fair day, and we went to labor that day in the building of our town, in two rows of houses for more safety. We divided by lot the plot of ground wheron to build our town. After the proportion formerly allotted, we agreed that every man should build his own house, thinking by that course men would make more haste than working in common. The common house, in which for the first we made our rendevous, being nearly finished, wanted only covering, it being about 20 foot square. Some should make mortar, and some gather thatch, so that in four days half of it was thatched.

A good idea of the lay-out of the fort and the first street of Plymouth may be gained from the miniature reconstruc-

8

tion made there in 1888. It is, however, incorrect in representing the houses as having been built as log cabins, with the logs laid horizontally on each other. This kind of construction was probably not introduced into America until the Swedes and Finns came and settled on the Delaware River in 1638. The English adopted it later for forts and prisons, and then frontiersmen found it the best construction for them.

A vivid idea, and probably a correct one, of these first shelters, both the English wigwams and the earliest houses, may be obtained from the 1630 Colonial Village erected at Salem, Massachusetts, in 1930. Captain John Smith refers specifically to tents at Jamestown. Tents were natural first shelters there, as the weather was much warmer in Virginia in May than in New England in December, 500 miles farther north.

It will be noticed that in the very first work done at Jamestown, "some provided clapboard to relade the ships." Further, on the 15th of June, "we wrought upon Clapborde for England." This may seem like prompt exporting of lumber. It was. These first voyages or expeditions to Virginia were commercial ventures. This was one of the commodities with which the London Company hoped to load the ships on the return voyage and make a profit. Lumber had been in demand in England increasingly for fifty or sixty years, as wood had been the usual building material for houses, until the drain of the oak for the Royal Navy had made it scarce and until the Great Fire in 1666 had brought other materials, stone and brick, into greater favor. In the American Colonies the tall pine was reserved for the Royal Navy until nearly the time of the Revolution. For the return cargoes the eagerly preferred gold and silver and pearls did not prove to be immediately abundant. But the valuable lumber did, exceptionally fine lumber. So the planters or settlers planned forthwith to return the ships to the London Company with cargoes of lumber and of course loaded it on board dressed as clapboard rather than in log, which would waste so much space in the hold.

These first houses were of boards driven vertically into the ground or fastened upright like the palings of a fence or a palisade. Indeed, the walls of wooden houses and back-yard fences—and so garden fences in general—undoubtedly had a common origin. The roof, sloping front and back, was of thatch; and the chimney was of branches woven together and heavily plastered with mud or clay. Where heat was an important consideration, as in New England with its long winters, the chimney was put up in the center and the house built around it. The fireplace at the base of the chimney afforded a special place to cook in and to keep warm in.

When one or two rooms were added, the development toward a second, more durable type of house distinctly advanced. The extra rooms were used to sleep in, and the fireplace room became or continued to be the common room, where all gathered during the day—the kitchen-living room. This naturally was always larger than the other rooms. When a second story was added, a steep flight of stairs, often almost as steep as a step-ladder, provided access out of a little entry between the chimney and an outer door. When the family grew and still more room was wanted, the back roof was extended to cover a sort of lean-to addition to the common room. This was often called a leanter. And so the salt-box house came into being!

With the lean-to extension or without it, such was the type of house that developed in New England. There may be earlier houses than the Boardman House still extant in New England, but their dates cannot be proven; and there are no doubt many salt-box houses in New England equally typical which are considered as of subordinate importance only on account of later date. They will be found, however, of equal interest, especially if connected with the reader's own family. *The Salt-Box House* by Jane deForest Shelton is the biography of an actual house of that kind, built by Daniel Shelton near Stratford, Connecticut, in 1758. It gives a vivid account of the daily life there through five generations in the two hundred years of its existence and makes one realize how human a house can be!

There is more than humor in the saying that New England is a state of mind. There is New England, wherever New Englanders go. They crossed over to Long Island and settled their way a long ways down from Montauk toward Brooklyn, making drama and trouble wherever they came in contact with the Dutch. An authentic example of a New England salt-box house on Long Island, and one with which every one ought to be familiar, is the old Robert Dayton

House at East Hampton, built about 1650. This is the house in which long afterward John Howard Payne was born on June 9, 1791; and this is the house that inspired his immortal song, "Home, Sweet Home." At this time the house was occupied by Aaron Isaacs, whose daughter, Sarah, married the schoolmaster, William Payne, and bore him nine children, of whom John Howard was the sixth. The structure of the house is still the same as when first built. The frame is of heavy oak fastened with oak pegs. The corner posts slope slightly inward to strengthen the house against the winter ocean winds.

An essential element in building is the means of fastening the parts together, whether walls and roof, or beams and brick and stone. There have been two lines of development in this within the period of our study—one of wood and for wood, the other of stone and for stone. In the first line of development, for the wigwams, it consisted of lengths of vine—woodbine or grapevine—tying the branches into place in making the frame, and tying the thatch onto the roof. When the frame a little later was made of beams, the thatch on the roof was still fastened in place by tying with vines, but the beams were fastened to each other by notching the ends and dovetailing them. Then the fastening of the beams was made still tighter and more secure by adding wooden pegs. These lasted until what we might call the "iron age" arrived and hand-wrought nails were used, in some places by 1650.

The second line of fastening development started about

as far back as the first. In the day of wooden shelters, as has been noted, chimneys were made immune to fire by daubing mud or clay heavily on the interwoven oak or hardwood branches of which the chimney frames were made. The purpose was to keep the sparks as they went up the flue from setting the chimney and so the whole house on fire. But this was not always successful. The mud dried and fell out, leaving the branches exposed to the heat, with the natural consequences. Fire will spread; and the wind, especially in winter, will carry burning embers. The matter soon got into the strict colonial legislation. Thomas Dudley, Deputy Governor of the Massachusetts Bay Colony, in a letter to England wrote in March, 1631,

Wee have ordered that noe man shall build his chimney with wood nor cover his house with thatch, which was readily assented to, for that divers houses have been burned since our arrival (the fire always beginning in the wooden chimneys) and some English wigwams which have taken fire in the roofes with thatch or boughs.

Every one likes to go to a fire! Governor Bradford has preserved for us the details of a fire in 1623.

This fire was occasioned by some of ye sea-men that were roystering in a house wher it first begane, makeing a great fire in very could weather, which broke out of ye chimney into ye thatch, and burnte downe 3. or 4. houses, and consumed all ye goods & provissions in ym. The house in which it begane was right against their storehouse, which they had much adoe to save, in which were their comone store & all their provissions; ye which if it had been lost, ye plantation had been overthrowne. But through Gods mercie it was saved by ye great dilligence of ye people, & care of ye Govr & some aboute him. Some would have had ye goods throwne out; but if they had, ther would much have been stolne by the rude company yt belonged to these 2. ships, which were allmost all ashore. But a trusty company was plased within, as well as those that with wet-cloaths & other means kept of [off] ye fire without, that if necessitie required they might have them out with all speed. . . . And shortly after, when the vemencie of ye fire was over, smoke was seen to arise wuthin a shed yt was joynd to ye end of ye storehouse, which was watled up with bowes, in ye withered leaves whereof ye fire was kindled.

The settlers at Jamestown seem to have been similarly exposed to fire danger, when ships were in port, at that. But on the following serious occasion at least it was reported much more briefly, almost casually.

Within five or sixe dayes after the arrivall of the Ship, (14 or 15 January, 1608) by a mischance our Fort was burned and the most part of our apparell, lodging and private provision.

So came the first Jamestown to an end!

Under the leadership of men like Captain John Smith, Sir Thomas Dale, and Sir Thomas Gates in Virginia, Governor William Bradford in Plymouth, and Governor John Winthrop in Massachusetts Bay, progress in housing went steadily forward. In 1615 Ralph Hamor, Secretary of State, wrote of Jamestown:

The Towne itself by the care and Providence of Sir Thomas Gates is reduced into a hansome forme, and hath in it two fair

14

rowes of houses all of Framed timber (two stories, and an upper garret, or corne loft, high);

and of the City of Henricus, the successor of Jamestown for a while:

There is in this town three streets of well framed houses.

The complete transition in New England by 1654 is recorded by Edward Johnson in his *Wonder Working Providence* with a grateful reverence not inconsistent with the idea that fire is an Act of God.

The Lord hath been pleased to turn all the wigwams, huts and hovels the English dwelt in at their first coming into orderly, fair and well-built houses.

Fire hastened the use of stone for building, where it could be obtained, and the introduction of mortar as a fastening. The settlers got lime to make their mortar either from limestone beds, as in Maine, in Rhode Island, where Roger Williams made it a trade commodity, and on the Schuylkill River near Philadelphia, where it was abundant, or from beds of oyster shells by the shore. The quality of this oyster-shell lime varied; sometimes it was excellent. When the lime was good, there was little delay in using it, wherever stone was available, as near Philadelphia So too with brick. Good clay for making brick was fairly abundant in the American colonies. The Reverend Francis Higginson of Salem wrote home to London in 1630:

15

It is thought here is good Clay to make Bricke and Tyles and Erthen-Pots as needs to be. At this instant we are setting a Bricke-Kill on worke to make Brickes and Tyles for the building of our Houses.

For a time it was thought that at first brick were brought from England and Holland, but only a few brick were ever brought across the ocean, to the New Netherland. The set-

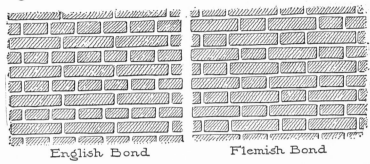

English Bond   Flemish Bond

Early brick work, English bond, had alternating courses, one with headers and the other with stretchers exposed. Flemish bond, courses alike with headers and stretchers alternating

tlers brought with them the mason's art and there was no need to import brick. The expressions in early records, "English brick" and "Dutch brick" meant the way of laying the brick, not the location of the kilns where they were made. English bond and Flemish bond (binding) are terms still used for the pattern in laying brick.

William Penn's great Experiment was not put to the test until 1682, sixty and seventy years after Plymouth and Jamestown. The other colonies had progressed quite a ways before the Quakers arrived at Philadelphia. When we turn to Pennsylvania, we come to a colony that had three special advantages: abundance of the best of building material— brick clay, fine ledge stone, and lime for mortar: prosperous commercial facilities well established; and an equally well-established policy of peace with all, both Indians and Europeans. What we might call the prehistoric conditions of home-making in Virginia and New England existed in Pennsylvania for only a negligible time. Accordingly it is not necessary to turn to the beginnings of Pennsylvania in the matter of housing before we have considered the daily life in the earlier years of the earlier colonies, and have also noticed the special circumstances in the case of New York.

"The Latch-string Is Out"

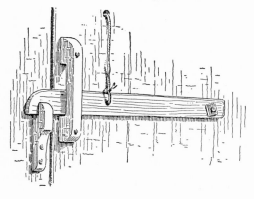

CHAPTER II

The Fireplace Center of the Home

THE daily life in the old houses, those which remain being mostly in New England, centered in the fireplace, the fireplace in the common room, more lately called the kitchen. The common room was the big room and needed a big fire to keep it warm. When fireplaces were made in the other rooms, which were smaller, the fireplaces were made smaller too. When John Adams extended his house by adding a lean-to with a larger kitchen, he also made a larger fireplace as a matter of course, and incidentally built a separate chimney for it.

But these large kitchen fireplaces were not of New England invention. They were of good English descent from Plantagenet times. Indeed, until the fifteenth or sixteenth century the fires were made on the floor in the middle of the great hall, the smoke escaping through an opening in the roof. Then the fire was made against an outer wall, and by the time of Queen Elizabeth a regular fireplace was built with a hood to keep the smoke from going out into the hall, and a flue to carry it out through the wall or a chimney to carry it up above the level of the roof. But there was no occasion for making the fireplace any smaller.

So when the settlers in America planned their dwellings they reverted to the warm memories of their English homes and very naturally and necessarily built large fireplaces. All the household gathered in this room where the fire was. The food was cooked there and it was eaten there. It was in fact the common living room and it had to be a large room. It was much later and in city houses that the cooking appropriated a whole separate room to its own exclusive use. In houses of this period what we call the kitchen fireplace was usually eight and frequently ten feet across.

Any one who in the summer cooks at an outdoor fireplace knows how the early American colonists prepared their food. They cooked at an open fire indoors. No sympathy need be felt for the early settler of New England or of any of the colonies because of any unappetizing flavor of the meat. A steak or a split chicken broiled over a live bed of coals! An egg or a potato baked in hot wood ashes! We also on our twentieth-century kitchen ranges sometimes broil a chicken or a sirloin steak quite successfully, but it is really something different. "Fresh-killed" and "well-hung" are expressions that have distinct meanings, just as corn "fresh" in the city market is one thing and corn fresh picked in the field twenty minutes before dinner is quite another. If this important distinction be recognized, it is possible to go on and consider the early colonial cooking of ducks and venison and wild turkey respectfully and intelligently —with the mouth watering. Their cooking was worth eating! No wonder they ate enormously!

In the seventeenth century there were three kinds of cooking—boiling, roasting, and baking. Boiling is cooking the meat or whatever food it be in hot water. For this the early colonists had first a lug-pole, a wooden bar across the fireplace, and later an iron crane fastened into the chimney on one side of the fireplace. On this crane pots and kettles were hung by pot-hooks or trammels, as they were also called. The housewife could swing the crane out into the room to hang the pots and kettles on it and swing it back over the fire, and out again to take the food off when it was cooked. Lids on the pots and kettles economized the heat and made the water boil harder. In these two and three hundred years boiling has changed the least of the ways of cooking.

Roasting has changed most. There is little roasting done nowadays except under the name of broiling. Roasting is cooking before the open fire. For this the early housewife had a spit. This was a sharp iron rod which she thrust through the meat and supported in front of the fire on two forked uprights. By a handle on one end of the spit some one, usually a small boy, turned the meat continuously so that it was cooked evenly on both sides. A pan underneath caught the juice of the meat, the drippings, as it ran out, for the gravy.

Baking was cooking with dry heat in a closed receptacle, as distinct from roasting, which is cooking with dry but open heat, and boiling, cooking with wet heat. Steaming, a refinement of boiling, did not come until later. No utensils adapted for that kind of cooking have come down from that period.

The earliest utensil for baking was a heavy covered pan

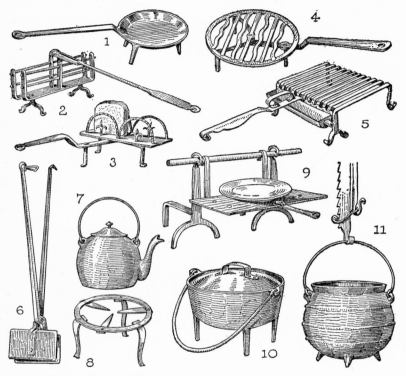

Some of the cooking utensils used with an open fireplace

1. Skillet. 2 and 3. Bread toasters. 4. Rotary broiler. 5. Gravy-drip broiler. 6. Waffle-iron. 7. Tea kettle. 8. Trivet. 9. Plate or food warmer, hangs from bar of the andirons. 10. Bake kettle. 11. Cooking pot

with legs, called a bake-kettle, which sat right down on the red embers, and on which more red embers were also piled. There were a number of different shapes and sizes of these.

Baking also came directly from roasting. One of the difficulties about roasting was that the meat was cooled off on the side toward the room almost as fast as it was cooked on the side toward the fire. This was what made the turning of the spit necessary. To meet this the roasting kitchen was devised. It combined spit and dripping pan and added protection from the cold drafts of the outer room. It was like an open shed of metal placed with the open side directly in front of the fire while the metal back reflected much heat onto the meat. A lid on hinges in the top made it easy to baste the meat while it was cooking. These roasting kitchens considerably shortened the labor of the turn-spit and improved the flavor of the roast!

As the chimneys and fireplaces came to be built of brick and stone, and even before thatch had been done away with for the roof, the brick oven came into its own. It was a good-sized hole in the massive chimney itself with a little flue of its own connecting with the main flue from the fireplace. The opening into the room was closed by an iron door. About once a week a hot fire of special dry wood, and therefore called oven wood, was built in the oven and kept going until all the bricks were hot. The wood and ashes were then swept out, the flue closed and the food to be baked put in—baked beans, brown bread, pies, as much as the oven would hold, pushed in by the long-handled shovel they called a peel. The iron door was closed and the oven left to do its wondrous work, until experienced instinct said it was time to get the peel again and draw the baking forth within reach of the appreciative consumers. So good was the cooking of the brick oven that before long meat also was put into the oven instead of onto the spit in the roasting kitchen, and to this day, after the remarkable development of the up-to-date kitchen range, roast beef and all roast meat are really baked. A slice of steak, laid over the end of a forked stick and broiled over a summer or autumn campfire, and then eaten without ceremony and without a fork on a slice of bread, is all that you and I, hungry reader, know of the roast meat of the early settler, with which he grew strong in heart and mind and body, able to meet trouble and to like it!

Meantime lighting was progressing as a practical art, a development of increasing radiance. At first the camp fire or the hearth fire in the common room supplied the only light after sundown. This encouraged the wholesome habit urged on the young in the rhyme:

Early to bed and early to rise
Makes a man healthy, wealthy, and wise!

But rush lights, consisting of the pith of certain rushes soaked in household grease and supported by an iron holder, soon undertook to specialize in the lighting function of the hearth fire. Then wicks of flax and cotton thread dipped and re-dipped in melted sheep tallow and cooled produced the candle and advanced the art of light and extended the hours of day. Beeswax and spermaceti, the white crystalline wax from the head of the right whale improved the

23

candles and supplied the demand until oil brought lanterns and lamps into their own.

As the common room increased in size, the chimney increased too. It pushed out farther into the room. The hearth was raised a little from the floor; the hood for the smoke asserted itself; jambs were built out on either side of the fireplace. All this might be assigned to kitchen architecture, but with the appearance of the settle kitchen arrangements broke away from the building and called for attention in and for themselves. Furniture became quite as distinct a development as utensils. Curiously, the roasting kitchen and the kitchen settle were cousins. Both originated in the desire to cut off the cold draft. The bench and the stool were at the first the only seats, affording the minimum essential for that purpose. Benjamin Franklin told how his great-grandfather at his home in the old country kept the Bible strapped on the under side of his stool and held it on his knees upside down when reading it; but on the slightest alarm of intrusion by the authorities he would instantly turn it over and sit on it. Such stools the settlers were accustomed to in England and may have brought with them; they certainly made them for themselves after they arrived. Of course the settlers were familiar in England with chairs and sedia in all their elaborate comfort and beauty, from the plain forms of the farmhouse and cottage to the carved and upholstered elegance of palace and cathedral. These indeed within a century they freely adopted and adapted. But the first native advance was planned to keep the draft off the backs of the settler and his wife. High plain board wings were put at either end of the long bench and a high plain board back behind it. Convenience was furthered by a clever improvement. The large broad back was pivoted on to the arms where they joined the back-posts. It could then be tipped forward and the settle became on occasion a good broad table, often called quite simply and naturally a chair-table.

The chair-table was a very practical piece of furniture for the same reason that the folding bed of the present small city apartment is practical. It saved space. The common room was indeed the warm room and the room where almost all the indoor work was done. There everything was apt to be wanted and there everything was kept. The common room was soon crowded. The family increased steadily. The common room became more and more crowded. This led inevitably to the extension of the roof for a lean-to and the addition thereby of an extra room. Usually, as has been noticed in the Adams houses at Quincy, the extra room became a new common room and kitchen, larger than the old, with a larger fireplace and a second separate chimney. The old kitchen, which still could be warm and comfortable with its own fire, became a "sitting room" and was so called. Smaller groups gathered there; it became more specially a social room. There were now two warm rooms in the house. It was not a very novel idea to build a fireplace in still another, a third, room. Originally there was a bed in the common room, usually occupied by the master and mistress of

25

the house. Before long this was moved to one of the other "firerooms." The specialization of rooms had begun. The original compact little house had started to grow into something else, more elaborate by far, but still retaining its simplicity and practical quality and therefore its dignity and beauty.

In the old common room and in turn in the lean-to there were, besides the settle, a regular table, chairs and stools, and the bed in the corner, a dresser with its array of pewter, a cupboard with a supply of wooden plates and trenchers, a water pail, a wash bench, a chest for the corn meal, a barrel for the salt beef and salt pork, a row of iron or copper pots and kettles and pans on the fireplace with a flint-lock rifle or two in their midst, convenient for either protection or hunting, a spinning wheel for flax or wool, a reel, and often a loom for weaving the household linen and the homespun for the family's garments. And then always—the people, the family and the neighbors. Yes, indeed, it was crowded!

The table may seem neglected. There were not many of them, and those were small. There was comparatively little use for a table in the old common room except during meals, and even then there were "two tables." The housewife, and the women generally, did not care to serve the men and to eat both at the same time. It was not convenient. So the space of even a fair-sized table could be much more advantageously used. The settle had led the way in the direction of real convenience and what was practical. Accordingly the idea of putting part of the board top of the table on hinges so that it could be turned up and pushed back against the wall, out of the way, gained in favor, and the gate-leg table, with its successive varieties, joined the chair-table in customary use. In its simple, what we would call its regular, form, it was called a standing-table, because it was kept standing. At best tables were purely practical affairs, like the boards and trestles that preceded them. They were not carved or otherwise decorated for some time. Nor were they brought over from England in the days of small ships.

It was quite otherwise with chests. Chests were both practical and centers of sentiment, and in addition were very inviting for artistic ingenuity. As the growing young English or American woman made and collected the sheets and other linen for her future home, it was in a chest, her hope chest, that she kept them. On the day when she married and her husband carried her off to the new home, the chest of linen went with them. All their married life the linen was kept in the chest. It was a permanently useful article of furniture—the chest. And if, as had been the case with many of our settlers, the family later moved again, across the ocean, the chest was a specially useful thing. It was their trunk. They lavished pride and affection on their chests and decorated them abundantly. Many, probably most, of the chests that were brought across the Atlantic were carved, with a shallow but often very elaborate design, all over the surface. Later the carving was deeper, until the decoration included a turned treatment, lathe-work, of some of the parts of the chest.

The early settlers also made chests for themselves. They had joiners or cabinetmakers as they called them rather than carpenters, who did any work with wood for them that required skill in the mortise and tenon construction from building a house to making a chest or a stool. John Alden and Kenelm Winslow were the "joyners" of Plymouth. They made chests and chairs and other furniture no doubt for the Pilgrims. There was not in those days plenty of cheap wood to knock together into crates for transporting their goods when they travelled. Indeed the law required for the safeguarding of life that on every voyage there should be a cooper to take care of the casks in which the meat and drink were carried. On the *Mayflower* John Alden was taken in this capacity. He had the privilege of staying in America or returning to England, as he wished. When the time came, on this question at least he spoke for himself and decided to remain. He was New England's first cabinetmaker, and probably did much of the earlier fine work for the Colony, not only in construction but in carving as well. We cannot know, however; there is no piece signed with his name or initials.

The chest as a form progressed. The housewife frequently wanted to get out some sheets or blanket at the bottom of the chest; and she inevitably wanted more room in her chest. Before long a drawer was put into the chest, at the bottom, and the chest was made higher; then two drawers, and three. And so finally with the lid of the chest fastened down permanently at the top, there had developed a chest of

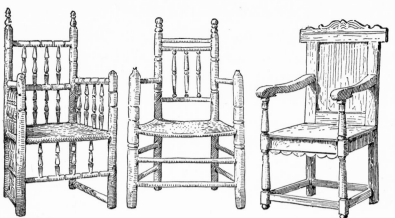

The Brewster chair   The Carver chair   A wainscot chair, 1630

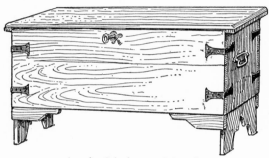

A colonial chest, 1675–1690

A trestle table

drawers, and a bureau; and for the dining room a sideboard. Desks and secretaries came by a similar line of furniture descent. But we are ignoring the passing of years, of many years.

The development of chairs, curiously enough, seems to have been in a way related to that of chests. There was an old form of chair quite familiar in England called the Great or Wainscot Chair. Its seat, back and sometimes even sides were of solid wood. The carving of its decoration was much like that of chests. The Wainscot Chair was a descendant of the mediæval throne. The atmosphere of authority also came down from the throne and surrounded it; likewise the spirit of exclusiveness and special privilege. It was a very aristocratic, not to say autocratic piece of furniture. The Governor, the Bishop, the presiding officer of any body had a chair. That was why the last-named functionary was called the Chairman; he had a chair. It was an official symbol of authority, and to some extent it still is. When the presiding officer of a Legislature rises from his chair, the Legislature is no longer in session.

So too the head of a family in his degree had his chair; it symbolized his dignity and authority as such. Others sat on stools—whether the others were, at Court, Ministers of State, or at home, wife and children. It was no indignity for a wife to sit on a stool, when not standing. It merely signified that she was not the head of the house. So too, a Prime Minister, in the presence of his King, sat on a stool. (Nor, one suspects, was a stool any more uncomfortable than a Wainscot

A New England chest of drawers, 1690–1700

A Flax-wheel. A bunch
of flax is on the distaff
ready for spinning

A wool wheel

A Quilling-wheel to wind bobbins or
quills for the shuttle

Chair with its hard oak board seat and back! But they were handsome things, just to look at!)

There are extant in America today only a few of these patriarchal chairs. They are treasured as President's Chairs in a few universities or colleges, or are in museums. If there ever were many of them in this country, they seemed durable enough to last for centuries, but they have disappeared, gone with civil autocracy and Puritan theology, long before many more delicate and democratic forms of furniture like the Windsor Chair and the Hitchcock Chair.

From Plymouth Colony mostly there has come a type of chair, or two similar types of chair which are indeed instinct with dignity and a certain formality but not so repellent in their magnificence. These are the Carver Chair and the Brewster Chair. It seems reasonable to believe that John Alden and Kenelm Winslow made quite a number of these, especially for the older leaders of the Colony. There are chairs of these types extant ascribed to the ownership of Governor Carver, Elder Brewster, Captain Miles Standish, and Edward Winslow. Though it is impossible to be positive, the ascription may well be correct.

The form was an ancient one originating in the Byzantine Empire. In making these chairs much of the work could be done with the turning-lathe. In the earlier examples from the neighborhood of Plymouth, the main posts and some of the cross pieces were evidently made by hand, and the decorative spindles by lathe. The main difference between the two types is that the Carver Chair is much the simpler, having for example only 3 spindles, in the back, while the Brewster Chair has many,—8 in the back, 12 on each side, above and below the seat, and 4 more in front, below the seat,—36 in all, quite a complement! The Carver is certainly the earlier form and the more beautiful. The modification

A colonial loom—at the right is a reel of yarn and upon the floor are bobbins and shuttles, the brushlike implements are cards for carding wool

of these chairs came with the substitution of horizontal slats for the spindles in the backs, according to the general tendency in the middle of the seventeenth century, towards greater comfort in home life. This was followed by a change to vertical slats in the banister-back chair, and then to a single broad piece in the fiddleback chair.

When the exclusive spirit so dominant in the Great or

Wainscot Chair gave way, the change produced a distinct and beautiful variety in all succeeding styles of chair to the present day. The arms were abandoned, and the general proportions were lighter and more graceful. For the earlier days these chairs also had the advantage of taking up less room. This may have helped to introduce them into favor. As the wife usually sat in one of these, they were called, especially in Connecticut, "Lady Chairs." They are also very appropriately called Side Chairs. The banister and fiddle kinds of backs seem specially suitable for these Side Chairs. One or two armchairs and four or more Lady Chairs make a beautiful set. Later in the eighteenth century came the more pretentious leather-back. With these, and with the graceful New England slatback chairs there came very handsome carved work on all parts of the chair, very elaborate and very handsome indeed. But again we are getting ahead of our story.

Beds we naturally follow out from the common room as well as every other kind of furniture. All started in the common room. And there space was before long begrudged the bed too and ingenuity was used to limit it. When the man and wife started keeping house, they started with their one bed comfortably located in the corner of their one common room. As the children came, a cradle was provided for the new one, and then a crib or two as each grew a little older and a little longer. By the time there were two or three children space was becoming valuable. The folding bed came into the family at about this time. Its bed frame folded on hinges back against the wall and the blankets went into the chest during the daytime. There was another device to save space, when the bed was a heavy one—the trundle bed. This was a low bed of quite good size, which

A four-post bed with trundle bed

would slide under the parents' bed during the day and could be pulled out for the children to sleep on at night. When the lean-to came and the larger common room permitted the first of the fire rooms, the bed of the master and mistress was moved in thither, and it stayed up all day long. The trundle bed went along with it, but the folding bed was forgotten until the latter part of the nineteenth century.

Meantime that other spirit in the development of furniture had been exerting its irresistible influence—the cold draft. Even in the earliest folding bed extant we can see the provision for shutting off drafts. A frame was put up over the bed, sometimes six feet high from the floor, from which to hang curtains. This also provided some privacy after retiring, but that was not the chief motive. It was the draft. Nonetheless these curtains brought in their train a wonderful result. The posts of that frame afforded excellent opportunity for skillful carving. At first the curtains themselves occupied all the attention that growing taste could give, but it was inevitable that artistic appreciation should soon recognize its opportunity and the four-poster came into its own!

The dress of people expresses their character in even more individual detail than their houses and their furniture. Probably only the expression of their faces and their carriage tell more about them. For this reason general statements about historical costume should always be made guardedly, and only a brief reference will be attempted here. On the other hand, to what degree did standardization come in to dictate the dress of the people? Often in colonial times to a considerable degree, with statement in legislation and with fine and even imprisonment attached on occasion. Costume in the seventeenth century followed the dress of England and Holland quite closely. In New England the English Puritans set the styles. In Virginia and the South the Cavaliers and the Court. In New York the styles of the Dutch naturally prevailed. But within these general styles the fashions continually changed, and with the fashions individual tastes continually demanded differences in dress of both men and women, and the changes were made more and more rapidly. Accordingly the best suggestion in this illimitable field is for the interested reader to look up contemporary portraits. As usual the reward will be the great fascination found in the genuine knowledge gradually acquired.

There will be found nonetheless certain principles that seem to guide the most arbitrary standards imposed in dress. For instance—the hat never changes from being a combination of the cap to protect the head and the brim to shade the eyes, always subject to the rule of good looks, whether of beauty or of dignity. The permutations and combinations of these two elements may be followed in every particular hat found reproduced. What greater difference in effect can there be then between the hat of the Puritan with the wide brim stiffened to express the rigidity of principle and the hat of the Cavalier with the brim purposely kept supple to sweep in the flowing lines of social adaptability. Then consider the three-cornered hat of the latter part of the eighteenth century with the brim pinned back to conform with the more crisp manners of the time.

A warming pan and foot-stove

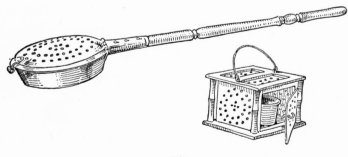

37

CHAPTER III

In Dutch New York

THUS far the everyday things considered have been found largely in New England. There the development was simple; there the material of that development has been preserved. When the study goes on to the Middle Colonies and the South it is interrupted by New York. Dutch New York in the succession of English Colonies extending from Massachusetts Bay to Georgia. Nieuw Amsterdam was indeed an island, a Dutch island in an English wilderness, and no less was the region claimed as its territory and called Nieuw Nederlandt.

In 1609 Henry Hudson, sailing where he pleased in the service of the Dutch East India Company, entered the River of the Mountains. By 1613 the Dutch had built only four small houses on Manhattan as a fur-trading station. It was not until 1623, ten years more, that they started a real settlement. In that year Cornelis Jacobsen May, with the title of Director-General, brought thirty families of Walloons, Protestant refugees from the southern provinces of the Netherlands, to Nieuw Amsterdam, and settled them there and at outlying points, to mark the extent of the Dutch claim—up the North River (where Albany is now), on the

South River (the Delaware, near the present location of Camden), across the East River (at Wallabout Bay on Long Island), and on the Fresh River (at Hartford), where they started to build a fort. In 1625 two shiploads of live-

The *Half Moon*

stock arrived, cattle and horses, sheep and swine, 103 in all, properly cared for to ensure their safe transportation. The same year, 1625, family life declared itself established by the birth of the first child in Nieuw Amsterdam, Sarah Rapaelje, into the family of Jan Joris Rapaelje. Twelve years! A long time to be reaching the full status of a settlement of families!

From the beginning Nieuw Amsterdam was a trading post. That was the distinctive fact. What interested the Dutch in Henry Hudson's reports was the fur trade awaiting the first comer, not the possibilities for a self-sustaining colony of families. The purpose was commercial. The settlers sent across the ocean included many fine Dutch

The Stadt Huys

From an engraving after a drawing by J. Danckaerts, 1679, at what was later called Coenties Slip

people, but they were traders rather than farmers, and at first they were all men. Further, the management of the colony was always primarily commercial. The people were there for the benefit of the trade, not the trade for the benefit of the people. And so it continued to be until the people compelled old Governor Pieter Stuyvesant most unwillingly to haul down his flag and surrender to Colonel Richard Nicolls, Groom of the Bed-Chamber to the Duke of York, and anticipatorily Governor of the new Province of New York. Briefly stated, the majority was 120 guns in the four black frigates flying the red flag of England to 20

Nieuw Amsterdam
Broad Street, 1663, with canal inlet back from the old shore line

whose fuses were ready to be lighted at the order of the Dutch Governor, and the Dutch people had no sentiment in favor of the minority.

Charles II, on account of personal memories, had no love for war. He felt it always a gain when a purpose could be achieved by diplomacy or duplicity rather than by bloodshed. Those of us who are of English blood may, if we wish, vicariously confess the sins of our king and need complain of no lack of occasion. Nonetheless the fact remains that the general outcome could never have been different from what it was. King Charles simply took the most obvious short-cut. As long as the Dutch Government and the Dutch West India Company blandly ignored the chief principle of successful colonial development in Nieuw Ned· erlandt, Dutch trading stations could not long maintain

Indian and Dutch traders bargaining over furs

themselves within reach of English settlements. The Dutch people and the English people were too closely related in blood, in traditions, in instincts for this to be possible. Governor William Bradford and Director-General Pieter Minuit conducted their negotiations and controversies with each other in a very friendly and successful manner. Granted that the English Government was tainted with the same commercial insanity in the administration of its colonies and persisted in it to the end. Still the English settlers had a stake in the homes they had established; for these they could fight. The Dutch traders had only their ledgers, their credit and debit accounts for which to fight, according to the theory of their government, and even these were not theirs. The great heritage the people of New York have received from their Dutch ancestors came from the Dutch people, but the heirs had to become Englishmen before they could inherit.

But there was a cleavage between the Dutch governors and the Dutch people as well as between the Dutch and the English regimes. Racially the English people and the Dutch people were closely related. Commercially also they had been closely related for hundreds of years. The English wool trade with Flanders in the reign of Edward I (1272–1307) and the importation of Flemish weavers into England in the reign of Edward III (1327–1377) are instances of the fact. In government too the instincts of the Dutch people were democratic.

When, however, a settlement is made purely for commercial purposes, the standard of management, which includes the government of the settlers, is apt to be one conducive to profit and quick turnover rather than the welfare of the people. Nonetheless Pieter Minuit was a successful and beneficent Director-General, and Cornelis Melyn was a successful and beneficent Patroon of Staten Island. But Willem Kieft and Pieter Stuyvesant as governing officials were near-sighted by character. They could not see beyond the commercial ideal they held close to their eyes. Accordingly when the caprice of affairs snatched the government of Nieuw Nederlandt away from the Netherlands and tossed it to England, the Dutch people of Nieuw Amsterdam had no special objection. They would be in good company with the English people, and their commercial relations would have a chance to grow, by land as well as by sea.

The colony that centered in the town at the mouth of Henry Hudson's river was for a long time hampered by this trading history. It is well to understand this clearly and to bear it in mind even in connection with minor matters. In these everyday things we may find tokens of the sturdy individual quality of these related people. The everyday things in use in New York and in New England were in many ways similar, in some ways different, and these distinctions may be found in the houses, in the furniture, in the clothes and in the food. As the years passed the differences became less and the similarities greater. At first many of the houses in Nieuw Amsterdam and later in New York were like those in Holland, of brick with the gable ends toward the street, some with the slope of the gable in steps or treated in curves. Another type of house was usually of only two stories with a gambrel roof, the upper story, under the roof, being used chiefly for storing goods for need later in the year or for trading. The Dutch gambrel differed from the New England gambrel in having the upper slope shorter and the lower longer, whereas the New England gambrel had the lower slope shorter and much steeper.

A widespread contribution the Dutch made to the American house was the stoop or porch. With the gambrel-roofed house this developed from an extension of the eaves beyond the house wall. The Dutch door also was a genial addition, making it natural to carry on a social conversation with the neighbors without the formality of a long visit in the house. The trading habit modified the use of one of the rooms

From Bryant's "History of the United States"

The Beaver Street side of Fort Amsterdam, Pieter Stuyvesant leading the evacuation on September 8, 1664, after the surrender to the English

other than the common room, making it more of a display room. In the eighteenth century many of the houses of the storekeepers were still quite like the other town residences, only one of the front rooms was used for the purposes of trade and so developed into the store of later days. In their furniture the Dutch were apt to make their chairs, for instance, noticeably a little more sturdy, as they themselves

English New York waterfront in 1760

were apt to be a little more stocky in build than the English. Their clothes also were more full-bodied. The skirts of the women hung very full, and the knee-breeches of the men were baggy. These differences can be recognized better when studied in detail. At that the differences tend gradually to disappear as time advances until the styles, the customs and the daily life in one and in another of the colonies are evidently very much the same.

The love of color, especially the greens, the blues, and the reds, and the love of flowers, are of course by no means confined to the Dutch, yet if a flower has race or nationality where is the Tulip to be found but among the people of Holland and among their descendants, whether by inheritance or by the love of gardening! There are many other indications of the Dutch heritage to be found in the neighborhoods of the ancient Nieuw Nederlandt. Even in our own familiar names, there is the pronunciation of "uy" with the sound of long "i," as in Schuyler, or in Huyler's candy, or in Spuyten Duyvil. The diphthong has however strayed over to Quaker Philadelphia and lost all its character on the banks of the Schoolkill River. One can make a serious mistake in New York to this day in taking Hell Gate to refer to the entrance to a terrible place instead of a specially "Beautiful Approach" to Manhattan. There is probably still need for a standard to be raised in such matters. This is no doubt the reason for the old Dutch colors —blue, white, and orange—in the flag of the City of New York.

CHAPTER IV

Penn's Quaker City

THREE great men were the founders of the Colonies to which we are chiefly giving attention: Captain John Smith at Jamestown; Governor William Bradford at Plymouth; and William Penn at Philadelphia. Captain John Smith was hampered by the impractical character of so many of the settlers, not of his own choosing, who were sent with him. Governor William Bradford was handicapped by the inclement weather and rugged terrain in which, through no fault of his or of theirs, they had to make their beginnings. Both of them overcame their difficulties by virtue of their superior character, the power of their innate leadership, and their practical ability. Governor John Winthrop of Massachusetts Bay also commands respectful recognition with these great leaders, both for his ability and for his extraordinary success.

William Penn was equally successful. He also overcame his difficulties. He overcame them beforehand. He did invincible planning. He became familiar with the conditions of the region in the course of his firm and wise action as arbitrator and administrator of the affairs of East and West Jersey, between 1673 and 1680. He secured excellent condi-

A brief Account of the

Province of Pennsylvania,

Lately Granted by the

K I N G,

Under the GREAT

Seal of England,

TO

WILLIAM PENN

AND HIS

Heirs and Affigns.

Since (by the good Providence of *God,* and the Favour of the *King*) a Country in *America* is fallen to my Lot, I thought it not lefs my Duty, then my Honeft Intereft, to give fome publick notice of it to the World, that thofe of our own or other Nations, that are inclin'd to Tranfport Themfelves or Families beyond the Seas, may find another Country added to their Choice; that if they fhall happen to like the Place, Conditions, and Government, (fo far as the prefent Infancy of things will allow us any profpect) they may, if they pleafe, fix with me in the Province, hereafter defcribed.

I. *The* KING'S *Title to this Country before he granted it.*

It is the *Jus Gentium,* or Law of Nations, that what ever Wafte, or uncultred Country, is the Difcovery of any Prince, it is the right of that Prince that was at the Charge of the Difcovery: Now this *Province* is a Member of that part of *America,* which the King of *Englands* Anceftors have been at the Charge of Difcovering, and which they and he have taken great care to preferve and Improve.

A   II. William

William Penn Document, 1681

tions in the charter from his father's friend, King Charles II, both in the matter of settling and of government. And he gathered an excellent class of people, practical, home-loving, and industrious, to go to America and take up the work of settling and developing his province.

Penn's common sense, his foresight, and his simple, humane spirit are evident in the prospectus he wrote in 1681 to invite settlers to his Colony, *A Brief Account of the Province of Pennsylvania*. It is a practical document. In it he says:

> But they that go must wisely count the Cost, For they must either work themselves, or be able to imploy others. A Winter goes before a Summer, and the first work will be Countrey Labour, to clear Ground, and raise Provision; other things by degrees.

He then gives specific information about the cost of passage to Pennsylvania and advice as to what the settlers should take with them.

> 1st. The Passage for Men and Women is Five Pounds a head, for Children under Ten Years Fifty Shillings, Sucking Children Nothing. For Freight of Goods Forty Shillings per Tun; but one Chest to every Passenger Free.
>
> 2ly. The Goods fit to take with them for use or sale are all Utensils for Husbandry and Building, and House-hold-stuff; Also all sorts of things for Apparel, as Cloath, Stuffes, Linnen &c. Wherein all that desire may be more particularly informed by Philip Ford, at the Hood and Scarf in Bow-lane in London.

The emigrant is then told something of the conditions of

his life and work after he reaches Pennsylvania. So definite is this prospectus that one feels sure it states the actual experience of many of the early settlers on the Delaware, and incidentally illustrates Penn's foresight.

Lastly. Being by the Mercy of God safely arrived; be it in October, Two Men may clear as much Ground for Corn as usually brings by the following Harvest about Twenty Quarters; In the mean time they must buy Corn, which they may have as aforesaid; and if they buy them two Cows, and two Breeding Sows; with what the Indians for a small matter will bring in, of Fowl, Fish, and Venison (which is incredibly Cheap, as a Fat Buck for Two Shillings) that and their industry will supply them. It is apprehended, that Fifteen Pounds stock for each Man (who is first well in Cloaths, and provided with fit working Tools for Himself) will (by the Blessing of God) carry him thither, and keep him, till his own Plantation will Accomodate him. But all are most seriously cautioned, how they proceed in the disposal of themselves.

The prospectus closes with an injunction that sounds amusing 250 years or more later but which was quite as practical and indeed as resultful as any of the advice about tools or live stock.

And it is further Advised, that all such as go would at least get the Permission, if not the good Liking of their near Relations; for that is both Natural and a Duty incumbent upon all: And by this means will natural Affection be preserved and a Friendly and Profitable Correspondence maintained between them. In all which God Almighty (who is the Salvation of the Ends of the Earth) Direct us, that His Blessings may attend our Honest In-deavors; and then the Consequence of all our Undertakings will

51

be to the Glory of His Great Name and the true Happiness of
Us and Our Posterity. Amen.   WILLIAM PENN.

The response to this opportunity offered by Penn was
remarkable, greater than the migration to any of the other
colonies. They came in three streams. First, there were the
Quakers, many of whom were from Wales and from across
the Bristol Channel in Cornwall. Second, the Germans,
from the Palatinate and from along the Rhine, most of
whom belonged to the mystic German sects. And third,
there were the Scotch-Irish, aggressive Presbyterians, who
came originally from the Border, from the Scottish Lowlands and the North of England, and who had sojourned
a generation or two in Ulster on the way. As convenient
dates, we might say that the Quakers began to come in
1682; the Germans (although some came almost as early
as the Quakers) in 1709; and the Scotch-Irish in 1720.
The three were very different. Their settlements and equip-
ments, their houses, tools and utensils were in the beginning
very naturally quite different. But soon all three were living
within range of one another, vigorously emphasizing those
differences and rubbing their rough corners smoother within the present limits of the State of Pennsylvania.

Another fact should be borne in mind. The stage of
development attained in building, in farming, in ways of
living, advances much more slowly on the frontier than
at the center of the settlements. This would be more
primitive out among the Pennsylvania-German farms near

the Susquehanna River than in Philadelphia, and much more primitive still out in the forests of the Allegheny Mountains among the Scotch-Irish pioneers.

The Quakers settled in the town of Philadelphia and in

The Letitia Street house from an old photograph made while upon
its original site

The photograph is in the possession of the Historical Society of Pennsylvania

the immediate vicinity. The town grew rapidly. Few of their houses before 1700 remain. A house was started for Penn before he arrived but it was not finished when he reached his colony in October, 1682. So he did not occupy it that winter. He gave it later to his daughter, Letitia. There is a house which for many years was believed to be this first house of William Penn's and to be the house he gave to his daughter.-As such it was moved in 1883 from Letitia Street, its original location, to Fairmount Park. In the historical research attending the Sesquicentennial Celebration in 1932, however, it was found that the evidence did not support this belief. So it is now simply called the Letitia Street House. In the judgment of Fiske Kimball, the house now in Fairmount Park was built sometime between 1703 and 1715. Historical haloes are often impulsively conferred.

There was another house in which Penn lived. When he returned to Philadelphia for his second visit, in 1699, he lived in what was called, on account of the new material used for its roof, the Slate House. This was built in 1698 by Samuel Carpenter, the Treasurer of the Province. It stood at the southeast corner of Second Street and Norris Alley, later called Gothic Street. Of this house we know something, from the statement of a descendant of Samuel Carpenter written in 1828, while it was still standing.

Its dimensions are about 45 feet front by 55 feet deep. It is of brick, two stories in height with large projecting eaves and a square turret at each of the front corners. . . . In the centre of the front may still be seen the Gothic arched doorway, opening into a narrow entry, which is rendered curious by the heavy old-fashioned wainscoting and which communicates with the principal rooms below stairs. From these you pass into the smaller rooms within the turrets, which were perhaps intended for offices or studies. It is many years since the diamond shaped sash still remained in some of the windows; at present however all are of modern construction. What renders the original appearance worthy of some attention is the fact that James Logan (Penn's

The Slate House, Philadelphia, 1699. One time residence of William Penn

secretary) in one of his letters to Penn speaks of it as the choicest house for a Governor in the Province of Pennsylvania and strongly urges him to purchase it for that purpose.

But neither does this house survive to our day. It was pulled down in 1867.

Penn also built himself a fine house on a country estate of 6558 acres twenty miles up the Delaware River, which he called Pennsbury. He furnished this house in the style of no mean palace. His silver was exceptionally fine. There was nothing ostentatious about him, but he liked handsome comfort. Hannah Callowhill, his second wife, was a devoted and competent woman, who managed his houses and estates well. So there at Pennsbury he lived in unrestricted comfort and enjoyed his state for two years, the last he spent in America. He liked good food, venison and shad especially. He loved to sit and talk over some ale or wine with a not too complacent friend.[1]

Especially he enjoyed being rowed in a barge by six oarsmen down the river to Philadelphia, and back again —quite in the manner of English royalty on the Thames. Once on a squally day a friend overhauled him on one of these trips and expressed surprise at his venturing out in such weather. Penn immediately replied, "I have been sailing against wind and tide all my life." Pennsbury too is gone. Of Penn's three houses none survives.

---

[1] An instance of this is told in Dean Swift's letter to Stella, September 30, 1710, when Penn was in London. Queen Anne was on the throne. The "First Minister" was Sir Robert Harley, later Earl of Oxford; Mr. St. John was Henry St. John, later Viscount Bolingbroke.

"They had just done dinner. Mr. Harley came out to me, brought me in, and presented me to his son-in-law, Lord Doblane (or some such name), and his own son, and among others, Will Penn the Quaker. We sat two hours, drinking as good wine as you do; and two hours more he and I alone; where he heard me tell my business, entered into it with all kindness, asked for my powers, and read them, and read likewise a memorial I had drawn up, and put it in his pocket to shew the Queen; told me the measures he would take, and in short said everything I could wish; told me he must bring Mr. St. John (secretary of state) and me acquainted, and spoke many things of personal kindness and esteem for me, that I am half inclined to believe what some friends have told me, that he would do everything to bring me over. He has desired to dine with me. (What a comical mistake was that), I mean, he has desired me to dine with him on Tuesday; and after four hours being with him, set me down at St. James coffee house in a hackney coach. All this is odd and comical if you consider him and me. He knew my christian name very well. I could not forbear saying thus much upon this matter although you will think it tedious."

But the Letitia Street house is nonetheless very interesting. It is one of the few houses remaining from the early Quaker days. It is a small house of brick laid in Flemish bond, compact and businesslike in appearance. There are two rooms on each floor. It is rather tall in proportion to its front, and therefore has a somewhat vertical effect, as do many of the houses in this region. The Letitia Street house is definitely a town house.

The Quaker was a citizen. By preference he lived in a town and generally engaged in business or in some other distinctly town occupation. He saw things in a large way and was capable of large management. William Penn himself laid out the streets of Philadelphia. It was the first instance of city planning, in the modern sense of the term. Only Washington, laid out by Major L'Enfant, or to give it the original name, the Federal City, was laid out as definitely and with as permanent success from the beginning as Philadelphia. William Penn was a city planner. There may be very few buildings remaining from before 1700, if any, but the plan of the city of Philadelphia as a whole survives straight through from 1682 unchanged.

The Welsh Quakers, many of them, settled out to the west of Philadelphia, where Welsh names still remain. There they had bought 40,000 acres from Penn in advance. They called the holding the Welsh Barony. There they kept up the use of their own language for some time and maintained their own local government under the proprietorship of the Penn family, civil as well as religious affairs being taken care of by the Friends Meetings. These arrangements were quite in accord with Penn's belief in self-government and were therefore readily made. The Quakers prospered. They were simple, thrifty, and able. They did not maintain their original superior proportion in the population as time went on and other peoples poured in, but they did maintain their influence and their political control in the Province. In 1750, when the population of Pennsylvania was 150,000, the Quakers numbered only 50,000. Nonetheless though so decidedly in the minority they still continued to dominate the Provincial Legislature, and they continued to dominate it down to the Revolution.

Wynnestay is a Welsh Quaker house, one of the oldest houses remaining in the neighborhood of Philadelphia. It was erected only seven years after the coming of Penn, which shows how rapidly these people prospered. Thomas Wynne was in 1683 the first speaker of the Provincial Assembly of Pennsylvania. He was a chirurgeon or surgeon, a friend of Penn's and came over with him in the *Welcome*. He had a town house in Philadelphia, at the corner of Front and Chestnut Streets. Chestnut was at first called Wynne Street. He bought 5000 acres in the Welsh Barony and in 1689 built at the center of his estate a two-story stone house, which he named Wynnestay. This he made his home and there he lived until he died in 1692 at the age of sixty-two years. As he built it, Wynnestay was a two-story stone building with a single room on each floor. His son, Jonathan Wynne, extended the house to its present

From a painting by Stanley M. Arthurs

The arrival of the first woman in Jamestown, Virginia

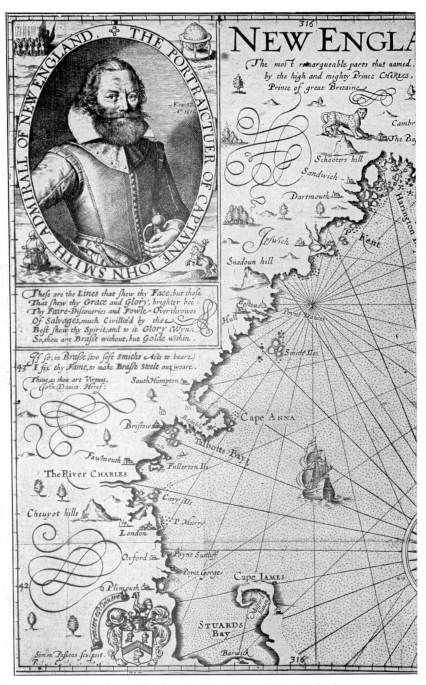

A section of Captain John Smith's Map of New England
From a copy of the fifth state of the map in the New York Public Library

Plymouth in 1622 as constructed by W. L. Williams

English wigwams, first two covered with bark

This view and the one above are from the 1630 Colonial Village erected in Salem, Massachusetts
in 1930
Both pictures are from "Everyday Life in the Massachusetts Bay Colony," by George Francis Dow

Salt-Box Houses

Top. The Boardman House, Saugus, Massachusetts, 1651
Middle. The birthplaces of John and John Quincy Adams, Braintree, Massachusetts
Below. The John Howard Payne Memorial at East Hampton, Long Island

This kitchen in Washington's Headquarters at Morristown, N. J., was selected because there are gathered together so many colonial utensils including those which went with the fireplace itself

Cavalier   Puritan   Hollander   Quaker

Costumes of the early settlers

In the Stocks

An attempt to enforce morality in the Puritan settlement

From drawings by Darley for Lossing's "Our Country"

Wynnestay, Lower Merion, built by Doctor Thomas Wynne in 1689
From "Colonial Homes of Philadelphia," Eberlein and Lippincott

From a drawing by Howard Pyle

Colonial school days in Pennsylvania

Lower Merion Friends' Meeting House
From "Colonial Churches and Meeting Houses" by Philip B. Wallace

From "Nord Amerika seine Stadte und Naturwunder," by Ernest von Helle

A Quaker meeting in Philadelphia

St. David's Episcopal Church, Radnor, Pennsylvania, 1715
From "Colonial Churches and Meeting Houses," by Philip B. Wallace

Barn on the Kauffman Farm, Berks County
From "Early Domestic Architecture of Pennsylvania" by Eleanor Raymond

Log house at Lititz   The spring-room door, Fort Zeller

Log house, Berks County

All three are from the Pennsylvania German Society Proceedings, Volume XLI

Saal and Sister's Home, Ephrata Cloisters, Ephrata, Pennsylvania

From "Colonial Churches and Meeting Houses" by Philip B. Wallace

The Ephrata Printing Press

The earliest known Ephrata imprint bears the date 1745, but the Press was undoubtedly set up before that time. This is known as a "Blaeu" press after William Jansen Blaeu, of Amsterdam, who first improved the original Gutenberg press. It stands 6′ 2½″. The inside measurement of the chase is 23⅞″ x 19⅝″

The house and mill of the miller at Millbach, Lebanon County, Pennsylvania

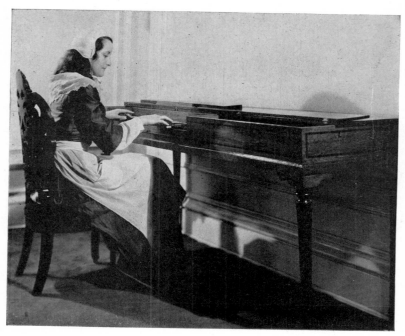

Old spinet of 1754 at the Moravian Seminary and College for Women,
Bethlehem, Pennsylvania

Nº 3879

Ten Shillings

This Indented Bill of Ten Shillings current Money of America, according to the Act of Parliament, made in the Sixth Year of the late Queen Anne, for Ascertaining the Rates of foreign Coins in the Plantations, due from the Province of Pennsylvania, to the Possessor thereof, shall be in Value equal to Money, and shall be accepted accordingly by the Provincial Treasurer, County Treasurers and the Trustees for the General Loan-Office of the Province of Pennsylvania, in all Publick Payments, and for any Fond at any Time in any of the said Treasuries and Loan-Office.

Dated in Philadelphia the Second Day of April, in the Year of Our Lord, One Thousand seven Hundred and Twenty Three, by Order of the Governor and General Assembly.

Ten Shillings

MERCY JUSTICE

Indented bill used in lieu of money in the province of Pennsylvania. The original is in the collection of the Historical Society of Pennsylvania

From Julius F. Sachse's "German Sectarians of Pennsylvania"

A settler listens to the warning of a friendly Indian

From a painting by N. C. Wyeth

Colonial forces recruited from the people of the mountain regions

length. In so doing, he raised the roof of the old part of the house a little. Otherwise the house has not been changed at all. Thomas Wynne's town house has of course gone long since. We do not know what it was like.

But it would not be correct to think of the distinguished mansion of Wynnestay, even in its earlier form, as an example of the average homes of the Quakers in and around Philadelphia, though there were others no doubt quite as fine. Such an impression might well be balanced by the attitude of John Woolman toward "superfluities," when taking passage on board ship for London. Some of his friends were protesting against his taking passage in the steerage instead of in the cabin. In his *Journal* he wrote:

I told the owner (of the ship) that on the outside of that part of the ship where the cabin was I observed sundry sorts of carved work and imagery; that in the cabin I observed some superfluity of workmanship of several sorts; and that according to the ways of men's reckoning the sum of money to be paid for a passage in that apartment had some relation to the expense of furnishing it to please the minds of such who give way to a conformity to this world; . . . and that I felt a scruple with regard to paying my money to defray such expenses.

He went in the steerage. People who held to such simple ideas and made it such a strict matter of principle would not in general build elaborate mansions, even in a style as moderate and dignified as Wynnestay.

Rather we should look at the Merion Friends Meeting House, built by the people of the Welsh Barony in 1695, for an example of architecture that would meet their approval and gain their use. Solid, compact, consisting of the essentials only, no "superfluities"! It was built of stone quarried near by on the estate of one of the members of the Meeting. Indeed, it might seem that the dignified magnificence of the fine stone work came to be regarded with doubt, for in 1829 when the building needed some repairs the whole beautiful stone work was covered with rough cast, with plaster. This certainly did not strengthen it any. May it not have been a case of Quaker asceticism? As such it may be characteristic and interesting.

But neither can we assume that the Merion Meeting House was an absolute expression of Quaker life and taste, any more than Wynnestay. The law of averages and the influence of environment were sure to have their effect. Strict loyalty to principle, so admirable in John Woolman, may have satisfactorily counteracted the seasickness for him, and may have rebuked the handsome stone walls of Merion, but the æsthetic vanities of the Church of England made inroads on the Quakers of the Welsh Barony. Even William Penn's own sons became Anglicans and the great Founder himself modified his dress, to the grief of many of his followers, and wore clothes of richly colored velvet with lace ruffles, and furnished that country estate Pennsbury, on the Delaware River, in the style of no mean palace. It was a stern struggle between the power of principle on guard in every detail and the insidious beauty of holiness, ever present in abundant detail and leading toward the unrestrained belief in the holiness of beauty. In the Welsh Barony itself St. David's Church at Radnor is a witness, built in 1715, so Welsh, so simple and restrained, so truly Quaker in spirit, so beautiful. To their religion men and women give the best in their life and their uttermost to the death. Among the trees around the Merion Meeting House and St. David's, Radnor, imagination can still hear the echoes of sincere strife two hundred years ago.

The Quakers in general were characterized by an instinct for the truth. The truth can be perceived only by a quality that has something of the stern in it. It was this sense for what is essential that made them leaders in good management and in sound business. It was this that through the century made the diminishing Quaker minority nonetheless retain the political control of the Province straight through to the Revolution. Not only in the city of Philadelphia, so to speak their headquarters, but no less out through the farming regions and on far out through the mountains the Quakers guided and molded the public and commercial life of the Colony.

These people—what did they look like? We can hardly find a better description than Doctor S. Weir Mitchell gives us in his novel *Hugh Wynne* as the young man and his father start off for meeting. Doctor Mitchell knew them.

We set off soon after in silence, he walking with hands behind his back clasping his gold-headed cane, his collarless coat and waistcoat below his beaver, and the gray hair in a thick mass between. He wore shoes, fine drab short-clothes, and black silk stockings, all without buckles, and he moved rapidly, nodding to those he met on the way to the Bank Hill Meeting-house in Front Street above Arch.

We can soon get a vivid idea of them by following the two into the Meeting.

There were many drab-coated men, and there were elderly women, in gowns of drab or gray, with white silk shawls and black silk-covered cardboard bonnets. Here and there a man or woman was in gayer colors or wore buckles, and some had silver buttons; but these were rare. The meeting-room was, so to speak, a large oblong box with whitewashed walls. A broad passage ran from the door to the farther end; on the right of it sat the men, on the left the women; against the remoter wall, facing the rude benches, were three rows of seats, one above the other. On these sat at the back the elders, and in front of them the overseers. The clerk of the Meeting had a little desk provided for him. . . . When the doors were closed I sat silent in prayer; for some ten minutes a perfect stillness fell upon one and all of the three or four hundred people here met together.

Such they were—in character, in standpoint, in manners, in dress—the leaders in working out a dream, to make in behind the Delaware River (and probably in front of it too) a great peaceful Quaker nation. Did they fail? Or in their extraordinary contribution did they accomplish even more than they dreamed, more than they could have dreamed?

CHAPTER V

Pennsylvania German Farms

THE term Pennsylvania German came to cover the
Germans from along the Rhine, the Huguenots
from France, and the Swiss, who came over in
response to Penn's invitation and under the impulse of succeeding events such as the Revocation of the Edict of Nantes
in 1685. William Penn's missionary trip with George Fox
through the Rhine country and into Germany in 1677 made
his name and the character of any enterprise with which he
might be connected somewhat familiar in that region.
When copies of Penn's prospectus reached the land organization at Frankfort, of which Francis Daniel Pastorius, the
learned German, was agent, the means was already effective
for turning the steps of many emigrants in that direction.
Huguenots and Swiss followed the organized German lead,
who in general went down the Rhine to Rotterdam and em-
barked there for Philadelphia direct. This stream of migration continued in large numbers until 1735 and later, and
constituted an exodus of some of the best people of the continent of Europe to new homes. Some also went by way of
England to the Mohawk Valley, but of these quite a number came down the Susquehanna in 1723 and joined their
fellows. In religion they were all Protestants, most of them

belonging to the Lutheran and Reformed churches and to the mystic German sects. Industrially they were farmers, as the Quakers were in general business men. Any one nowadays travelling through their country whether by train or by automobile has noticed the beautifully laid out farms and the large red barns and houses of the Pennsylvania Germans.

These agricultural immigrants did not stop in Philadelphia. The first party under Pastorius settled Germantown in 1683, at that time some six or seven miles out in the country. In general the Germans went on farther, up the Delaware River and up the Schuylkill and out into the rich farm lands, back of the Swedish settlements around Upland or, as renamed by Penn, Chester. The Pennsylvania German country may be roughly indicated as the square bounded on the northwest by the Blue Mountain range, on the northeast and southeast by the Delaware River, and on the southwest by the Susquehanna River (with of course the exception of the section in the immediate vicinity of Philadelphia).

In this region the beginnings of fine agriculture and cattle raising were made, such as a hundred years later led to the great agriculture of the West, and also through their love of beauty to the beginnings of much in native American culture, such as the fine glass of Baron Stiegel at Manheim, the fine printing and choral singing at the Cloisters at Ephrata, and the choral and orchestral music among the Moravians at Bethlehem. Quite as notable as the hundred-

64

mile semicircle around Puritan Massachusetts Bay, this colonial country of the Pennsylvania Germans, but how different!

But we must not allow ourselves too idyllic an idea of these people. We must consider the situation into which they came. They were a menace! or were suspected of being a menace by some of the responsible citizens of the town of Philadelphia. Governor William Keith became apprehensive lest these foreigners, coming in such steady numbers, speaking a foreign language and unfamiliar with English rights, liberties and customs, should swamp the countryside and make of it a foreign colony. Accordingly he issued a proclamation ordering all Masters of Vessels who had brought any such immigrants to appear and render an account of their numbers and character, and another proclamation ordering all such immigrants to appear before a magistrate within one month of their arrival and take oath (or make affirmation) that they were well affected toward His Majesty King George I and toward the Government. Considering the state of affairs on the continent of Europe, Governor Keith's nervousness was not unreasonable. Considering the entirely pacific and indeed agricultural hopes and purposes of the immigrants his anxiety was certainly unwarranted. New points of view were being introduced into the colonies, making new combinations possible and leading to a new variety of civilization in the future, which now we call American. These new qualities were evidenced distinctively in all sorts of ways from the building of their homes to the decoration of their dishes and the working of their tools.

In their building the Pennsylvania Germans carried on

Rear view of Moravian Seminary buildings, Bethlehem, Pa. Note steep roof with two stories of dormers, also German gambrel roof in background

Redrawn from *Pennsylvania German Society Proceedings,* Vol. XLI

the essential methods and repeated the main characteristics of their home country along the Rhine, adapting them to the materials and conditions they found in the new country. For the first settlements they quickly learned from

the Swedes and the Finns who preceded them on the Delaware River to use the horizontal log construction which
soon became characteristic of the American pioneer. Practically all their temporary settlements were log cabins,
though so solidly were they built that to call them temporary is almost humorous. Indeed, some of them last in
fairly good condition to the present day, as for instance
a log house near Landis Store in Berks County. With a
desire for greater permanence and a less primitive appearance came the sheathing of the logs with boards, frequently
vertical, especially in the gables, as seen in the log house
opposite the Moravian Seminary in the town of Lititz.

Stone cabins followed the log cabins when a real intention to put up a permanent home came to them and led
to the erection of considerable buildings. These stone cabins
usually stood on the slope of a hill, so that one side would
be one story high and the other side two stories. They
almost always covered a spring in the basement. Why is
not known. It was not to ensure a water supply in case of
attack by Indians, as has been said. Under Penn's friendly
attitude toward the Indians, there never were any Indian
attacks for seventy years, until 1755, after many of these
had been built. Further, there was in most of them no inside access from the spring room in the basement to the
rest of the house above. The purpose may have been to keep
the water pure from contamination by the farm animals
and to provide ample space for keeping the milk and vegetables cold in the summer.

An interesting and typical instance of these stone cabins is Fort Zeller, near Womelsdorf. In this may be seen the basement spring room, the plain wall surface, the small windows, the vertical gable sheathing, the diagonal molded door and other characteristic features. It was the home of a Huguenot settler named Henri Zellaire, who changed his name, when he cast in his lot with these Germans, to Heinrich Zeller. His cabin got the traditional title of Fort about the time that Indian attacks began, when a young daughter, left alone in the house, noticed three Indians skulking around with malicious intent. She locked and barred all the doors and windows and slipped around down into the spring room. The three Indians tried to crawl through the little passage by which the water flowed out, but the girl brained each one with an axe as his head came through, and dragged his body inside so that none outside might suspect the fate awaiting him.

These spring-rooms and spring-houses played the same part in those days as ice in our later day, whether the winter ice cut and stored, or the artificial ice made when wanted in the refrigerator. Indeed they still do on many farms throughout the country. There the pans of milk are set to rise and the tubs of butter to keep. What more do you want? It was not until the nineteenth century that ice was cut in the North and shipped to the South for use. The liking for ice-cold food has become a passion which few Englishmen can understand. The thick walls sometimes built by the early settlers were not entirely to keep out

Indians. The thick walls of European castles and cathedrals did considerable air-conditioning, rendering them of a fairly even temperature, cooler in summer and warmer in winter, as well as more defensible from enemies and more impressive to the view.

Another stone cabin of pertinent interest is the house of John De Turk or Johan De Tirck in the Oley Valley, not more than eight or ten miles northeast of Reading. It is a small house with a spring room in the basement, whose walls rise two stories to the eaves at the back from the edge of Kaufman's Creek. The main floor is all one room. The cabin is historically noted as the place where the Oley Conference gathered for its three-day session in February, 1742. This conference was called by Count Zinzendorf in the hope of bringing about a union of all the German sects of that region into one denomination. There were present delegates from at least seven religious bodies—Dunkers or Baptists from Germantown, Mennonites from Skippack Valley, and Schwenkfelders from the Perkiomen, Lutherans from the Tulpehocken, mystical monastics from Ephrata, Quakers from Philadelphia, and Zinzendorf's own Moravians from Bethlehem. Though all were intensely Protestant at heart, they were by no means homogeneous or even remotely harmonious in point of view, except the Mennonites and the Quakers. So the conference was conscientiously foredoomed to failure.

On the lintel of an upper door, like the upper door of a grist mill, is carved "JOHAN DE TIRCK 1767 DEBORA

DE TIRCKEN." Twenty-five years after the conference!
This suggests a fascinating question for research. There is
no question of the date of the conference, nor of the fact

Hood and Lintel inscription over second-floor door, John De Turk
House, 1767

Redrawn from *Pennsylvania German Society Proceedings*, Vol. XLI

that this is where the conference was held. The proceedings
were printed, by a Philadelphia printer whose name is a
guarantee of simple reliability—Benjamin Franklin.

John De Turk also may have been a Huguenot. The
De would indicate a French origin but he did not give it
up when joining the German migration. Maybe he came
from the village of Turkheim in Upper Alsace. In 1742

he was already a man of influence widely known for his broad and humane interests, so that Count Zinzendorf knew of him and regarded his house as a good place to ask the delegates of the contentious German sects to come to discuss uniting with each other. It seems probable that John De Turk and his wife Debora lived together here, thrifty and prospering, for at least twenty-five years until in 1767 they replaced a log house with this strong well-built stone house, joyously lavishing their artistic taste on it and proudly carving their names and date on the lintel stone over the second-floor door. In the peak of the gable they placed a decorative feature, and on the window shutters they painted roses in the upper panels and tulips in the lower with a border pattern around the stiles and rails. They had accomplished something in their many years of life and work together!

The painted flowers and decorations on the old stone houses are hard to find now, not so much that they were not common enough two hundred years ago among the people who came from or through the Rhine Valley, as because they have faded away. But the gay decorative instinct still continues among their descendants. Painted decorations are common on the barns to this day in all the Pennsylvania German region. The rose and the tulip were their traditional emblems and are found still on the chests, the benches and even on the dishes that their descendants have preserved or reproduced to this day.

Masonry is itself an art, and among these settlers out in

the country it was one of the home arts, brought with them from the home land. In the cities—in Philadelphia, for instance—doubtless the building of stone and brick houses

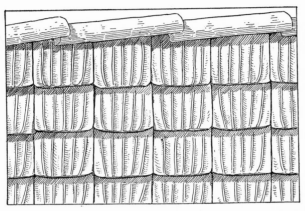

Hand-made roof tiles showing grooves to deflect water to center of tile and away from the vertical joints which is typical of old German tile
Redrawn from *Pennsylvania German Society Proceedings*, Vol. XLI

had soon become a specialized industry. A man wanting to have a stone house, like Thomas Wynne at Wynnestay, doubtless supplied the plans to a builder, a sort of middle-man, who hired the masons and carpenters, and on contract became responsible for the erection of the house according to directions. But out in the country, a man like John De Turk in the Oley Valley put up his stone house himself with the help of his neighbors, to whom he in turn lent a hand on occasion.

There is one detail in the building of these early stone houses which is still found in some of the old stone cabins, the tile roofs. These tiles were hand-made. They were cleverly designed so that, while they were not staggered in laying, grooves in the surface of the tile guided the water to the center of the tile below. The tiles were fastened in place on the roof by means of a hook molded on the under side of the tile which hooked over the horizontal lath of the roof structure. In most instances these tile roofs have worn out and been replaced by other and cheaper materials. The same native artisans made square tiles for the floors of their houses and other buildings.

So through shelters such as these the Pennsylvania German settlers progressed from the status of pioneers to being farmers, established in their typical and permanent occupation to the present day. Several of what we might call the historical Pennsylvania German farms still exist. How they grew, as one house or barn was added after another, may still be seen, from the original stone cabin to the great house and the large barn of prosperity. The Kaufman Farm near Pleasantville is a most interesting example.

The Pennsylvania Germans instinctively gravitated to the best farm land in the Province of Pennsylvania. The family is the agricultural unit. But with increased acreage the farm unit directly tends to exceed the family. The hired man and "the hands" are added to the family household and it grows in the direction of a limited community.

CHAPTER VI

Handwork at Ephrata

AMONG the Pennsylvania Germans there grew up an extreme instance of such community life which was quite notable—the monastic Cloister or Kloster of the Seventh Day Baptists at Ephrata in Lancaster County. It is easy to overestimate this movement and it is easy to underestimate it. As has been said, many of these Palatines were of the mystic German sects. This means that they were not only emphatic Protestants but they were strong individualists. They did their own thinking, whether it was able thinking, as in the case of Peter Miller, the most learned German in the Province, or whether it was but a stubborn devotion to certain peculiar notions. Like all persecuted people, they were strongly emotional. Let us imagine a farm community growing up among "the hands," without a family unit as the nucleus, around a gifted leader and teacher. Being sincere and instinctively moral, these people would readily believe in the spiritual superiority of celibacy. Being loyal in heart and desire, they would implicitly obey their accepted leader and follow literal interpretations of some revered system such as the Bible—and quarrel over the correct interpretations. Such were the Brethren and Sisters of the Kloster at Ephrata and its affiliated branches.

They were extremists, but nonetheless we must bear in mind that most of all they were good Pennsylvania farmers like their relatives, the Pennsylvania German families cultivating the neighboring farms. They were able builders, even if for ritual reasons they refrained from the use of iron as the metal that symbolized darkness and evil, fastening their rafters and beams and frames together with wooden pegs instead of nails. Their buildings have lasted nearly two hundred years. Within their limitations they joyed in the arts and crafts and showed creative originality in what they did, and lived an honest, placid, earnest human life.

The Kloster at Ephrata grew up around a remarkable man, Johann Conrad Beissel. In its buildings and in everything else the community showed the impress of the character of this leader. Conrad Beissel came to America with a party of Palatines, landing in Boston in 1720 on their way to "the Quakerthal in the Island of Pennsylvania." He was born in Eberbach, a small town on the River Necker, in 1690. He was short and well-knit in figure, had a high forehead, a prominent nose and piercing eyes. He was an ascetic of sincere culture and strong character. He inspired and directed the community in all its activities, at times withdrawing from his official leadership to live as a solitary, farther back in the forest. He died, greatly and justly revered by his followers, in 1768.

The main buildings at Ephrata were large, as was natural, inasmuch as they were to house not single families but the large associative families of which such communities consist. They were impressively tall in proportion to their area, as has been noted was common in this region. And they were distinctly German, with high steep roofs, often emphasized by two rows of dormers, indicating two stories in the roof structures. The windows were uniformly small, whether in the roof or in the walls; and the doors were similarly low and narrow, which seemed to them peculiarly fitting as thereby they symbolized the idea that the perfect life with its greater space and larger opportunities could be reached only by humility and self-denial.

The construction of their buildings was of hewn beams, filled behind the boarding or stucco with rubble and clay. They preferred wood to masonry, it may be, partly because when they started to build they had gone out into the wilderness where wood was abundant and of fine quality and they could use what they cut in making the clearings for their farms. The practice also won their approval as, symbolically considered, the use of wood entailed less of the use of iron tools, only the simple axe and adze, than the working of the hard stone into smooth blocks. Further, during these same years of the eighteenth century it was more and more stone with which the worldly men of Philadelphia and other towns, the Quakers who had fallen from grace and abandoned the simple life, were building their splendid mansions. Inside also the buildings were very plain and bare, in accordance with their renunciation of all the physical amenities of life.

That they attached an ultrasignificance to details may be instanced by a dispute that arose in the planning of one of their larger buildings. The question was whether the length of the building should be 66 feet, or 99 feet, or 100 feet. This was the occasion for a long and intense controversy. It was decided in favor of those who favored 99 feet. The argument that won was that in its symbolism the circle represented God, and the down stroke, narrow and prone to fall, represented Man. If they decided on 66 feet, they would be putting Man over God; if they decided on 100 feet, they would be putting Man before God; if they decided on 99 feet, they would be putting God over Man, which was right.

But make no mistake, while ascetic the Brethren and Sisters at Ephrata were not inæsthetic. Their buildings had a severe beauty of their own, the beauty of fine proportion and ascetic expressiveness, as may be seen still. So too in their dress, which at first was simply that of the German farmers and peasants they were when they came over. As the example of the most ascetic was followed, as the number of those who vowed themselves to celibacy increased, and those who betook themselves to living alone as Solitaries, the adoption of special costumes for ritual occasions and for daily use was desired. These costumes were rather similar to those of the White Friars or Capuchins, modified to meet the ideas of Conrad Beissel (or Father Friedsam Gottrecht, his spiritual name) and others of the congregation. Designed by Martin Bremer, the community tailor, they were made of unbleached linen or wool, according to the season of the year. For men it consisted of a shirt, trousers and vest, with a long gown to which was attached a pointed cowl or hood. For women it consisted of a shirt and narrow skirt with a long gown covering all, to which was attached a rounded cowl or hood. Then the Spiritual Virgins, the extreme order in the community, requested a special costume, and it was granted them. Even the "domestic householders," as the secular members who lived with their families were called, adopted a special gown of a gray color to distinguish them at divine service and on public occasions from the Solitary. There can be no doubt that these pietists in their simple garb, going about their farms, working at their crafts, and meditating in their cells or near their cabins in the forest, presented an appearance that was harmonious with their Cloister buildings, and that was practical from their own point of view and helpful to their own spiritual purposes.

It has been said that the interior walls of the buildings were plain and bare. So they were, except for one kind of decoration, which can be described only as large illuminated German texts hanging on the walls. Penmanship was an art which no doubt began with them on a purely practical and amateur basis. Brethren and Sisters both wrote, copying papers and manuscripts for the use of the members of the congregation, doing their work conscientiously until gradually, the reward of conscientious work, it attained, from crude beginnings, the quality of an art. Even

Ephrata script alphabet—Each letter said to have been created by a
continuous pen line or flourish

From *German Sectarians of Pennsylvania* by Julius F. Sachse

the flourishes and decorations they added at the ends of their writings became skillful productions of line drawing, and their initial letters were examples of simple beauty. The barrenness of their life of renunciation compensated itself by particular æsthetic activity in those arts which they felt served religious consecration. So it always is. Life,

Ephrata pen work
The mystical tulip, pomegranate, and lily of Ephrata
From *German Sectarians of Pennsylvania* by Julius F. Sachse

like water, seeks its own level, and insists on finding it, in art.

This handicraft of penmanship, called fractur, it should be remembered, started in the practical industry of simply making enough copies of books of instruction and ritual and hymns for the members of the community. They were necessarily thrifty people, and would not buy, whether by cash or by barter, what they could make themselves. The care with which they did this work developed it into an art. The practical purpose of manifolding their texts launched them into another craft, which also by the same simple devotion they developed into another art. They needed more copies than they could make themselves by hand. So they betook themselves to the Philadelphia printer, Benjamin Franklin, and for a while he did quite a good deal of printing for them. But disagreements arose between them, and the outcome was that Conrad Beissel soon after, surely before 1743, set up a printing press at Ephrata. He also set up a paper mill. Before long the Brethren and Sisters of the Kloster were supplying most of the paper and were doing some of the best printing in colonial America. They had a bookbindery which was the largest and best in all the colonies. One of their presses is now in the Historical Library of Pennsylvania in Philadelphia.

There were other industries, not a few, in which they engaged. At first the cultivation of the ground was their chief activity, and so primitive were their methods and so limited their resources that as the *Chronicon Ephratense,* the official history of the Brotherhood, says:

They were their own horses; when they traveled they went heavily laden like camels, and sometimes the whole Brotherhood might be seen trooping around the hill of Zion.

The first industry of which there is definite record was the building of a bakehouse; it was erected in the interest of the poor settlers, no charge being made either for the baking or for the bread itself. As they progressed, they planted a large orchard and a row of fruit trees around the whole of the Kloster property. Then came a gristmill, a sawmill, the paper mill, an oil mill, the oil from which was used to make all the printer's ink used in the Province, a fulling mill, a tannery. And looms were set up for weaving both linen and woollen. And yet with all this advanced industry with excellent production they still avoided the use of iron as far as possible, even "ironing" their garments with blocks of wood.

The development of industry also caused division and controversy. Some of the community wanted to develop these industries so they could be a source of financial support through trade as well as of immediate service to themselves. To the mind of Conrad Beissel this was to depart from the purely spiritual life of renunciation and to go in pursuit of mammon. There was bitter because sincere contention. This was brought to an end on a winter night in 1747 when several of the mills burned down, proof as Beissel said that God did not approve of this profitable labor.

In contrast with these practical industries, which from the standpoint of Conrad Beissel were in danger of becoming profitable, there was the art of singing. This was possibly even more exclusively associated with their spiritual

Display initial "G" from
the Kloster font

A decoration for chapter
ends

Watermark used in Ephrata paper mill for commercial work

Display type from the Kloster font made at Ephrata prior to 1748

From *German Sectarians of Pennsylvania* by Julius F. Sachse

life than the art of printing and bookmaking. It was directly associated with their worship and consisted altogether in the writing, composing, and singing of hymns and anthems.

This art originated out of the severe German and Genevan chorales of the Reformation. In America its development was first influenced by the learned Peter Miller who joined the Brethren of Ephrata in 1735 and by Ludwig Blum, a trained musician, who was a master singer and was also skilled in composition. He came in 1738, and to him much credit is due. Somewhat later Conrad Beissel himself, with his versatile originality, took charge of the singing and incorporated into the singing much of his theoretical symbolism, thus uniting it more closely to their religious beliefs and at the same time giving it a peculiar cast of technique both in writing and in execution which was quite consonant with their daily community life.

The peculiarity of the Ephrata music in its composition was that though barred like modern music in its notation it was free and that the accent of the word was observed but not the accent of the bar. The first and other notes were sometimes lengthened. It seems to have been somewhat like chanting. It was written sometimes in two or four parts, but usually in five, six or seven parts. There was a folio volume of anthems all of which were set in seven parts. Many of the Brethren and Sisters composed hymn-tunes; there were in all more than a thousand pieces of original music in their collection. The rendering of the music also was specially adapted to the effect desired. It

GOTT ein Derrscher aller Heyden, der sein Volck bald wird herrlich leiten, und ihr Recht lassen hoch hergehn: wenn ER Zion schön wird schmücken, ihr Heil wird lassen näher rücken, so wird man Freud und Wonne sehn

an Seinem Eigenthum, das nun giebt Preiß und Ruhm GOTT dein König, der sie erhöht, ihr Völcker sehet wie GOttes Braut nun einhergeht. 196.

Seven Part Ephrata Choral

The original MS. is called *Paradisisches Wunder-spiel*

From *German Sectarians of Pennsylvania* by Julius F. Sachse
The Historical Society of Pennsylvania have in their archives many manuscripts and documents bearing upon the life at Ephrata

was sung in a falsetto voice without opening wide the lips, which, wrote one of the Brethren, "throws the sound up to the ceilling and the melody, which seems to be more than human, appears to be descending from above and hovering over the heads of the assembly." There was also an elaborate antiphonal singing introduced into the singing.

Conrad Beissel further carried his discipline as choir-master to the extent of requiring each of the singers in the seven voices to observe a distinct diet adapted to the perfecting of those voices. He taught no less that purity of heart and spirit and a clean godly life was essential to the proper rendering of this music. Accordingly he required that all the singers appear at all rehearsals and services in snow-white garments, a rule which he also followed himself. It would be difficult for us to judge the musical effect of these principles and practices, but when we consider the fine results achieved by these same people in their building, in their printing, and in their bookmaking, we will be ready to believe they achieved similar distinctive results in their music. Nonetheless the eminence of Ephrata has passed, though in history it is remembered, and more than that, is treasured.

CHAPTER VII

At Moravian Bethlehem

EPHRATA was an instance of the extreme in community life. The extreme always sacrifices. At Ephrata the extreme sacrificed the normal to its own special ideas. But the normal while seldom very striking is more beneficent, and lasts longer. Among the many German sects in Pennsylvania there was one which while having a strong community character was distinctively normal —the Moravians of Bethlehem. "Blessed is the country that has no annals." Bethlehem, "at the Forks of the Delaware," as it used to be described, was a community that had quiet annals. The ways of the Moravians were the ways of peace, not only with others, but among themselves. They were apt to think things over and to correct their course when it was not leading in the right direction. They instinctively understood that there were standpoints other than their own, and their impulse with others was to bring people together and to try to harmonize the attitude of all in mutual understanding and co-operation. Accordingly they made substantial and lasting progress in many lines.

The great leader of the Moravians was Count Nikolaus Ludwig von Zinzendorf (1700–1760), who carried on in

Europe and in America the standards of their heroes, Jan
Hus (1369–1415) and Johan Amos Comenius (1592–
1670). Zinzendorf impressed his character on his people as

The staircase in the great hall—Millbach, Lebanon County,
Pennsylvania, 1752

Drawn from *The House of the Miller of Millbach* © Pennsylvania Museum of Art

truly as did Conrad Beissel on his monastics at Ephrata,
but more truly, he expressed in himself the stronger and
finer characteristics of the Moravians. The life of the
Moravians under his inspiration had great results. They
produced buildings of a specially monumental character;
their leading institutions were strongly educational; their
public construction boldly advanced in the direction which

later was to be called engineering; their prevailing interest —indeed habit—was musical; and in all these lines what they have done has continued with increasing influence down to the present day.

The first house in Bethlehem, 1741
From a sketch copyrighted by August H. Leibert

The first house erected by the Moravians was built of logs. It was 40 feet long and 20 feet wide, one story high. It was divided into two parts: in the larger part the people lived; in the other their animals were sheltered. The Moravian settlements were as truly church organizations as were the Puritan settlements of New England, but the Unitas Fratrum or Moravian Church was not antifestal in its principles and traditions. On Sunday, December 24, 1741, which was Christmas Eve, they had all gathered in their single log house on the edge of the forest, and with them had gathered a number of neighbors from some miles distance, for a special service. Count Zinzendorf had arrived in America and had come to visit them and commune with them.

89

With the Christmas theme uppermost, their devotions were protracted until after nine o'clock. Their humble sanctuary, with beasts of the stall sharing its roof, brought the circumstances of the Saviour's birth vividly before their imaginations. It stirred the quick fancy of the Count, always keenly responsive to such impressions. Acting upon an impulse he rose and led the way into the part of the building where the cattle were kept, while he began to sing a German Epiphany hymn, "Jesu, rufe mich," of which two stanzas went:

Nicht Jerusalem,	Not Jerusalem,
Sondern Bethlehem	Rather Bethlehem
Hat bescheret	Gave us that which
Was uns naehret;	Maketh life rich;
Nicht Jerusalem.	Not Jerusalem.
Werthes Bethlehem,	Honored Bethlehem,
Du bist angenehm;	Pleasant I esteem;
Aus dir kommet	From thee springeth
Was mir frommet,	What gain bringeth;
Werthes Bethlehem!	Honored Bethlehem!

By general consent the name of the ancient town of David was adopted and the place was called Bethlehem.[1]

These ancient buildings of the Moravians at Bethlehem, now nearly 200 years old, are a monumental group. They are of stone, of durable structure, and fine mediæval character, with high two-story roofs, small windows and nobility of design. The monument of the whole monumental group is the Bell House, completed in 1745. Originally the Bell House was a tower, built directly across a street with

[1]Abbreviated from the account of Bishop J. F. Levering.

a passage through it, the doors of which were and still are kept unlocked from sunrise to sunset in honor of the old-time right of way. The tower was that part of the present building which extends from one chimney to the other, the two chimneys rising on the sides of the tower. Later, additions were built on either side and the Bell Tower became a connecting element between these two newer buildings and thus itself an integral part of the group. Even so, the Bell House, as it was thereafter called, was hardly less monumental. The group is a monumental unit with its various parts contributing to the whole, as do the various parts, chapels, cloisters of an English College or Gothic Cathedral.

From the day it was completed the Bell House was the center of their life. "Watch and Pray!" The entire congregation was divided into 19 Prayer-Bands, to maintain the "hourly intercession," changing every hour on the hour between 5 o'clock in the morning and midnight. Then the night-watch went on—a man in the Chapel, a woman in the woman's dormitory, and another man patrolling the premises outdoors—until 5 o'clock. They called out the hours until July, 1742, when a bell was procured and hung to a tree near by. Then a timekeeper and bellringer was appointed, the first being Joachim Senseman. In June, 1746, the six-sided Bell Turret was erected and in it three bells were mounted, one large and two small, cast by Samuel Powell at his foundry on the south side of the river. The first Town Clock, constructed by Augustine Neissen of

Germantown, was installed in this cupola also, in 1747. The beautiful weather vane on top of the Bell Turret, enfiguring the Lamb bearing the Banner of the Cross, the

The Bell House, Bethlehem

The first girls' boarding school in America, established in 1746

emblem of the Moravian Church, was also cast by Samuel Powell from a design by the young Bishop Cammerhoff (1721–1751).

This little Bell House is truly the center of Bethlehem!

It is easy to see that the central window on the second floor, the one having four panes of glass across instead of three, originally went down to the floor line and was a door. There

The weather-vane on Bell Tower

Redrawn from Albert H. Sonn's *Early American Wrought Iron*

was a balcony here over the main entrance to or through the Bell House, for the use of musicians. Zinzendorf and the first settlers named the place with the singing of a Christmas carol. Zinzendorf very soon organized Sing-stunden when the people of Bethlehem came together regularly to sing hymns and chorales under trained musicians and to rehearse systematically in the art. Not a few of those

93

who came in the earlier ships brought musical instruments with them in the use of which they were skilled, and later there were twilight serenades consisting of instrumental concerts. At the early 4 o'clock Easter morning service in

Count Zinzendorf. After a print in Levering's *History of Bethlehem, Pa.*

1744, the beautiful Moravian custom was started of all going in procession singing hymns with instrumental accompaniment to the little God's Acre, then containing only three or four graves, there to greet the rising sun. Thus was started the noble tradition of the Trombone Choirs of Bethlehem and its Oratorio Societies.

The trombones became the sacred musical instruments

of Bethlehem. It is said that at the time of the Indian massacre at the Moravian missionary post of Gnadenhutten on November 24, 1755, Bethlehem was naturally the place of refuge from the raids of the savages. Thither fugitives poured in from all along the frontier. In one day 208 children were brought in. There was intense anxiety among the vigilant but peaceful people. Definite information had been received that the Indians were determined to make an end of the two towns, Bethlehem and Nazareth, and clear the region of white people by the time of "their great day." At four o'clock on that dreaded Christmas morning, the music of the trombone from the roof-terrace of the Brethren's House ushered in "the great day." The people rose quietly and began their daily routine; and the night watch went off duty. There is a tradition that the music of that Christmas morning chorale breaking the dead silence in the darkness was wafted to the startled ears of the savages lurking on the hillside ready to attack, and that the strange sweet sounds struck fear into their hearts. So they slipped away into the woods, in dread of some unearthly power guarding Bethlehem. Other Indians, to whom the prowlers had spoken about it, told the Bethlehem people of it.

Among the larger musical instruments in Bethlehem the first was a spinet, which came over in the *Little Strength,* landing in New York, and transported by water with all the other heavy baggage to New Brunswick, and thence hauled by wagon to Bethlehem early in 1755. It was given by an English member of the church, a fanmaker of London, William Peter Knolton by name. The spinet, it is recorded, "looked very delapidated" on arrival but skilled hands at once got busy on it and "put it together," so that they could use it the next day in worship.

Bethlehem's first pipe organ was made and set up by the Moravian organ-builder, John Gottlob Klemm, in 1757. He then came to Bethlehem to live, and made a number of organs for towns and villages in that part of Pennsylvania. He associated with him a skillful joiner or cabinetmaker named David Tanneberger, who after Klemm's death in 1762 continued the making of organs and became one of the best known organ builders in the Colonies long before he died in 1804.

Bethlehem had the first symphony orchestra in America. In 1748 their orchestra numbered 14, consisting of

2 first violins	1 double bass
2 second violins	2 flutes
2 violas	2 trumpets
1 cello	2 French horns

By 1771, it numbered 20, having added five woodwind and started the tympani with

2 bassoons	1 clarinet
2 oboes	1 kettle drum

It then included all the instruments used in the European orchestras of the time. The Forks of the Delaware have always been pre-eminently a center of the musical art.

Zinzendorf was a planner of vision and of practical common sense, quite of the type of William Penn. So too some of his associates, such as Henry Antes, who suggested to Count Zinzendorf for the developing of the region around their station of Nazareth the opening of six "plantations" or settlements, each with a complete set of buildings and occupied by six families living and working together in a co-operative agriculture their fields, stockyards, dairy, and orchards. In this way would be established an important source of food and of support for their people wherever they were, in Bethlehem or out in the mission field. Nazareth was to be the center of their farming, and Bethlehem the center of their manufacturing and trade. The families selected for these locations were such as would be suited to the special work to be done there. In October, 1743, the sites for these farms were selected, each one where there was a copious spring flowing at that time. If the spring was apt to run dry at any time during the year it would be in October; accordingly they were reasonably certain of a steady water supply.

With the approach of the first harvests, both around Nazareth and around Bethlehem, agricultural expansion began. A large barn was built; it was "raised" on October 15, 1742. A threshing floor was constructed also. In August they began to cut rye and wheat at Nazareth and at Bethlehem, and giving thanks therefor with a special service. Then while the men mowed the oats, the women pulled flax. A grist mill was started near the spring at Bethlehem on January 25, 1743, and the first grist was ground on June 28. The industries of Bethlehem were now definitely started.

Education was among the first definite interests of the

A Lebanon County decorated dower chest and German pottery of the late eighteenth century from the Edwin Atlee Barber collection

Drawn from *The House of the Miller of Millbach* © Pennsylvania Museum of Art

Moravians as soon as they settled. They provided for a home for the children as well as for their teaching. In June, 1742, these schools started with a number of children brought from Moravian families in Germantown. In a few years all was running well. In the Bell House that first little boarding-school for girls in America was quartered from 1746 to 1790, with the more mature title of The Seminary for Young Ladies. It still continues its work under the

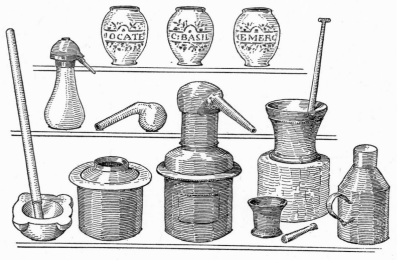

Apothecary's utensils, 1752

At the top are porcelain drug-pots of which the early apothecary had many on his shelves

name of The Moravian Seminary and College for Women.

In the summer and autumn of 1742 several small log houses were built for various emergency uses. One had a room in which meals could be served to strangers who stopped at Bethlehem. These strangers were not always pleasant to welcome into their homes; they were not always respectful to the Moravian ways of life and thought and religion. This room in the log house was then the first step toward a hotel. On July 11, 1743, the congregation considered providing for a regular tavern on the other side of the river, both as a convenience for the strangers and as a means of keeping undesirable people out of their own homes. In the same year a Swedish neighbor named Yssel-

The Crown Inn near Bethlehem, Pa., 1757
From *The Crown Inn near Bethlehem* by W. C. Reichel

stein arranged to give such accommodations. In March, 1745, "The Tavern over ye Water" was really started, a few rods east of the ferry (about where the passenger railroad station is now), and it was opened in charge of Samuel Powell, the same who cast the bells and the weather-vane for the Bell House. Samuel Powell also had charge of the first bookstore, which he maintained in the tavern, both enterprises being at first under public authority. Later, the tavern was given the name of the Crown Inn.

The Crown Inn was 40 feet long and 28 feet wide, compactly built of white oak logs. It had two stories and a high gable roof. There were four rooms on each story, floored with 1½-inch white oak planks. The posts of the studding were grooved to receive cross pieces with a filling

The Sun Inn, Bethlehem, 1763

From J. M. Levering's *History of Bethlehem, Pa.* © Congregation of United Brethren

of cut straw and clay. The posts of the doors and windows also were worked out from solid timbers. The latches and bolts were of wood. There was not a nail in the entire inn but had been wrought by hand from horseshoes by the nailsmith over the river in Bethlehem. When after standing for 113 years it was finally demolished by an unappreciative generation in 1858, the whole structure was still sound to the core.

Bethlehem was the center of industry and trade for that region. Travel increased. In 1758 another tavern was built, up in the town, called the Sun Inn. At first there was some preference given to Moravians here at the Sun Inn, while strangers were still encouraged to stop at The Tavern over ye Water. For crossing the river the means was until 1758 the ordinary ferry. In that year a rope ferry was instituted, the same year the new inn was built. Both improvements were naturally connected with the increase of travel that had also demanded a highway between Easton and Reading in 1754. Bethlehem however took quite the modern stand toward through traffic and objected to the highway going directly through the town, and urged that it be routed a little to one side. It is of the nature of through traffic ultimately to have its way. In 1786 a bridge was built across the Lehigh River leading straight to the Sun Inn. It was this bridge incidentally that put an end to the Crown Inn as a hostelry.

Hospitals and hotels had a closely common origin at Bethlehem. The fitting up of a room in one of the early little log houses resulted in the Crown Inn and the Sun Inn. A room in another of these little log houses was fitted up in 1742 for the care of sick men. Sick women were taken care of in the Community House. At this time eight men and seven women were appointed as nurses under the direction of the physician of the settlement, Doctor Adolf Meyer. Certain of these he designated and trained to be assistants in the dispensary and to collect medicinal roots and herbs for his primitive pharmacy. It was all systematic.

One result of this intelligent interest in the care of the sick, and also of their experience in living the community life for a while, was that in time of need the Moravians

Bethlehem September the 22d 1777

Having here observed a humane and diligent attention to the sick and wounded, and a benevolent desire to make the necessary provision for the relief of the distressed, as far as the powers of the Brethren enable them. We desire that all Continental Officers may refrain from disturbing the persons or property of the Moravians in Bethlehem, and particularly that they do not disturb or molest the Houses where the women are assembled. Given under our hands at the time and place above mentioned.

Nathan Brownson, Richard Henry Lee
Nathl. Folsom
Richard Law
John Hancock
Samuel Adams
Elipht Dyer
Jas. Duane

Wm. Duer
Cornl. Harnett
Henry Laurens
Benj. Harrison
Jos. Jones
John Adams
Henry Marchant
Wm. Williams

Subject to Congress

Order of Safeguard

From J. M. Levering's *History of Bethlehem, Pa.* © Congregation of the United Brethren of Pennsylvania

of Bethlehem, without departing from their non-combatant principles, were twice able to render humane service of very great value. At the time of the Gnadenhutten Massacre in 1755 they organized the whole town as a place of refuge with a population double its normal size. Benjamin Franklin wrote to the Governor from Bethlehem:

We found this place filled with refugees, the workmen's shops and even cellars being crowded with women and children, and we learned that Lehi [Lehigh] Township is almost abandoned by its inhabitants.

One report said that a total of 639 refugees were received. But the Moravians took care of them all.

Again in the Revolutionary War practically the whole town became a hospital, and a very efficient one, for the Continental Army during two periods, from December 3, 1776, to March 27, 1777, and from September 17, 1777, to April 14, 1778, including the months that Washington and his army were at Valley Forge. The autograph letter of grateful appreciation that General Washington wrote to the citizens for this patriotic service is treasured in the archives of the town. In both cases when the emergency had passed the people returned without delay to their normal methods of living on a family and individual basis.

Another industry with which these people rendered important service in the Revolution was the manufacture of rifles. The British Army used a smooth-bore musket, as did the European armies generally, and most of the American colonies. It was well adapted for European warfare, which consisted largely of volley firing at close range, and in which rapid loading was important. The rifle was a Swiss invention. The Swiss and Palatine immigrants brought with them to Pennsylvania a knowledge of the rifle. It was

Henry Young's gun factory

From *The Gun Makers of Old Northampton* by William Jacob Heller
Pennsylvania German Society Proceedings, Vol. XVII

specially well adapted to hunting and to the individual fighting of the frontier in which slow loading was not a serious disadvantage. The backwoodsman was a sharp-shooter. The Americans steadily improved the rifle from the beginning. One of the chief improvements was finding that if the bullet was made slightly smaller than the bore and was inserted with a bit of well-greased cloth, which was called a patch, the rifle could be loaded faster; the fabric was pressed into the rifle-grooves, preventing the escape of gas at the side of the bullet and so increased the force of the shot; and it gave the bullet an extra spin which kept it on a straight course for a longer distance. Whereas the smooth-bore was effective at 100 yards, the rifle was effective at 200 yards. Naturally it became the great American backwoods weapon.

Often a frontiersman cared for his rifle with a personal feeling, as a musician for his violin, and decorated it himself, carving out a design on the stock, melting a piece of silver or gold, and pouring it into the design.

The Scotch-Irish, when they began to pour in about 1720, were just the men to use the weapon the Pennsylvania Germans made. Accordingly when Daniel Morgan —in blood, incidentally, part Scotch-Irish and part Pennsylvania German—came up from Virginia through Pennsylvania, recruiting as he came, to join Washington before Boston in the summer of 1775, he brought a force equipped with the rifle, every man carrying not only a rifle but his own rifle. It was a force of sharpshooters. The Pennsylvania craftsmen now simply increased their output. The Committee of Safety of Northampton County, Pennsylvania, for instance, passed a resolution debarring from combat service all men having knowledge of the making of any part of these rifles. Such men must work at that occupation. This they did, at Allentown, Easton, Bethlehem, Nazareth, and elsewhere in Pennsylvania-German land as far down as Lancaster County. At Durham they also made cannon. The result told with effect, not only before Boston, but

Drawn from photographs furnished by Captain J. G. W. Dillin, Media, Pa.

1-2. Early Pennsylvania flint-lock rifle, showing both sides. 3. Hunting bag and powder-horn. 4. Pennsylvania Indian powder-horn reproduced large enough to show primitive decoration. 5. Mechanism of a flint-lock rifle, note flint held in jaws of hammer. 6. A 1729 Pennsylvania rifle

before Quebec, and at Saratoga, Kings Mountain and the Cowpens.

Akin to their hospital work, and distinctly an advance in their peaceful development, were the measures the people

The water works at Bethlehem said to be the first in the country

of Bethlehem took to provide for a pure and sufficient water supply. This was engineering. The site of Bethlehem in the first place was chosen at a good spring. There beside this spring the first tree was cut to mark the location. In March, 1747, the spring was enclosed by a fence to keep domestic animals and barnyard fowl away, and two men were instructed to clear the spring out under the most favorable circumstances, which was stated to be in the conditions found "in the light of the moon." This condition was not imposed again in 1754 when the Brethren undertook to find a better way to bring the water up the hill to the town and a better way to distribute it than by buckets in carts. Water power ran the oil and bark mills near by. Let it do more work. A water tower up on the hill and one or two tanks it would be quite possible to construct. Pipes to carry the water and a pump would be essential. Bethlehem had in Hans Christiansen and John Boehner two men who were equal to the problem, and should be recognized as pioneer engineers. Carefully selected trunks of hemlock were rafted down the Lehigh River from Gnadenhutten. From these the water pipes were made. On June 21, 1754, the water was successfully forced through them as high as the homes in the square on the bluff above. On May 25, 1755, water flowed into the tower, and on June 27, 1755, from the water tower into the tanks. The operation of the first American public utility of its kind, the Bethlehem Water Works, had begun!

On religious occasions the played from of Moravian and solemn trombone is the belfries churches

CHAPTER VIII

Scotch-Irish in the Mountains

THE third great immigration to Pennsylvania started in or about 1720—the Scotch-Irish. The difference between these people and the Pennsylvania Germans was not merely in whence they came or in their blood; it was in their temperament. The Scotch were of the Nordic race—conquering, alert, roving, fiery; the Pennsylvania Germans were of the Alpine race—contented, steady, domestic, agricultural. Any one who expected them to get along well together would not comprehend the nature of either; also, he would fail to comprehend the great achievement of the Melting Pot of America which was then and there beginning to accomplish its work.

The chief entrance of the Scotch-Irish into Pennsylvania was by way of the Chesapeake Bay, around the Quaker settlements, and up the west bank of the Susquehanna River, past the Pennsylvania Germans, and turning the corner to the southwest up the Cumberland and the Juniata Valleys. So on up into the mountains in pursuit of the receding frontier.

To the Quakers and the Germans the aggressive Scotch-Irish seemed a wild lot, savage, relentless, trouble-seeking and trouble-making, untamable. To the Scotch-Irish the Quakers and Germans were a spiritless, land-grabbing, money-loving lot of unpatriotic cowards. The Provincial officials seemed to have changed their view of the Scotch-Irish with the circumstances. They had poured into the interior and settled where they pleased, with a disregard for regulations that must have been distinctly annoying to the government clerks. James Logan, William Penn's trusted representative, in 1730, though he was himself an Ulsterman, complained of them that they had "in an audacious and disorderly manner" intruded into the Conestoga Manor, a district of 15,000 acres, reserved by the Penn family for themselves, without leave gained or asked, and settled there. To this the Scotch-Irish opposed the argument that "it was against the laws of God and nature that so much land should be idle while so many Christians wanted it to labor on and raise their bread." Later generations may thank them for saving Pennsylvania from the curse of absentee landlordism, but the Penn family and their able and eminent representative did not appreciate the value of this consideration at the time.

A year earlier, in 1729, at a less prejudiced moment, James Logan said of these same people:

About that time (1720) considerable numbers of good sober people came in from Ireland who wanted to be settled. . . . At the same time it happened we were under some apprehensions from the Northern Indians (the Iroquois). . . . I therefore thought it might be prudent to plant a settlement of such men as those who formerly had so bravely defended Londonderry and Inniskillen as a frontier, in case of any disturbance.

Very perspicacious! James Logan knew his countrymen! Not only in time of trouble but in time of peace, or let us say in quiet times, for they could change their behavior very quickly. He went on to say:

These people however if kindly used will, I believe, be orderly, as they have hitherto been, and easily dealt with. They will also, I expect, be a leading example to others.

Can one find anywhere a better description of a Scotchman filtered through Ulster into the Allegheny Mountains!

The attitude of the Scotch-Irish toward the Indians was very different from that of the Quakers and the Germans. They did not distinguish between one Indian and another, which was a grave mistake. But neither did their critics. They knew nothing of the politics of the Indian tribes, of the wars of extermination among the Iroquois, the Algonquins, the Abenaki, the Ojibways, the Lenni-Lenape, and the Shawnees, with the French all along the mountain frontier pressing them down upon the English settlements. When an Indian suddenly appeared out of the forest with his tomahawk in hand, the Scotch-Irishman saw only imminent danger for his wife and children, and there was no time for inquiry or debate. He killed him.

Their theology also proved, indeed authorized, this attitude toward the Indians. John Knox Presbyterianism was the great revelation of righteousness to them. They knew that they were the spearhead of the new white man's civilization in America. They did not shrink from the responsibility; they were proud of it and intent on making a record. Accustomed no doubt to ascertain the will of God in particular emergencies by closing the eyes, opening the Holy Bible at random and putting the finger on a passage, it seems probable, especially as more than three-quarters of the Bible is in the Old Testament, that the finger fell upon some passage in the belligerent Book of Joshua often enough to be quite convincing as to what the general attitude should be. And the women were of the same stuff as the men, which confirmed the clear directions of Holy Writ. Imagine stealthy Indians skulking about in the forest outside your cabin looking for a chance to murder and torture your brave wife and precious children, and then read these words at the end of your finger:

And when the Lord thy God shall deliver them before thee, thou shalt smite them and utterly destroy them; thou shalt make no covenant with them, nor show mercy unto them.

During all the eighteenth century, until after the Revolutionary War, the Allegheny Mountains were the frontier. In the daily life of the Scotch-Irish there were just four things that were essential—the rifle, the backwoods axe, the fort or blockhouse, and the trail, later to become a road, connecting them with their source of supplies and their markets back east and following their spearhead farther and farther on toward the Ohio and the West. Heroic equals with them as well as of them were such men as Daniel Morgan (1736–1802) and George Rogers Clark (1752–1818) and Daniel Boone (1735–1820). But there were plenty others—Simon Kenton, Campbell, Shelby, Robertson, Sevier. The woods were full of them. These were the men who used the rifles they made in the eastern part of the Province, who made a fine art of their use.

Fearless, taciturn, silent historically, there was one boy of them who grew up to be a minister among them, but who knew them himself and who made some *Notes*—the Rev. Joseph Doddridge (1769–1826). These *Notes* give a first-hand account of the daily life of his father and mother, his brothers and sisters, his grandfather and grandmother, their relatives and neighbors, the Indian attacks and outrages, and their defenses and revenge.

Settlers began to come over to the western slope of the mountains along the Monongahela River in 1772. They came from Maryland and Virginia by Braddock's Trail, or from Pennsylvania along the military road through Bedford. Doddridge's father brought his family in 1773 on horses with their few things on pack-saddles. The Indian meal they had did not last until they could raise some corn or grain. For six weeks they had to live by the rifle. Lean venison and the breast of wild turkey the parents called "bread," bear's meat was "meat." Eagerly the children watched the growth of the potatoes, corn, and pumpkin vines, and when they ate the first young potatoes they celebrated the new supply of real bread.

By general understanding and consent there was an extra way of acquiring land which dispensed with some of the legal formalities. It was called the "tomahawk right" and consisted of deadening a few trees near a spring and marking the bark of one with the initials of the settler. This was

On horseback with his few belongings on pack-saddles the settler invaded the western slope of the Alleghenies

quicker than the more formal way by "taking up." This consisted of building a cabin and raising a crop of grain, which gave legal right to 400 acres with a valid claim by certain further procedure to 1000 acres more adjoining.

When a cabin was to be built, whether for a new couple or for a newly arriving family, the neighbors gathered; and distance was no interference. The first day a party of choppers went out to fell trees and cut them into proper lengths, while one man with a team hauled them to the place and piled them where they would be used, at the sides and ends of the future cabin. Another man searched the woods for a proper tree for making the clapboards for the roof; it must be straight-grained and from three to four feet in diameter. Others got together puncheons for the floor, made by splitting trees about eighteen inches in diameter and hewing their faces with a broad axe. The first day supplied the timbers.

The first thing to be done the second day was to elect the four corner men, who notched and placed the logs as they were brought to them by the others. This required skill. The door was made by cutting an opening through the logs about three feet wide and putting up timbers for the sides of the doorway. A place for the chimney was made in the same way at the end of the cabin, only it was a wider opening with room for a back and jambs of stone. The roof was made by shortening the logs at the ends until a single log would form the ridge.

The third day some made mortar and filled in the chinks between the logs, while others made the door itself of clapboards, levelled off the floor, and made a built-in bed, a table and a few stools. Some pegs around the walls supplied a convenient place to hang the "coats" (petticoats) of the women and the hunting shirts of the men. It also showed people who came by how well off they were in clothes. A pair of buck's horns fastened to a joist for the rifle and the shot-pouch completed the structure. Then came the housewarming before the owners were given possession. This was a dance which lasted all night long, when the neighbors all had a good time.

With most "farms" consisting of 400 acres, it will be seen that neighbors were not very near each other. This would be all right in quiet times, but in case of Indian attacks, neighborliness had a more serious part to perform in the daily life. Doddridge tells how in case of an alarm, the "express," one of the neighbors, came softly in the night to the door or the back window and by a gentle tapping aroused the family. Care was taken not to waken the youngest child. The whispered word "Indians!" was enough to ensure quiet with the others. Getting quickly together rifle and ammunition and what else they could, they made off silently through the forest to the fort.

The fort was a place of co-operative defense. This is summed up by Doddridge in one sentence.

The fort to which my father belonged was, during the first years of the war, three-quarters of a mile from his farm.

It was not only a place of defense in time of emergency but a place where several settlers had their cabins together, each building as it were on the corner of his farm. In time of trouble there was thus always a group on hand to whom others could gather. Indian warfare, and sometimes Indian amusement too, consisted of indiscriminate slaughter of all ages and both sexes by means of the most fiendish cruelty. Preparedness, co-operation, and vigilance were their only protection!

The fort consisted of cabins, blockhouses and stockades. A range of cabins commonly formed one side at least of the fort. Divisions or partitions of logs separated the cabins from each other. The walls on the outside were ten or twelve feet high, the slope of the roof being turned wholly inward. A very few of these cabins had puncheon floors, the greater part were earthen. The blockhouses were built at the angles of the fort. They projected about two feet beyond the outer walls of the cabins and stockades. Their upper stories were about eighteen inches every way larger in dimension than the under one, leaving an opening at the commencement of the second story to prevent the enemy from making a lodgment under their walls. In some forts, instead of blockhouses, the angles of the fort were furnished with bastions. A large folding gate made of thick slabs, nearest the spring, closed the fort. The stockades, bastions, cabins and blockhouse walls were furnished with portholes at proper heights and distances. The whole of the outside was made completely bullet-proof. . . . In some places less exposed a single blockhouse, with a cabin or two, constituted the whole fort.

Bedford has been spoken of as a town. It was at one period Fort Bedford; it had a notable as well as typical history for the mountains. There in 1751 a Scotch-Irishman named Ray built one and then two or three cabins, on a bluff about thirty or forty feet above the river. The place was a natural crossroads. Within a mile or two at most, trails following streams went in five or six directions—down to Fort Cumberland, up to Fort Ligonier, across to Carlisle and Chambersburg in the Cumberland Valley, across the mountains to Fort Duquesne, and down the Juniata to Pennsylvania proper. The three cabins that Ray built became a fort, probably at first with the name of Rays-

118

town, as the stream is still called the Raystown Branch of the Juniata. In 1758 Brigadier-General John Forbes (1710–1759) camped at Bedford and made it the rendezvous for his expedition against Fort Duquesne. There Colonel Montgomery with his Highlanders, Lieutenant-Colonel Henry Bouquet with the Royal Americans, and Lieutenant-Colonel George Washington with the Provincials, 7000 troops in all, assembled. From Bedford General Forbes started his quite modern campaign, building a road through the mountains with forts at intervals that soon resulted in changing Fort Duquesne to Fort Pitt and then to Pittsburgh. He himself was suffering from a very painful sickness, but he never flinched; he had himself carried the whole way on a stretcher. In December he was taken back to Philadelphia, and he died there the following March, 1759. Major George Armstrong of the Pennsylvania forces was in command of the roadmakers. It was at this time that Fort Bedford was built. In 1761 the town was laid out for the Penn family by John Armstrong. Additions were later made to the original log fort, first of stone and then of brick, and the parade ground became finally a public square. The noted old fort was destroyed by fire on December 14, 1885.

The dress of the people in these mountain regions was very different from the splendid uniforms of the European soldiers. The men universally wore a hunting shirt reaching half way down the thighs, with large sleeves, open in front, and so wide as to lap over a foot or more when belted. Over this they wore a cape which was sometimes handsomely fringed with ravelled cloth of a different color. The hunting shirt was generally made of linsey-woolsey, a cloth made of linen and wool, or sometimes of a coarse linen; a few were made of dressed deer skins, but these were very cold and uncomfortable in wet weather. On the feet they wore "moccasins" made of a single piece of deer skin and bound around the lower part of the leg with thongs of deerskin, so that no dust, gravel, or snow could get inside the moccasin. In cold weather the moccasins were well stuffed with deer's hair or dry leaves to keep the feet comfortably warm.

The belt, which was always tied behind, served more than one purpose. It held up the breeches. It fastened in the hunting shirt and thereby also made of the large overlap a wallet to carry a chunk of bread, a good-sized piece of "jerk" or dried meat, a bunch of tow for wiping the barrel of the rifle, which was always kept clean and highly polished inside and out, and anything else they wanted to carry and have conveniently at hand for the hunt or for the fight. On the right side the tomahawk hung on the belt; on the left the knife in its leather sheath. In cold weather the mittens and the bullet bag hung in front.

For food, wild meat was plentiful and easily obtained. As the meat was wild some kind of bread and some vegetables were specially important. Every cabin had a truck garden of a half-acre or more close by, which the wife and the older children took care of. Later a small field of grain brought real bread to the table. But from the first settling they had potatoes, pumpkins, beans and corn, and soon a cow and a few pigs gave them milk and pork. So the table afforded them a diet of "hog and hominy," johnny cake and corn pone, and mush and milk within a short time. Supper usually consisted of mush and milk. When milk

Study on the frontier by light from the open fireplace

was not plenty, whether from scarcity of cows or of pasture, mush was eaten with sweetened water, molasses, bear's oil, or the gravy of fried meat. The standard eating for every log rolling, house raising, harvest day or whenever the neighbors got together, was a pot pie!

The dishes were mostly woodenware. How natural it was that the people themselves spoke of them as the table furniture! There were a few pewter plates and spoons but wooden bowls, trenchers, and noggins were what they used mostly everywhere through the mountains. The knives and forks and the pots and kettles were brought on pack horses from the eastern side of the mountains along with the salt, and the other ironware. When needed, utensils made of gourds and of hard-shelled squashes were used too. They did not have tea and coffee and did not want either, for quite a while. When they first came, the real pioneers said they were only slops, and complained that they did not stick to the ribs. When china first appeared they had no use for it. It broke so easily they felt any one selling it to them was cheating them; and besides it dulled the edge of their knives as compared with their woodenware.

Tea, coffee, and china they could do without. But salt, iron and steel they had to have. The pack-horse and the packer's trail were the means for acquiring the products of the East. Their only practical commodity for exchange at first was peltry. Every family collected what furs they could by hunting and trapping or by trading with the Indians through the year to send them in the fall over the mountains for barter. Later they collected also quantities of potash and alum from the wood ashes. And still later they raised cattle and horses for sale on the Atlantic coast.

In the fall of the year, after seeding time, every family went into a sort of association with some of their neighbors to make up a pack train. A master driver was chosen from among them, and he had with him one or more young men and sometimes also a couple of boys. The horses were fitted out with packsaddles, which were of wood and had high pommels and cantels, pretty cumbrous affairs. Every horse had a little bell on him and the bridle of each was tied to the tail of the horse ahead of him. The horses went in single file of course, as this was before the time of anything that could be truly called a road. The bags provided for the salt on the return trip were filled with feed for the horses. On the way east a part of the feed was left at convenient stages to be picked up on the way back. Large wallets filled with bread, jerk, boiled ham, and cheese supplied food for the drivers. At night the horses were hobbled with hickory withes and the bells were loosened before they were turned out into the woods, so that they could be traced easily if they wandered away.

The destination of the pack trains, whither they went to do their bartering for salt and for iron and steel, was in the earlier days Baltimore; then successively, as trading spread farther west, Frederick, Hagerstown, Oldtown, and Fort Cumberland, which was almost due south of Fort Bedford. Each horse carried two bushels of alum, weighing eighty-four pounds to the bushel. This was not a heavy load for a horse, but it was enough considering the scanty subsistence allowed for the journey. The common price for a bushel of alum salt in the early period was a good cow and calf, and until weights were introduced the salt was measured into a half-bushel by hand as lightly as possible. No one was permitted to walk heavily over the floor while the measuring was going on, lest it shake the alum down into overweight.

One of the chief packer's trails or paths crossed the Allegheny Mountains near where Altoona is now. From there it went down through Bedford and thence followed the Juniata River. Later developments broadened it so that a two-horse stage made regular trips over it and the journey between Pittsburgh and Philadelphia could be accomplished in eight or ten days. By 1817 such primitive conditions as this were left behind and what was formerly appreciated as a wonderful road was called "a mere mudpike." Benefiting by the genius of John Loudon McAdam (1756–1836), also a Scot, the old Packer's Path had become a Turnpike, and Troy coaches with relays of horses travelling eight miles an hour and going all night long made "real travelling" possible! But through sheer speed we are getting far ahead of our story!

The zest of the Scotch-Irish has taken us with them up into the mountains. We must go back through the farm regions below them to the towns and cities with their growing commerce on the coast. Water is ever a bond of union and a means of communication. It took the Scotch-Irish to advance the inland frontier beyond the mountains and thereby duplicate the eastern waters as a means of extending the line of English settlements and English civilization. But they did not accomplish this before the Revolutionary War.

CHAPTER IX

Georgian Mansions

IN ALL the Colonies creative ability through successive generations developed the local products into an important line of exports. This built up a large seagoing commerce both with the mother country and with each other. Started in the seventeenth century, this commerce increased and multiplied in the eighteenth century to the benefit of the people on both sides of the water. Politics unfortunately was to destroy this natural unity. Fishing was from the beginning, indeed from before the first permanent settlements, the great industry of New England, and itself developed considerable shipbuilding, especially in the smaller fishing vessels. Tobacco was the principal export of Virginia, and dominated the agriculture of all that region. Furs found their outlet to European markets through all the ports, from the north through Boston and Salem; from the Great Lakes and the Adirondacks down the great artery of Indian trade supplied by the Mohawk and Hudson rivers and out through New York; from the Allegheny Mountains and the Ohio Valley through Philadelphia. Lumber was a universal cargo from beginning to end; lumber was becoming scarce in England. Shipbuilding became a growing interest in Philadelphia. Capital accumulated rapidly in Philadelphia, from England as well as from the American Colonies, because of the excellent and well-

The one horse shay
From a drawing by Howard Pyle

From *Scribner's Magazine*, 1891

balanced economic procedure in force under the Quakers. The shipbuilding was conducted partly on goods sent over in advance to pay for purchase of timber and the building of ships. Before the Revolutionary War more than one-third of the tonnage afloat under the British flag had been launched from American dockyards, in which Philadelphia led.

In these ways the leading men of the Colonies were

during the eighteenth century acquiring means, and were able as they desired to build handsome houses. Land was inexpensive. Horses were of good breed and good speed. Roads within limited distances were not bad. Neighbors of comparable wealth were sufficiently numerous and near enough to afford a certain companionship with a stimulating touch of rivalry. These conditions made the building of fine houses a real pleasure.

There were no architects in the Colonies, but this lack was not a serious disadvantage. In ample time books on architecture with suggestions for designing new houses began to be issued in England and soon found their way across the ocean. A new spirit, with a new principle expressing it, was revolutionizing architecture in Europe. It started in Italy and was gradually making its way across the Alps, through France, and into England. In Italy the leader was Andrea Palladio (1518–1580). By 1700 it had, so to speak, arrived in America.

This new style of architecture, frequently called the academic, came from the standardizing spirit. Before, during the mediæval centuries, building had proceeded in accordance with the purpose that each part was to serve. A house was built, and if later another room was wanted, all right, another room was added, wherever the owner pleased, and maybe still another. Just as a lean-to was added to an early New England house when another room was wanted, which made it a salt-box house. Or a church was built and a chapel might be added to it, maybe several chapels. But when Palladio's ideas came into fashion, the house was built from the start with strict regard to its exterior symmetrical appearance as a whole. No extra room was tacked on afterward; no chapel was added the place of which in the design

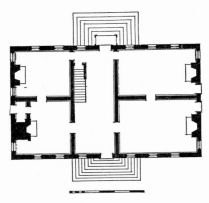

First floor plan, Westover, Va., about 1726

had not been planned from the beginning. Variety in the uses of the parts of the house was provided for by dividing up the interior of the building. Whatever variety there might be inside, it made no difference on the outside; the exterior made a design, single and regular in form by itself. This is strikingly illustrated in the beautiful mansion of Westover in Virginia, built soon after 1726. The exterior is absolutely symmetrical. There is a handsome entrance in the center of each façade, and it would appear that a broad transverse hallway passes between these two entrances through the center of the building dividing the interior into halves. But it does not. A partition passes from one entrance across to

128

the other, and the rooms on one side of the center of the building are half again as large as those on the other side.

It is easily seen that it would have been of no use to write a book about adding new parts to a house in the mediæval period, when people accumulated a house rather than built it all at once. In those days every new part would probably be different from what other people would want. But with the academic spirit in control, it would be quite practicable, quite important to raise a standard, and it was very useful to write books to state that standard, to explain the principles of such standardized building, and to suggest both general designs and details for planning buildings according to good standards. This was the great revolution in architecture. It meant that people were getting to be willing to be alike and to conform to each other's ideas somewhat, willing to be standardized to some extent.

So too the Americans of means and influence. They wanted to have "good architecture" in their new houses. They had seen the new styles in England when they travelled, or certainly had heard about them. They eagerly welcomed the books that described the new standards of residence architecture and that illustrated those standards with specific examples and suggestions. Those books came to all the Colonies, the same to all, and to one about as soon as to another. There naturally resulted a general similarity in the finer houses that were built during the eighteenth century from New England to Georgia. Further, as in their homes people strive to meet their ideals as well as their needs, this similarity in the homes of so many of the influential men of the Colonies made another common interest, one more tie tending to unite them as increasing facilities for communication whether by water or by land made it possible, and as the public questions in dispute with the mother country came inevitably to an issue.

These books should be held in grateful remembrance in America, though now they are only of curious interest. They rendered practical and valuable service. Without them the sightliness of our building and our development in good taste would have been seriously and long delayed. One of the most notable of them was William Halfpenny's *Modern Builder's Assistant,* 1747, which was perhaps the first to give general designs. Those who are interested will find a remarkable collection of these works in the Library of the Metropolitan Museum of Art.

It should be noted as one of the best results of these books that they impelled close attention and careful consideration to the problem of building on the part of those who wanted or needed to engage in new construction. There was no one for them to consult, no one to relieve them of detail questions. Consequently each one tackled his own particular problems with enthusiasm and with pride in what he accomplished. This resulted in a goodly number of amateur architects well distributed through all the Colonies. Of these Thomas Jefferson (1743-1826) was the most famous and one of the best. His study of architecture was both thorough and progressive. Only technically can he be called an ama-

THE

Modern Builder's Assistant;

OR,

A CONCISE EPITOME

Of the Whole

SYSTEM of ARCHITECTURE;

IN WHICH

The various Branches of that excellent Study are eſta-
bliſh'd on the moſt familiar Principles,
And rendered adequate to every Capacity ;
Being uſeful to the Proficient, and eaſy to the Learner.

Divided into THREE PARTS.

CONTAINING

I. A Correct View of the FIVE ORDERS, explained in ſeveral Sheets
of Letter-Preſs.

II. Conſiſting of REGULAR PLANS, ELEVATIONS, and SECTIONS
of HOUSES, in the moſt elegant and convenient Manner, either
for the Reception of Noblemen, Gentlemen or Tradeſmen with
large or ſmall Families, adapted to the Taſte of Town or Country.

To which PART is added,

A great Variety of other PLANS for Offices or Out-Houſes adjoining to
them of different Dimenſions for Domeſtic· Uſes ;

SUCH AS

KITCHENS, WASH-HOUSES, MALT-HOUSES, BAKE-HOUSES, BREW-HOUSES,
DAIRIES, VAULTS, STABLES, COACH-HOUSES, DOG-KENNELS, &c. &c.

Together with the

ESTIMATES of each DESIGN, and Proper INSTRUCTIONS
to the WORKMEN how to execute the ſame.

III. Exhibiting (ornamental as well as plain) a Variety of CHIMNEY-
PIECES, WINDOWS, DOORS, SECTIONS of STAIR-CASES, ROOMS,
HALLS, SALOONS, &c. SKREENS for Rooms, alſo CIELINGS, PIERS,
and GATE-ROOFS, &c. &c.

The Whole beautifully Engraved on EIGHTY FIVE Folio Copper Plates,

From the DESIGNS of

William and *John Halfpenny*, Architects and Carpenters,
Robert Morris, Surveyor,

AND

T. Lightoler. Carver.

LONDON

Printed for JAMES RIVINGTON and J. FLETCHER in Pater-noſter Row, and
ROBERT SAYER oppoſite Fetter-Lane, Fleet-Street.
MDCCLVII.

Title page of William and John Halfpenny's *The Modern Builder's
Assistant*, 1747

teur. It should also be recognized that the builders and artisans working under and with these interested owners were many of them skilled craftsmen. It was a fruitful combination for a new country!

In the building materials used in America during the eighteenth century, masonry became more usual in the houses of men of importance, especially south of New England. In New England wood continued to be used even in some of the finest houses, like the Royall House at Medford, 1733, for excellent lumber was abundant. In choice of masonry, between brick and stone, the local supply usually determined. Brick was so easily made, so convenient to handle, and so distinguished in effect. It was much used wherever there was good clay. Stone houses were really common only in Pennsylvania, where good limestone was abundant.

In the stonework there are two kinds easily distinguished. Rubble was the rough form of masonry, using unhewn stone. Ashlar was the later form, of finer finish, using evenly cut stone. Carving and any approach toward exterior sculpture came later, with the ashlar masonry, on account of the lack in the earlier period of men capable of doing the carving. Governor Thomas Hutchinson had a magnificent house on the front of which four pilasters rose the full three storeys to the eaves, the capitals of which were beautifully carved. For the reason just stated Fiske Kimball is inclined to believe they could not have been erected at the time the house was built by John Foster between 1681 and 1691, but were added by Governor Hutchinson when there was a fire in the roof of the house in 1748. One of these capitals is still preserved, in possession of the Massachusetts Historical Society. The house was gutted by the mob in the Stamp Act riots in 1765.

The Van Cortlandt mansion, at New York, 1748, one of the most important houses of the century, was built mainly of rubble masonry, with brick for the lintels over the windows. But not only so; brick was used also as a filler to even up the stonework to receive the window frames. This suggests that the finest skill in masonry was not here available. But there was no hesitation in attempting new things. Over each of the front windows the central lintel stone is not of brick but of brownstone carved to represent a head, every one different. These heads are worthy of notice and thoroughly enjoyable, the more so as they do not oblige one to acknowledge any attainment in architectural sculpture. Very likely they are the first step in this region.

The little wooden porch in front of the main entrance, not itself the original of course, was in idea an inheritance from the Dutch, who brought their stoop with them from Holland. Such a stoop and its greater development, the piazza, are common throughout the once-Dutch part of New York, and thence spread far. John Singleton Copley (1737–1815), the painter, helped to introduce the piazza to Boston. In a letter he wrote from New York on July 14, 1771, he said to a friend:

You say you dont know what I mean by a Peaza. I will tell you then, it is exactly such a thing as the cover over the pump in your

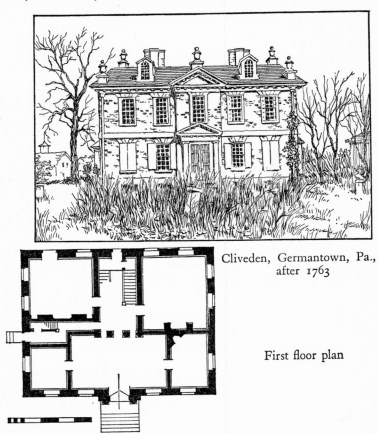

Cliveden, Germantown, Pa.,
after 1763

First floor plan

Yard, suppose no enclosure for Poultry their, and 3 or 4 posts added to support the front of the Roof, a good floor at bottum, and from post to post a Chinese enclosure about three feet high. . . . these Peazas are so cool in Sumer and in Winter break off the storms so much that I think I should not be able to like an house without.

134

Copley had "peazas" on his house very much like those we see on the John Vassall (Longfellow's) house in Cam-

John Vassall (Longfellow) house,
Cambridge, Mass., 1759

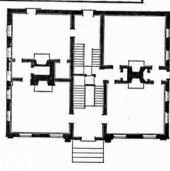

First floor plan

bridge. These are not in architectural descent of the same family as the Portico seen in the Miles Brewton house in Charleston, South Carolina, and in the Roger Morris or Jumel mansion, New York, both 1765, which can trace their more classic descent through the books directly back to Andrea Palladio.

135

With what might almost be called an instinctive compliance with the rule of exterior symmetry, there soon came also an advance in the planning of the interior, from houses one room deep to houses two rooms deep. Four rooms to the floor with a transverse hall became the usual Colonial plan. But the planning of the four rooms was usually quite irregular. The John Vassall house, 1759, where Washington made his headquarters while he was in Cambridge, and where Longfellow lived from 1836 to his death in 1882, was distinctly regular in its interior as in its exterior plan. So too was the Miles Brewton house in Charleston. But generally, inside their homes the men of the 1700's used to like to do as they pleased, however properly they might conform on the outside where they were to be seen of the public. We have noticed that Westover was deliberately unsymmetrical on the inside. So were Cliveden, under attack in the Battle of Germantown; Mount Pleasant in Philadelphia; Mount Airy in Virginia; and many others.

Graeme Park, at Horsham, near Philadelphia, built for Governor Keith in 1721, though dating so far within the eighteenth century, conforms so little, only in the general regularity of mass on the outside, that it may rather be considered as belonging to the earlier period before the books laid down the rule as to what was good architecture. There were, however, certain local tendencies in these various regions, certain emphases. Graeme Park illustrates the tendency of the Pennsylvania region to erect buildings that were high in proportion to their area. So does the old

Philadelphia Courthouse, 1707. This tendency appears sometimes even in farm buildings, in which certainly

Graeme Park, Horsham, Pa.
Built for Governor Keith, 1721

First floor plan

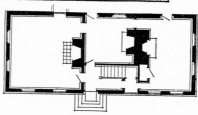

height would not be necessary on account of lack of land.

This local tendency, evident in many instances, was restrained into a solidity of form in Mount Pleasant among the finer mansions, and in the Letitia Street house and in the Isaac Potts house, Washington's headquarters at Valley Forge, among the smaller houses. It was entirely suppressed in the State House at Philadelphia, now called Independence Hall, built in 1733. This great achievement, appropriately to its services in the creation and development of the nation, seems to transcend all local emphases and to express a character that is simply Colonial and indeed also prophetically National.

But the contrast is marked between the tall Pennsylvania buildings and the low buildings of similar purpose, lying close to the ground, in East Jersey, near by. The reason was that East Jersey was settled from the Hudson, not from the Delaware; its building tastes and habits came from New York, which despite the events of 1664 was still largely Dutch. The contrast is equally marked if comparison is made with the similar buildings of Virginia to the south. Yet all are nonetheless of the same century and, barring the differing local emphases, all are of the style of architecture that has come to be called Georgian.

The widespread plan of the Georgian houses in Virginia and the South, with the transverse hall allowing the air to blow through, adapted them to the warm weather natural so much of the year in this region. Having detached buildings for the kitchen, the laundries and other work and for the offices for superintending all the work of the estate also made it cooler and more comfortable. These outbuildings were planned into a symmetrical arrangement with the main house, making a handsome and impressive whole. Washington's home, Mount Vernon, probably more familiar than any other such estate to Americans over the country, is of this type. Here the outbuildings are connected with the main buildings by arcades, as they are at Independence Hall, Philadelphia. At Mount Airy in Virginia, and at Montpelier in Prince George County, Maryland,

The John Hancock House, Boston, Mass.

they are connected by enclosed passages; at the Governor's Palace in old Williamsburg only by a wall; and at Mount Pleasant in Philadelphia only by paths and hedges. At Westover in Virginia again they are not connected at all, but they are placed so as to fit symmetrically into the whole.

These detached outbuildings were specially suitable and convenient for the large plantations in the South. They ensured the family more privacy. This was important with the increase of the slave population, and wherever there was class distinction. But the feature was primarily an adaptation to the weather. In the North where heat had to be provided during a large part of the year, the kitchens and laundries, which had means for heating in them, were kept within the same walls and under the same roof as the main house. The Van Cortlandt mansion in New York was an interesting example of this. It was predicted that it would have to be abandoned. It was so large it would never be possible to heat it. The Hancock house in Boston is another instance. It was built in 1737 by Thomas Hancock, a wealthy merchant himself and uncle of the famous John Hancock. It was when built and for fifty years afterward the most important and luxurious house in New England. It was of granite with trim of brown sandstone specially quarried and brought to Boston from Middletown in the Connecticut Valley. Magnificence was intended and anything that could be thought of would be included in the plans. When the Stamp Act was repealed in 1767 John Hancock placed a pipe (126 gallons) of his best Madeira wine on a platform in front of the house for all to enjoy who would celebrate with him. Uncle and nephew alike were lavish in their ways. And yet there were no detached outbuildings. There were two large wings as long as these two lived. The one on the east side of the house was a ballroom; the balancing wing, on the west side, contained the kitchen and other working quarters. As before, the question of detached outbuildings was primarily a matter of the weather.

Modification of the roof structure, coming along through the century, had practical effect in increasing the available

The stairway at Westover, Va.

space for rooms. These modifications added to the house a good third story which was not as formerly a mere attic. They also gave greater artistic value and dignity to the house as a whole. Different forms of roof structure were the gambrel roof, such as is seen in Graeme Park (1721) near Philadelphia; the hip roof, seen in Westover (1726) in Virginia; and the mansard roof as in the Van Cortlandt mansion (1748) in New York. Dormer windows provided adequate light for the new rooms; and a rail around the edge of the mansard roof sometimes added to the decorative effect, as in the Schuyler mansion (1761) at Albany.

Development in the interior planning of the house also ensured privacy for the family and greater convenience and efficiency in the management of the house. One such improvement consisted in additional hallways, so that it would be unnecessary, in order to reach any room in the house, to go through any other room. Another improvement consisted in providing a second stairway between the lower and upper floors. In the plans of the following houses these features will be found to be of special interest: Rosewell in Virginia, built before 1730; the Hancock house in Boston, 1737; the John Vassall house in Cambridge, 1759; Cliveden in Germantown, 1763; and the Chase house, Annapolis, Maryland, 1769.

The swift development of the stairway established it soon as a magnificent feature of the house. One tendency was to make the stairs broader, and ultimately to bring the stairway out into the center of the main hall. At the same time there was another tendency to clear the main hall of the stairs altogether and to relegate them to one or more side halls. This did not entail any neglect of them, however. Rather they were often treated as specially beautiful, encased in their own place, protected from any distracting competition. Again, the slope of the stairs was made more and more gentle.

But naturally the chief attention was paid to the balusters as they rise in a line of graceful motion from the newel post in the entrance 'hall below to the hallway and the more

The stairway at Graeme Park, Horsham, Pa., 1721

intimate part of the house on the floor above. In the earlier type, as at Graeme Park, the ends of the treads were enclosed and the balusters rose from the sloping string-piece. Later, the treads were left open and the balusters rose from each stair, at first two balusters to the stair, as at Tuckahoe

143

Virginia; and then three balusters to the stair, as in Cliveden, 1763, at Germantown, at Westover in Virginia, in the Jeremiah Lee house at Marblehead, Massachusetts, and in the Schuyler mansion at Albany with the mark of the tomahawk thrown at young Margaret Schuyler in the attack on the house in August, 1781.

The wainscoting and panelling followed the stairways in their magnificent development, beginning back in the seventeenth century with a practical purpose to make the walls tighter and the house warmer. Then the books brought suggestions and designs for making the interior walls and partitions beautiful in themselves with the classic effect and the use of the classic architrave, pediment, cornices, columns and pilasters. The panelling of the Georgian mansions is a study in itself with almost limitless detail. The advantageous approach, in the opinion of at least one enthusiast, is to look at the panelling first as it goes up along the wall by the side of the stairway—when it is in fact the staircase. Then it seems to have motion in it. In a room the panelling seems to keep still, not to express itself, almost to remain silent, unless one already understands it and enjoys it. But going upstairs it takes on something of the life of the stairway. Both are to be observed and can be fully enjoyed only when going up or down stairs. Then they will be found to have as much ever-changing motion in them as a brook. But ever the stairway more than the panelling.

To many people, and to all more than is realized, the stairway reveals the personality of the house and of its owner with inflexible truthfulness. It will emphasize the good manners or betray the bad manners of any lady or gentleman ascending or descending the stairs; indeed it

Detail of stairs in the Jeremiah Lee House, Marblehead, Mass., 1768

will accurately expose their characters. This is so of all stairways, cottage or palace. Can you not see the solemn, the stern but sterling young Puritan minister, Parson Capen, coming down those steep stairs in his Topsfield house? Irrespective of the discrepancy in dates, can you conceivably imagine him coming down the magnificent stairway of his

145

neighbor, only ten or fifteen miles away, Jeremiah Lee of Marblehead? His own house was built for him by his father-in-law when he married; he would not belong in the other at all, probably would not approve of it.

But the development of the stairways and of all the interior features of the Georgian houses went to extremes, and finally brought on a sweeping reaction. The balusters, for instance, through the elaboration of intricate details, became simply amazing pieces of carving and expensive-looking rather than beautiful. Good taste turned back toward a restful simplicity. Ultimately, in the early days of the next century, the curiously carved balusters and newel posts gave way to simple square or round sticks, unobtrusively contributing to the finer beauty of the sweeping lines of the stairway as a whole. Warnings of this change began to come as early as 1760. At about the same time panelling began to give way to tapestries, textile hangings, and wallpapers. The most luxurious period in the eighteenth century, with the unrestrained wood carver as its chief minister, was probably between 1740 and 1765. Building slowed down after 1765 as the colonial Americans of importance got together and prepared for the momentous stand whereby they brought into being a new nation. But first the charming furniture of the period, with its varied forms and uses fitting so perfectly into the panelled rooms and halls of these Georgian houses, calls for attention.

CHAPTER X

Eighteenth-Century Furniture

DURING the seventeenth century the furniture was a simple development of the chests, tables, chairs, and beds that the settlers made for themselves when they first landed. The chief quality was durability, progressing into some comfort; the chief improvement was in becoming less crude in workmanship, and thus progressing into fine workmanship. When this stage was reached there came a tendency in the more southern Colonies to rely on the northern Colonies for their better furniture. They bought it; and it was sent to them by the coastwise commerce that was growing up. Later the cabinetmakers in the North had agents in the South to sell their product, but this was hardly until after the Revolution. The story of the Pennsylvania-German furniture was different. They made their furniture for their own use on their farms and only so. It was different also in that they painted it in rich bold designs with brilliant colors; each was an individual piece.

By the time the standard of living and the means for maintaining that standard had advanced to the point that the Americans wanted good furniture there were carpenters here, "joiners" as they were called, cabinetmakers, capable of producing it. Their knowledge of furniture design came in the same way as the good architecture came—through books. This was somewhat slower in spreading than was the knowledge of building. Strong furniture was a necessity but fine furniture was not. In Puritan New England the prevailing ideas would be apt to class fine furniture as one of the vanities, especially if actual money were spent in buying it. In Philadelphia the Quakers, while not immune to the attraction of such refinement and even of out-and-out luxury, were apt to be moderate in their speed toward such dignified worldliness as they condoned. In Maryland and Virginia and in all the South the market for fine furniture was not a large one though a cordial one. There were few families of wealth and the large estates had but one big house and numerous small quarters for the indentured servants and the slaves. They could get whatever fine furniture they wanted from the northern colonies, or indeed from Europe for that matter, quite as easily as they could have the artisans on their estates make them.

Accordingly, while we know the names of some of the early furniture makers, such as John Alden of Plymouth (1599–1686), and Nicholas Disbrowe who worked in Hartford from 1639 to 1683, John Goddard of Newport (1723–85), and William Savery of Philadelphia (1721–87), those names do not convey the idea of a style of furniture as definitely as do the names of the authors of some of the books, such as Thomas Chippendale, George and Andrew

Hepplewhite, and Thomas Sheraton. These books were written and printed in England and came over here to be used by many a colonial cabinetmaker, often with modifications of their own.

Not the first but one of the most widely influential of these writers was Thomas Chippendale. He was probably the first to give general designs and to approach the subject deliberately in an advisory spirit. His book of directions, *The Gentleman and Cabinet-Maker's Guide,* was published in 1754, about the same time as William Halfpenny's *Modern Builder's Assistant.* It is quite the same kind of book and freely supplies the customer with directions and specific information. In 1788 Andrew Hepplewhite's book came out, and in 1795 the first of Thomas Sheraton's series of books.

The Chippendale style ran to ornate wood carving, quite in the same spirit as the stairways in the Georgian houses of the middle of the eighteenth century. It lasted through the Revolutionary War. Mahogany came into use in America in the second quarter of the century. It was well adapted to the Chippendale carving, hard in grain and rich in color. It rapidly became popular and kept its hold through various kinds of treatment. The Hepplewhite was the more simple style that followed in the reaction from the overelaboration of the later Chippendale. Hepplewhite was the response in furniture to the influence of Robert Adam (1728–92) and his classic design and ornament in architecture. The Sheraton style was also more simple than the Chippendale with

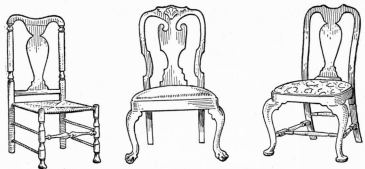

Three Dutch or Queen Anne chairs

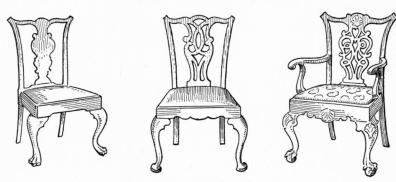

Three Chippendale chairs

These two at left Hepplewhite

These two at right Sheraton

a different variety. But this carries us beyond our period. In the entire subject of furniture, however, two things must be borne in mind. One is that there is continual adaptation of style to the purpose of the piece of furniture, chest, table, or chair, so that it would hardly be more than an exaggeration to recognize a chest-Chippendale, a table-Chippendale, or a chair-Chippendale. And it certainly is helpful to a beginner to study one of these at a time. The other point is that, as previously noted, every cabinetmaker devised his own variations in the style, so that reference may reasonably be made to Savery-Chippendale, to Goddard-Chippendale, or to Egerton-Chippendale. After it reaches the point of being a fine art, furniture is multiplicit in the detail variety of its style, just as are the canvases of the painter or the bronzes of the sculptor. That is the fascination of it.

We will here then note only a few characteristic features of two or three kinds—the chest, the table, and the chair—leaving the reader to follow the trail with entire freedom and infinite delight. Even so, the production of furniture in variety is so irresponsible in any adherence to the date that one feels like appending the old style accountant's reservation, E. & O. E.—Errors and Omissions Excepted.

Something has already been said in a previous chapter about the earlier developments of home furniture. The chest continued its development from what was at first simply a substantial box to the blanket chest of the William and Mary period, which was part bureau. The old Puritan

Bible-box was a chest in miniature. Ornament began to take liberties with the chest in the extraordinary bulbous foot, a good-sized ball bearing its burden by means of a very slight connection. In better taste brass mounts came into use. But the chest was still a chest, and had a straight front reminiscent of its ancestry in the packing box.

With the brief transitional influence of the Queen Anne style, the development continued and the chest of drawers and the chest-on-chest definitely appeared. In the telltale foot, the more substantial short turned leg or foot replaced the bulbous corner support, though a tendency to take the law of gravity not too seriously showed itself in the cabriole leg, probably derived from the shape of a goat's leg, coming out with something of a hip and then tapering quite gracefully down to some kind of a foot. This form of leg was adaptable to several kinds of furniture, especially tables and chairs, and also allowed variety in its detail treatment.

With the arrival of orthodox Chippendale, the chest and its successors were not higher but they were apt to be greater in length and in breadth, and so of more impressive proportions. Something of increase of wealth and of social dignity had come over the furniture. This too was the period when wood carving was turned loose to work its elaborate skill. There was often a carved recess in the front of the chest, and the front was carved with shells and similar figures, all which was far away from the original box of which all four sides were pretty much alike, the front being superior only in the lid lifting from that side

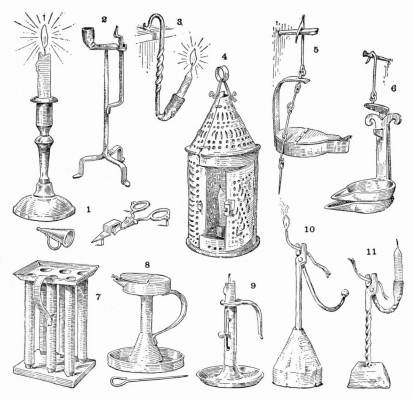

Early devices for illumination using grease-soaked pith of the rush plant, animal or fish oils and candles

1. Brass candlestick, snuffers and an extinguisher. 2. Tall wrought-iron candle holder. 3. Candle holder terminating in a hook. 4. The Paul Revere lantern: as it was popularly called. 5. Betty lamp and its pickwick. 6. Double Betty lamp, the lower receptacle catches drippings from lamp above. 7. Moulds for making candles. 8. Lard-oil lamp. The pickwick was used to pull out the wick. 9. Candlestick with hook for hanging. 10. Rush-light holder. 11. Combined rush-light and candle holder

and its having the responsibility of the lock and its keyhole. The most conspicuous mark of the Chippendale style was the claw-and-ball foot, which was used quite generally throughout this period.

When the more chaste style of George and Andrew Heppelwhite, demanding more grace and more simplicity, displaced that of Chippendale, there were no more claw-and-ball feet. The feet became a modification of the earlier bracket foot, only taller and more slender. The ornamentation of profuse carving was now replaced by a bow or slightly curved front, and while mahogany was still used there was with it not a little inlay of lighter-toned woods. Sometimes the Hepplewhite chest of drawers was a little taller, had a larger number of drawers, but in general more simplicity was the advance. When the Sheraton style followed, on the edge of our special period, it continued in the direction of more simplicity and of grace. The front of the chests was straight or bowed, and there was less of the lighter woods used, more pieces were entirely of the uncarved, uninlayed mahogany. The distinguishing mark of the Sheraton was the reeded column continuing the rounded leg up the corners of the chest.

Turning now to tables, and following the manifestation of these same influences, it seems that the making of tables took a new departure in the Queen Anne period. The cabriole leg was a very applicable idea in the making of tables, but also there were a good many made with simple turned legs. Practical uses suggested a variety in forms, such as the drop-leaf and the tea-table with the molded edge to keep the delicate little teacups from falling off.

The Chippendale style of course brought the claw-and-ball foot, and, as tables generally had longer legs than chests, put the claw-and-ball foot on the end of the cabriole leg. But there were also a number of straight-legged tables, such as the Pembroke, which is said to be Thomas Chippendale's own design. He also was personally much taken with what he learned about the Chinese and their art through the commerce that was springing up with the tea-ships and he introduced this into the designs that he acquainted the English people with. The Chinese features soon also came over to America and became popular here. Supplied with ships of increasing size and seaworthiness by shipbuilders in many of the seacoast towns, American merchants, often in partnership with ship owners and sea-captains, were carrying on a thriving trade with the Orient.

The Hepplewhite style, while criticizing the cabriole legs of former days, found much to approve in the simple straight table legs that frequently came adorned with the Chinese Chippendale. Hepplewhite improved by tapering the straight legs and sometimes decorating with inlay or with a simple fluting. In general the new dictum was:—no carving, no curves, right angles. Also there came the very practical long dining-room table, or banquet table, considering the burden which it was often called upon to bear. Very moderate with two parts set up together, it sometimes was made in three or even four sections and would seat from sixteen to twenty-four people, serving them hospitably in the way that the eighteenth century enjoyed being served with food and drink.

And Sheraton, coming as already noticed in the last years of our period, freed, as it were, its reeded column from the corners of its chest and made them the graceful reeded legs that are the distinguishing element of the Sheraton table.

Chairs traced their descent down from the Carver and the Brewster chairs through the horizontal ladder-back and the vertical banister-back to the refined and simple fiddle-back. About that time, under the reign of Queen Anne, there was introduced what might reasonably be called a throw-back to the idea of the old-time settle or table-chair with its comfortable protection against the draft,—the wing chair, now with all its woodwork handsomely carved and with seat, back and wings amply upholstered fore and aft. With Chippendale came the elaborate carving of the handsome roundabout chair, and other designs of many varieties. Hepplewhite extended the use of upholstery especially in the backs of the chairs and in the simpler forms used straight lines in most of the parts with curves for the back. For the carving of the usual Chippendale chair, restrained to a good extent by the fact that the single chair offers not very great opportunity for elaborate carving, the Hepplewhite presented various forms of shield-shaped backs, which harmonized beautifully with the tapering legs of the style.

There is something peculiarly personal about an antique

chair. You do not have to have a whole set of them; you can have just one. Chairs of various styles and kinds, of different centuries, will sit together in a room as companionably as people of different natures, interests, and characters. If one is going to have some friends in for the evening, one does not want to have them all alike. In the same way one does not want all the chairs alike. Around the dining-room table, yes; but not in the sitting room. It is more informal, much pleasanter if they are different. Fortunately too it is comparatively easy to pick up good single chairs at sales and auctions.

But this is not even a resumé of the styles through which these pieces of furniture passed their charming way. It is hardly more than a signpost pointing to a charming region of great interest.

A fireplace settle

CHAPTER XI

Iron Mined and Wrought

W ORK in the home and on the farm dominated the daily life of all New England well down toward the middle of the nineteenth century, more and more of course as one went back through the less settled regions toward the mountains. But the significant development, forecasting what was to be the prevailing character of the region and itself molding it, was industry, in the modern sense of the word, using its material in quantity, availing itself of mechanical manipulation and disposing of its products by widespread marketing. This began in the earliest period, probably with the iron industry. Lumber, peltry, and fish were all three occupations pursued on a large scale, but in method followed the individual method of the home industries.

The first attention paid to any iron ore on the Atlantic seaboard was on Roanoke Island in 1585 but the settlement was lost. In Virginia, at Falling Creek, about seven miles below Richmond there were constructed in 1620 a blast furnace and a "finery" for converting the pig iron into wrought iron, and a forge for working the wrought iron, but before these structures were put into operation they were destroyed in the Indian Massacre of 1622. Iron making in Virginia did not begin again until 1715.

In the Massachusetts Bay Colony bog iron ore was early

Ruins of the furnace at Roxbury, Connecticut
Redrawn by courtesy of the Connecticut Society of Civil Engineers

found in what is now the town of Saugus, and in 1642 "The Companie of Undertakers for the Iron Works" was formed in England with eleven stockholders and a capital of £1000. This company sent a number of practical iron-workers to New England. John Winthrop, Jr., the son of the Governor of Massachusetts Bay, took an active interest

159

in it and soon became the head. He secured for it a charter in 1644, giving it the right to take wood, ore and other material for ironworking wherever found in the Colony. Winthrop started these works in Saugus and also in Braintree for his company. They were the first ironworks to be actually operated in America.

Across the Saugus River a dam ten feet high was built, which flooded about 1000 acres, raised the water level six or eight feet and gave thirty feet of head to the thirty-foot water-wheel. The floor from which the charge was fed into the top of the furnace was nearly level with this pond. The raw material was bog ore; the fuel was charcoal; and the flux oyster shells. In 1648 the Massachusetts Governor wrote of its product:

> The furnace runs eight tons per week, and their bar iron is as good as Spanish.

There is specific record of the making of pots, mortars, stoves and skillets there. An interesting item is that the dies for the famous Pine Tree shillings were made for John Hull, the Mint-master, at the Saugus ironworks from drawings by the wife of Joseph Jenks, the master mechanic of the company. By virtue of these ironworks at Saugus John Winthrop, Jr., should be recognized as the first industrialist of America, the progenitor of the New England of the twentieth century.

But there were troubles. These ironworks were supplying so absolute a necessity to the people that the General

Court granted the members of the company special privileges, among them that of being absent from church without losing their voting rights. This caused bitter resentment

Iron mining at Salisbury, Conn.
Redrawn by courtesy of the Connecticut Society of Civil Engineers

and contention. Nonetheless ironworks increased and multiplied, and in 1720 Massachusetts was said to be the chief seat of the iron industry in America.

The industry spread to other colonies. Rhode Island built its first in 1675. The most important event in this field, however, came in 1657 when John Winthrop, Jr. (1606–1676) became Governor of Connecticut. Thither he took his interest in the iron industry. He found bog ore in a favorable locality near New Haven and built a blast furnace at the outlet of Lake Saltonstall near by. This was the first in Connecticut.

The most important iron mines in the Colonial period were those in the Salisbury district, which extended from

From the old "Scribner's Monthly"

Running pig-iron from an early type of furnace

southern Vermont, through western Massachusetts and Connecticut, and the adjoining part of New York east of the Hudson River, and down into New Jersey. This district was named after the Connecticut town in which the first mine into these ore-beds was opened, about two miles west of Lakeville in 1732. The first forge, or bloomery, for producing wrought iron, was built at Lime Rock in 1734, even before the settlement of the town, a confidence in the out-

162

come of the venture that was amply justified. This was the beginning of the Salisbury iron industry. There were forty-five important mines in this district which became famous not only in America but throughout the world.

There was one mine, one of the richest in the region,

Lime rock furnace in 1935

Redrawn after a photograph in the possession of Mr. and Mrs. Rutgers Fish. Courtesy of the Connecticut Society of Civil Engineers

which was a complete failure on account either of misapprehension or false management, or both. It was at Roxbury, Connecticut, where there was a vertical vein of siderite, carbonate of iron, six to eight feet thick, in a hill rising 550 feet above the river. In simple words, nearly half of the mass was iron. The local conditions for its reduction also were exceptionally advantageous. It was first worked in 1724. Again in 1760 a company was formed, and a German goldsmith was employed to operate the mine. This goldsmith either did not recognize its extraordinary value as an iron mine, or with confidence in dishonesty thought there was great gain for himself in pretending there was a large amount of silver to be extracted from the mine. He kept up his futile deception systematically until the company's capital was exhausted. So with one company after another, the hope, the false gleam of silver lured attention away from this great iron mine until it was too late.

During the entire colonial period Salisbury, Connecticut, was the synonym for Iron as Pittsburgh, Pennsylvania, is now for Steel. That region was the chief source of the iron-ware of the Colonies and of the Revolutionary War and for years afterward of the new nation. One instance: a blast furnace was built at Lime Rock in 1762 by a group of men of whom Ethan Allen was one. In 1768 this furnace passed into the hands of one Richard Smith, who later became a Tory and went to England. This furnace made cannon and shot for the American Army throughout the Revolution, and it has been claimed that parts of the great chain stretched across the Hudson River at West Point to keep the British ships from going beyond the Highlands was forged there too. Many such associations with the Salisbury mines could be told. But the day of the pre-eminence of the district passed. The science of mining engineering has made the art of making steel a precise art. Iron can no longer compete with steel for any purpose. All the natural advantages that the Salisbury district had for the iron industry, even the high quality of the ore, are no longer of moment. And the strange fact is that in this revolutionary science the greatest figure was a Salisbury boy, the metallurgist, Alexander Lyman Holley (1832–82).

Wrought iron gates at Westover, Virginia, north entrance
Redrawn from Albert H. Sonn's *Early American Wrought Iron*

Wrought iron is the basic craft of all the crafts. It is a real man's art. The ironworker is the blacksmith. He designs his hinges or his weather vanes, his balconies or gates, with his hammer in his hand. So too his work is appreciated, with the hammer in the hand. If the reader would *know* about wrought iron, let him make a nail—from the beginning, from the pig iron, just one nail. If he gets that nail done, it will be a great nail! He will know in his heart it is. Not only in the pride of creation. In the wonder of revelation also. With that nail of his own in his hand he can go and lift the latch of some 1750 door with understanding. He can swing the door of the fort at Ticonderoga on its hinges with admiration. He will look up at the two-hundred-year-old Moravian weather vanes at Bethlehem with a new reverence. He will see in the gates at Westover a Te Deum far beyond the owner-satisfaction of William Byrd, the Te Deum of the unknown man who created them and set them up, to sing the song of boundaries to future generations, the song of usefulness appreciated in iron beauty.

There are few whose names are known of the artists in wrought iron; very few pieces of their work that are signed and dated, and before the Revolution practically none. Who knows what was the name of any particular blacksmith; who would ask a blacksmith to put his name on a weather vane or even on a balcony? His business is to shoe horses. But that is skilled work; if it is not properly, nicely done, it may lame the animal and render him unusable. Before the Revolution the articles the blacksmith made were not numerous in kind. There were bolts, latches, door hinges of many shapes and kinds, such as tulip hinges, cockshead, spearhead, and serpentine hinges, foot scrapers, wall anchors, shutter fasteners, gutter supports, weather vanes, railings, balconies and gates. Within a limited range like this they made an infinite variety of forms, which are best suggested by a few illustrations.

Reverting to the actual making of a nail, Henry Chap-

Wrought iron gate at Westover, Virginia, side entrance
Redrawn from Albert H. Sonn's *Early American Wrought Iron*

man Mercer (1856–1930), the creator of the Bucks County Historical Museum at Doylestown, Pennsylvania, who knew just as much about such matters as if he were one of the original settlers himself, gave in 1924 this description of the making of a nail. Any reader who would like to do so may try his hand at it.

The wrought-iron nail was made from rectangular strips of malleable iron, several feet long and about a quarter of an inch thick, called nail rods, which were furnished to the blacksmith or nailer, who, holding one of them in one hand, heated its end in his forge and then on the anvil, pointed it with a hammer on all four sides. Next he partly cut it above the point, on the "hardy" (the blacksmith's chisel) with a hammer blow, and then inserting the hot point into the swage hole he broke off the rod and hammered the projecting end so as to spread it around the top of the hole; after which the cooling and shrunken nail was easily knocked out of the orifice.

Foot-scrapers, indispensable in Colonial days

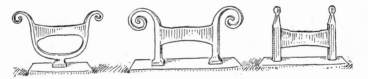

CHAPTER XII

Pewter in the Colonial Home

IN THE early days, the years of first settlement, the dishes were mostly of wood—trenchers, and bowls, and spoons, and noggins or mugs. The best were cut out from the knots or burls of tree trunks. Maple was considered the best. But sometimes a trencher was as simple as merely a square block of wood ten or twelve inches on a side, and three or four inches high, hollowed out like a bowl. From the one trencher a man and his wife would eat together; or two children would use the same trencher. Every one had his own knife, used for many things besides cutting his food. It will be remembered that the frontiersmen in the Allegheny Mountains had a decided aversion to chinaware when it was introduced, because it dulled their knives, as the wooden vessels did not. The people of the seventeenth century had no forks. They ate with spoons of wood or sometimes of horn; or they ate with their knives. And always of course the fingers were useful and always convenient. "Fingers were made before forks."

Wooden dishes were followed by pewter as the times progressed and as commerce across the sea increased. But at first only those who were comparatively wealthy could afford pewter; and that not before 1650, for it had to be brought from England and Holland. Later still, silver dishes and utensils began gradually to come into use. At this time pewter had become the usual material for tableware and continued to be so for many years. The well-to-do

Wooden mugs and trenchers

had, indeed, considerable silver, but nonetheless they had pewter for ordinary use, while ordinary people had only one or two pieces of silver, treasured and mentioned in their wills. Pewter had the place then that plated silver has with us now, in the treasured presence of solid silver. Wooden ware was still somewhat in use; it continued in use a long time. But it wore out rapidly, and once broken it was hardly worth while to mend it. There is little still existing that is very old, and there is practically no way to determine the date of what there is. It required skill to make a good trencher or bowl, and a wooden dish might be a beautiful piece of work, but the man who made anything of the kind for himself or for his wife would not cut his name or the date on it. So the story of tableware before the Revolution is the story of pewter, until it is glorified in silver.

Little pewter was made in America before 1750, although there were here and there those who were spoken of as pewterers, one in Boston in 1639, and another in 1654. But the early pewterers were more likely dealers in imported pewter ware or menders of pewter articles rather than professional makers of it. With repairing broken pewter there grew up considerable pewter-making as a home industry, and also considerable work for the itinerant tinker who made his rounds every year and repaired or melted and remade all the broken pewter ware that had been saved up for him since his last visit.

The composition of pewter varied a good deal, and with it the quality. The basic metal was tin. Tin was scarce in the American Colonies before the middle of the eighteenth century, and what there was had to be imported. To make clear the nature of pewter, it may be noted that bronze and pewter were in a way complementary metals. Bronze was 90 per cent copper and 10 per cent tin, while 80 per cent tin and 20 per cent copper made an excellent pewter. Lead was often used as the alloy instead of copper. Copper was used to temper the tin and harden it in making the pewter; lead to soften the tin and make it more malleable, and to reduce the cost of the pewter. Lead was the more common alloy in American pewter. When only 10 per cent or less was used with 90 per cent or more of tin the pewter was of a fine quality. When there was 25 per cent of lead or more with only 75 per cent or less of tin the pewter was dark and bluish and comparatively rather soft. Low grade pewter, sometimes with 40 per cent of lead in it, was called trifle. Pewter was a comparatively soft metal. The articles made of it wore out rapidly. But there was an artistic advantage in that this necessitated a simplicity in the design suited to the material, and forbade imitation of the intricate detail possible and beautiful in a harder metal like silver.

In England the Pewterers' Company in London maintained a high standard of quality both in the composition and in the workmanship of the pewter. In this country there was no organization of any kind to exercise a similar control. There were only general custom and public opinion, and the pride of the good workmen in the quality of their product. This made them willing and proud to put their names or marks on their work. In both countries therefore there were "touches," required in England, voluntary in America, corresponding to the hallmark in gold and silverware.

There were two kinds of pewter ware, according to the way it was made. Sad ware consisted of flat pieces, such as platters and trays. Sad ware was made by hammering the article out from a sheet of the metal. The hammering stiffened the metal and gave it a finer, smoother surface.

1. Measures.   2. Beaker.   3. Covered jug.   4. Teapot.   5. Tankard.   6. Flagon.
7. Mug.   8. Porringer.   9. Tankard.   10. Plates

Hollow ware, such as tankards, porringers, and bowls, was cast in molds. Many small articles also were cast in molds, such as spoons and small plates, since the work was simpler and cheaper. Once the molds, which were usually made of gun-metal, were made, any number could easily be cast. Often a family would lend its spoon molds to neighbors so they could make a new set of spoons for themselves or complete a set. In one village all the pewter spoons were marked with an L, as the molds belonged to a family whose name began with L and they had kindly lent them to every one in town. Hollow ware was usually finished either by hand polishing or by burnishing on a lathe. An article like a pitcher or a vase was usually cast in two or more pieces and then soldered together and finished. There seem to have been no pewter forks; the metal was not stiff enough. Pewter was limited to fairly cool use, on the table. It could not be put on the stove or close to the fire. It would melt. So there were no cooking vessels made of it.

There was nevertheless a long list of domestic articles made. Platters, chargers, plates and trays and porringers of all kinds. Saltcellars and sugar bowls had a prominent place. Tankards, pitchers, mugs and vases, tobacco boxes, inkwells, ladles and spoons. Almost everything that did not have to stand near the fire. A set of plates or of porringers of graded sizes was called a garnish, possibly because they were often placed or hung in a row and were very decorative. There was also much church pewter in the height of the period—flagons, cups, patens, and baptismal basons—what we nowadays would call "Communion silver."

The period of the common use of pewter was well launched by 1700, most of it imported. As has been said, after 1750 much of it was made in America, in Boston, New York and Philadelphia. Its decline set in with the Revolutionary War, when metal of all kinds, and especially lead, was needed for bullets and for making rifles and other arms. Up to this time pewter was the usual ware. In the Revolution General Washington's mess kit was fitted out with pewter ware. Thereafter silver gradually increased, with chinaware and porcelain among the well-to-do. With the deterioration of the quality of the pewter made in the first part of the nineteenth century, pewter lost its hold on the whole field of tableware.

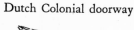

Dutch Colonial doorway

CHAPTER XIII

Silversmiths and Silverware

WITH silver style had a chance. Certainly the style of the artist showed in his pewter ware, but it was so circumscribed, so limited by the conditions of the material. Even in wooden ware the character of the worker will show itself, whether in the large or in the small. The neat clean cut of a sharp jackknife declares the man or boy who habitually keeps his knife sharp, who takes care of his tools. At Ephrata the magnificent bareness of character showed in the high steep dormered roofs and in the wooden latches of the doors alike. But only when we reach silver in tableware is the style of the artist no longer denied its will. Silver is hard enough yet not too hard, workable, malleable and ductile, and its beauty in color, in receptivity to form, in reflection to light when polished, is worth the work to attain. Therefore not only every silversmith has his distinct recognizable style, but every piece he makes responds with precision to the purpose and the circumstances that call it forth. With silver the delight of the artist in his work is turned loose on a holiday.

There was a great deal of silverware in the American

Colonies in the last quarter of the seventeenth century and during the eighteenth century. The reasons for this were curiously conflicting. There were no silver mines. The current silver was in the form of coin—English coin, Spanish and Portuguese coin. But there was not enough coin, certainly of English coin, which was of superior quality, to implement the trading. Accordingly domestic trade carried itself on in barter. Barter can get very complicated and inconvenient in its accounting. In the trading with the Indians, their wampum was used a great deal, and it was also used for domestic trade among the colonists. Exactly like paper money, as long as it was acceptable it was quite practical. In the trade with England the balance was usually in favor of Britain, and Britain wished to keep it so. This tended to drain the American Colonies of the coin, in other words, of their ability to trade advantageously. So the Americans did everything they could to keep the precious metals here and to further the acceptance of commodities in payment for British manufactured goods.

One thing they could and did do was to convert their silver coin into silverware. There were no banks in which they could deposit their hard money. As silverware they could keep, use, and enjoy their silver; as coin they could only keep it. They regarded turning it into silverware almost as we regard putting our money in the bank, or better still, as we regard putting it into good stocks and bonds. The silver did not lose value. It could be reconverted into coin by taking it to the mint. By Act of the

General Court of Massachusetts Bay, June 10, 1652, it was provided that

All persons whatsoever have liberty to bring in into the mint-house at Boston all bullion, plate or Spanish coin, there to be melted and brought to the allay of sterling silver by John Hull, master of the said mint, and his sworne officers, and by him to be coined into twelvepenny, and threepenny pieces [etc.].

Further, in case of the silverware being lost or stolen it could be more easily and positively identified than coin, and so it was a safer form in which to have their silver. But while it was not apparently against the law to convert coin into silverware, it was against the law to convert silverware into coin (except by and through the official agency of the mint), even into Spanish money.

One very fine silversmith, Samuel Casey of the Narragansett Country, a true artist, undertook to do some of this converting in the wrong direction with and for some of his friends and neighbors, and undoubtedly did do so over some two years or more. But on July 11, 1770, he was arrested for it, taken to Newport, indicted, tried, convicted and with a comet's tail of jail sentences for his associates was himself sentenced to be hanged. And he would have been, but the night before, a crowd of his aforesaid friends and neighbors, probably, broke into the jail and released all those therein imprisoned, and the last that was seen of Samuel Casey was on a horse going west. Therefore while it is fairly certain that Samuel Casey was born in Newport in or about 1724, it is not known when or where—or for

178

that matter if—he died. But of his work as a silversmith there is no question.

Nowadays a silversmith's customer pays him for the silver he uses in the work, and the silversmith supplies the material, as a matter of course. In those days the customer brought the silver to him, in any form that might be convenient, including coin. An instance of this practice is shown in an accounting memorandum of John Waite, another silversmith of the Narragansett Country, of date sometime after 1790:

> After receiving old Silver to Work up for Mrs. Potter and Returning Silver Wrought into Porngers [porringers] & mending one Remains Due to her 4 oz 2 pt [pennyweight].   John Waite.

It is evident that the commercial practice in the silversmith business was somewhat confused, as was the coinage practice, to which it was closely related. Silver was then, as it is still, a luxury, not a necessity. Silversmiths gathered where there was business and material with which they might thrive. That meant Boston, first of all, where in 1652 John Hull (1624–83) was officially appointed mintmaster, and he took Robert Sanderson (c. 1610–1693) into partnership with him. They were great silversmiths. Jeremiah Dummer (1645–1718) was a pupil of John Hull's under the apprenticeship system. By this the pupil acquired the instinct for the medium and the thoroughness of skill that resulted in the special quality of colonial American silver. Paul Revere, Sr. (1702–1754), and his greater and more famous son, Paul Revere, Jr. (1735–1818), of Boston and Lexington, also were masters of the art—and of what was not Paul Jr. a master! These all, and the many others of the time, benefited by the pouring of silver from the Spanish possessions in South America into Europe and thence into the English Colonies.

The attacks on the Spanish treasure ships had been extraordinarily lucrative enterprises. Through privateering they had led smoothly into piracy. Before piracy went to extremes and brought upon itself the popular reaction on land against the Knights of the Black Flag, many pirates came boldly, one might say frankly, into certain harbors where the merchants and in some cases the officials gave them a cordial though unofficial welcome. With us this would be diagnosed simply as the understanding that is sure to surround the disposition of stolen goods, but to those good citizens such a harsh judgment would be unfair. Oceanic warfare, so far as the Colonies were concerned, was hardly more than 100 or 150 years old. The advantage of oceanic warfare was that it kept the danger and destruction of war away from the home country while it brought in the spoils of victory just the same. Privateering was the legitimate child of oceanic warfare and inherited its emoluments. Piracy might be called the illegitimate child of oceanic warfare. It differed from privateering mainly in its indifference as to whether the ship attacked belonged to a friendly or to an enemy nation, or in its carelessness in determining this essentially political question. It was only five or six hundred years since a foreigner was *ipso facto* an enemy, on any coast. A principle is a principle always, but the appreciation of a principle and its practical application are usually matters of long and slow human development. There was still much confusion in all these matters and the dealing with them was not really just and accurate by any means. Queen Elizabeth was notably fortunate in her ventures into oceanic warfare, and into official and unofficial privateering. Sir Walter Raleigh was notably unfortunate in the result of his ventures into the same field of endeavor. The American Colonists must be seen as living in the same confused conditions; otherwise they will not be rightly understood.

The trade of the silversmiths is especially pertinent to illustrate this confusion in colonial life in New York. While the settlement was still New Amsterdam the Dutch West India Company planned such a management of the colony and of all the operations of the company as would bring in large dividends for its stockholders but such as would fail to develop the commerce of the colony and its long-time profits. New Amsterdam was to exist for the benefit of Old Amsterdam. It could not trade with the English Colonies on either side, nor with the Spanish Colonies to the south, only with the Netherlands. This not only handicapped New Amsterdam in its competition with the English; it cut New Amsterdam off from the stream of gold and silver coin that was pouring into the English Colonies and that was making Boston and Philadelphia and Charleston prosperous and wealthy. There was so much silver at hand that there was created a demand for some way by which the people could take care of their silver. In time it made an opportunity for the silversmiths. So Boston got a good head start. And so New York was delayed in its natural development.

The first real advantage that New York received was the monopoly conferred by Governor Edmund Andros in the bolting and exporting of flour (1676–1692). This bore hard upon the other towns of the Province but it trebled the wealth of the town itself. Then the lenient attitude toward trade with pirates brought in a great deal more silver than before, especially during the time of Governor Benjamin Fletcher. When there was business for the silversmiths, they naturally began to appear. And their work was excellent.

Probably the first of the New York silversmiths was Ahasuerus Hendrickse, who was born in Holland and came over to improve his condition. He swore allegiance to the King of England in 1675. With regard to these men dates are scarce. Another was Carol Van Brugh, sometimes called Cornelius Vanderburg, who made the silver cup presented in 1693 by the merchants to Governor Fletcher in appreciation of his liberal administration, and so forth; the value of silver in the cup was £106 Sterling, a fine and handsome piece of work, of course. Then there was the Huguenot, Bartholomew LeRoux (c. 1665–1713). But not all the silversmiths thought primarily of business advantage. LeRoux was a zealous member of the Leisler party. There was at this time keen fear of a Papist conspiracy. It was known that Louis XIV had given orders that in case New York were captured, "those of the pretended Reformed religion must be sent back to France." It was ascertained that there were a great many Catholics in the garrison in the fort, and an ordinance was passed that of the citizen soldiery only half of the company should ever be on duty in the fort at the same time. Bartholomew LeRoux, who was in command of the company, nonetheless marched the entire company in and took possession. Summoned before the Council, he made a very frank and complete declaration of the conditions in which the people found themselves and justified his action.

Among the lesser men also there was sincere and open independence. With the brave dignity of Bartholomew LeRoux we may give lighter recognition to John Wendover, or Windower, another silversmith, not comparable to Bartholomew LeRoux, either as a man or as an artist, but of interest. He got into trouble. The evidence against him as given in the trial records alleges:

The Examinant [witness] being duly sworn upon the holy Evangelists & examined Saith yt last night att seven or eight of the Clock or thereabouts he the Examint was in ye house of Edward Buckmaster of ye said Citty Inholder in Company with one John Windower of ye said Citty Goldsmith & severall others and that the sd John Windower did throw a piece of eight upon the Table & speaking to this Examinant did say there is your money or to yt effect, that he the examint did refuse to take it & said that would not doe; upon wch the said John Windower threw down another Piece of eight & said there take itt that's enough & called for ye scales, and said but Ille pay you for itt, & immediately did lift up his hand & did strike ye said examint upon ye face upon which the said Edward Buckmaster being then High Constable & hearing a noise came into ye Room & Commanded the Peace; & the said Examint further saith that after the peace was Commanded the said John Windower did say that Leisler & Milborne wer murdered which he would make appear & yt he would stand up for Jacobus Leisler while he had a drop of blood in his body and that their should be others hanged in a short time to Ballance the said Leisler & Milborne.

Garrett Onclebaugh, another eminent silversmith, came of a prominent family and stood high in the community. The city was divided into six wards—North, South, West, East, Dock, and Out—from each of which there were elected an Alderman and an Assistant Alderman, who together formed the General Court of the city. Onclebaugh was a number of times elected the Assistant Alderman from the North Ward. In 1713 he was elected again. As a result of factional disputes a majority of his colleagues passed the following resolution:

Whereas Garrett Onclebaugh who was lately Elected to serve in the Office of Assistant of the North Ward of this City for the year Ensueing is A Person of Evil fame and Reputation and hath been Convicted of Coyning the Current Money of the Province & since hath also been Convicted of Champetry, it is therefore the Opinion of this Court that the said Garrett Onclebaugh is not qualified to serve in the said Office and it is ORDER'D (Nemine Contra Dicente) that the Mayor and Recorder do refuse to swear him into the said Office.

184

But this was as far as it went. Though the offense was the offense of Samuel Casey, this time it was apparently only a political matter. Onclebaugh was unseated from his place in the General Court. That was what his enemies wanted. The incident affected his standing in the community no more than it did his work as an artist. Silversmiths were not a lot of knaves. Conditions were simply as confused and as unsettled as were their rules of spelling and capitalization.

One more of the New York silversmiths and we will leave others for our readers to discover for themselves. Charles LeRoux (1689–1745), the son of Bartholomew LeRoux, was one of the most prominent. He became the official silversmith of the city, and made the snuff boxes and the gold and silver boxes in which the freedom of the city was presented to distinguished visitors. One of these was presented in 1723 to Captain Peter Solgard,

who Pursued & Engaged two Pyrate Sloops Commanded by One Low (A Notorious and Inhumane Pyrate) . . . twenty Six of which Pyrates So taken being lately Executed at Rhode Island, not only Eased this City and Province of A Very great trouble but of A Very Considerable Expense &c.

The purse was always a sensitive organ, and probably always will be. To balance the cup presented to Governor Fletcher with its suggestion of piratical associations, we may mention the gold snuff box, 5½ ounces in weight, presented to Andrew Hamilton of Philadelphia, the great lawyer who acted as counsel for John Peter Zenger, when the jury vindicated the freedom of the press and established the principle as law that the truth is not libel. The resolution pays tribute to the service,

which he chearfully undertook under great Indisposition of body & Generously performed, Refusing any fee or Reward.

There is in this presentation one circumstance indicating an informality which nowadays we should consider an irregularity, if not an impropriety. It was at the same time a mark of appreciation of the silversmith as an artist. The resolution formally required that the box be made by Charles LeRoux; and Charles LeRoux was one of the Council who voted the resolution. It was in fact simply an informality in the point of view of the times.

In Philadelphia there were silversmiths within a few years of the starting of William Penn's settlement. This testifies both to the almost sudden rise of the town into prosperity, on account of its commercial character as a seaport from the beginning, and to the cultural character of its citizens shown by their appreciation of the artistic quality of the silverware produced for them. Cesar Ghiselin (c. 1751) and Philip Syng (1676–1739) were both artists of eminent ability, leaders in the craft. Philip Syng, Jr. (1703–1789), was an even greater silversmith than his father. His most noted piece of work was the inkstand he made in 1752 for the Assembly of the Province of Pennsylvania, at a cost of £25 16s, consisting of the inkwell, the quill holder, the sand shaker, and the stand itself. This

Top. Westover, Virginia, symmetrical in design and built soon after 1726
Below. Van Cortlandt Manor House, New York, 1748. Built mainly of rubble masonry

Mt. Vernon, showing outbuildings connected with main building by arcades

The Roger Morris or Jumel Mansion, New York, 1765. Its classic descent can be traced back to Andrea Palladia

Top. The State House, Philadelphia, now Independence Hall, built in 1733
From an old engraving
Middle. Old Philadelphia Court House, built in 1707, demolished 1837
*From a water color sketch by J. M. Kelley in the collection of the Pennsylvania
Historical Society*
Below. The College of Philadelphia
From a painting by Lifferts. Courtesy of the University of Pennsylvania

Top. Washington's Headquarters at Valley Forge built by Quaker Isaac Potts, 1760
From "Colonial Houses," by Philip B. Wallace. © *Architectural Book Publishing Co.*
Middle. The Zabriskie or von Steuben House, 1752, Hackensack, N. J.
Below. Ackerman (Brinckerhoff) House, 1704
The lower two by courtesy of the "Architectural Record"

Two New England rooms prior to 1750
Above. A room from Newington, Connecticut
Below. A room from Hampton, New Hampshire, with panelling in unpainted pine
Both rooms are in the Metropolitan Museum of Art, New York City

Above. Interior at Almodington, Somerset County, Maryland, circa, 1750

Below. A yellow brocade costume imported from France about 1775 with a Philadelphia interior of same period showing a richly carved highboy

Both are in the Metropolitan Museum of Art, New York City

Colonial Silver

The three pieces at top are the work of Paul Revere. They are from the collection of A. T.
Clearwater in the Metropolitan Museum of Art. The Standing Salt (center) is the work of
Edward Winslow in the collection of Philip L. Spalding of Boston, Massachusetts. The
Salt (lower left) is the work of Bartholomew Le Roux in the collection of F. A. de Peyster.
That on the right is by John David in the collection of the Pennsylvania Museum of Art

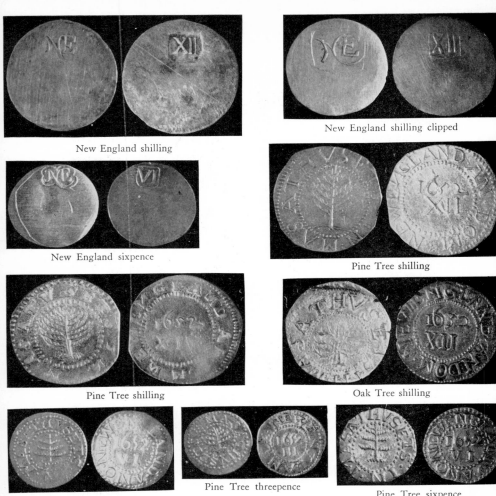

New England shilling

New England shilling clipped

New England sixpence

Pine Tree shilling

Pine Tree shilling

Oak Tree shilling

Pine Tree sixpence

Pine Tree threepence

Pine Tree sixpence

Willow Tree twopence

Pine Tree threepence

Willow Tree Twopence

In each case obverse is on left—reverse on right

The Spanish Milled Silver Dollar or Piece of Eight (Eight Reals)
All by courtesy of the Chase National Bank

From a painting by Ray Brown

New England early took the lead in shipbuilding

From Abbot's "Story of Our Merchant Marine," courtesy of Dodd, Mead & Co.

Sengat   Martin   **Long Wharf**   Hancock's Wharf   North Battery   *Bonetta*

           Glasgow   *Mermaid*   *Romney*   *Beaver*   *Launceston*

On September 30, 1768, British warships and transports anchored in Boston Harbor and settled themselves as for a siege. Next day two regiments and a detachment from a third, together with an artillery train, landed on Long Wharf. Each soldier received 16 rounds of powder and ball, after which they paraded up King Street.

From an engraving by Paul Revere, in the Stokes Collection, New York Public Library

Philadelphia from the Great Tree at Kensington under which Penn made his treaty with the Indians, drawn by G. Beck, engraved
by T. Cartwright about 1800
From the Stokes Collection in the New York Public Library

Arch Street Ferry, Philadelphia

Drawn, engraved and published by W. Birch and Son just prior to 1800
Courtesy of the Historical Society of Pennsylvania

The highlands on the Hudson River, when the river was a great highway for small sailing vessels

From a painting by F. F. Palmer lithographed by Currier and Ives

Road near Peekskill running down to a river landing on the Hudson. While the scene is post colonial and the road much more developed than in colonial days the rest remains as it was in earlier days

From a painting by Stanley M. Arthurs

Benjamin Franklin in his printing establishment

In the Seventeen Seventies Post riders went in all directions

inkstand was later made famous by its use in 1776 in the signing of the Declaration of Independence, and in 1787 in the signing of the Constitution of the United States. This historic and no less beautiful piece of silverware has always been and still is preserved in Independence Hall, Philadelphia. He was a personal friend of Benjamin Franklin, and a member of his Junta; he was one of the two or three who experimented with Franklin in his electrical work. He was one of the early members of the American Philosophical Society, and one of the charter grantees of the College and Academy of Philadelphia, which later became the University of Pennsylvania. Another of the excellent silversmiths of early Philadelphia was Joseph Anthony (1762–1814), a cousin of Gilbert Stuart, the painter (1755–1828). Anthony's father, a merchant in Philadelphia, ensured to both of them their training and start in their careers.

The making of colonial silverware was a personal matter, by which is meant something a little more than hand wrought. How little anything mattered beyond the silversmith himself is strikingly indicated by the small size of shop (size is an absurd word here) in which they did their work. John Hull and Robert Sanderson created their masterpieces in a little shack 16 feet long by 16 feet wide and 10 feet high—the two of them. They say that after death a man needs but six feet of earth. Before death a silversmith, it seems, needed but little more. Were these little sheds safe for the keeping of such valuable stores? Well, the turnover was fast. The customer brought his metal, the silversmith did his work, and delivered his ware; then another customer came. The silversmith sold his skill, his craftsmanship; he kept but little silver on hand. And yet, Judge Sewall in his famous diary noted on June 21, 1707, that William Cowell's shop had been entered by the chimney and some plate stolen. Evidently a burglar's occupation was not a very difficult one.

According to anthropology, the invention of tools was an extension of the hands. This is a peculiarly apt characterization of the silversmith's tools. His equipment could not have been very large or there would not have been room for its storage in factories 16x16x10 (for two or more). It was all in the instinctive ability with which the tools were used. Briefly stated, the processes began with the melting of the silver metal and refining it to the desired character, rolling it into sheets, cutting out the forms, and then hammering it into the design, molding and soldering the handles and ornaments, and finally polishing. But this list of operations tells nothing. The craft was learned by the apprenticeship system as already noted. This instilled two all-important conditions for good work. The first was a familiarity with good design, which the apprentice saw made, and assisted in making year in, year out, until he was himself also a master. This good design was throughout the Colonies almost entirely of the English tradition, except in New York in which there was also much of the Dutch tradition. The second condition the apprenticeship system fostered was an instinctive feeling for the metal as a medium, for what could be done with it, and how it could be done. This living with the work got it not only into the head but into the hands. There was no machinery used, no merely mechanical operation from beginning to end. The tools were extensions of the hands. The piece of silverware in the making never escaped from out of the control of the hand. The result was that colonial silverware had a texture of metal which was not merely of the surface, but, so to speak and also literally, of the material through and through. This is the reason for its special beauty.

It is further a natural consequence of the apprenticeship system that practically no two pieces made were alike. No piece came under the imputation of being a mere duplicate. Continuous originality gives a zest to a man's work which reproduction cannot bring. It also puts general comment at a disadvantage. But there is one suggestion that may be helpful to those who are interested in following these studies on for themselves. They will find a distinct similarity of style in the architecture, the furniture, and the silverware of this whole period, and the tracing of these correspondences will prove to be of fascinating enjoyment. Nor is this limited to these three arts and crafts.

The kinds of articles that were made were almost endless and to try to enumerate them would be well-nigh hopeless. Variety of form was encouraged by the freedom of reconversion into coin and back into silverware again according to the circumstances. If the customer had only a small amount of silver to "put in the bank," the order to the silversmith might be for only a single spoon. Or a wealthy customer might give an order for a large punch bowl or a full set of tableware. For domestic use there were cups and beakers, tankards and flagons, teapots and coffee-pots, pitchers large and small, spoons innumerable, vases and ornaments. For ecclesiastical use some of the finest work was done in the chalices and patens, the communion flagons and the alms basins.

Knives and forks and spoons: Knives go back to prehistoric times, to the stone age. Man evidently always wanted to cut up his food or his enemy or both. Spoons go back to antiquity, when soups and stews were eaten, and they were a regular article of the silversmith's and the pewterer's production. But forks did not make their appearance in America until nearly the beginning of the eighteenth century, and took about forty or fifty years to get well established in daily use. The first forks had only two tines; their main use was to hold the meat still while carving. The handles only were of silver, as silver tines were not strong enough to serve the purpose. Indeed when the whole fork came to be made of silver, they bent easily and wore out fast, and accordingly soon went back to the melting pot for remaking. Early silver forks are rare.

The saltcellar has about as significant history as any article of tableware we use. The name is a redundant expression. The "cellar" is a misspelling of the French word, *saler,* for salt-holder. Literally we call it a salt-salt-holder.

At about 1700 this article was a large and handsome piece of silverware and was called a standing salt, as a cup with a base and stem or goblet was called a standing cup. It had ceremonial importance, marking at the table the distinction between persons of rank and guests of honor and the others. It had a large and heavy base, not only because of its great significance but because salt was scarce and it would be unfortunate to spill and lose any of it. From these times no doubt came the genial superstition in regard to spilling salt at the table and also the custom forbidding hostility against any one to whom one had given bread and salt. As salt became a more common commodity, the small or trencher saltcellars were made and put on the table at the individual places in addition to the great or standing salt, which later was omitted altogether in setting the table.

Silverware, beautiful, interesting, distinctively individual, was abundant in the American Colonies all through the first three quarters of the eighteenth century. But with the Revolutionary War a serious depletion set in. Money was needed, and more money to finance the struggle. The reconversion of silverware into coin was a natural resource under the circumstances. Reconversion was almost a habit. What individuals had done in personal hard times, the Colonies joined in doing in the public hard times. The melting pot transformed personal treasures into the general welfare. Pewter was melted for bullets, and silverware for money. But fortunately there is still a great deal of colonial silverware extant.

CHAPTER XIV

Measures of Value

IT IS only an exaggeration to say that in the colonial days silverware was near-money. Now it was money; then it was a tankard or a teapot; and then it was money again. If the distinction between privateering and piracy was confused, the distinction between converting one's silver and counterfeiting was even more confused. The difference inhered chiefly in the prerogative of the Government over the private individual. Insofar as the Government was the organization fairly representing all the people of the country, this was well, right and proper. Insofar as the government was the representative only of the most privileged individual or class, whether king, political party, or dictator, the distinction was not well; it was unjust, and impossible as the basis of business prosperity or of any kind of prosperity.

Recognizing that the legality of money is an artificial quality, it will help our understanding of the matter to bear in mind a definition that comes from Francis A. Walker:

Money is that which every one receives without the slightest reference either to his own need or to the credit of the person who offers it. When an article reaches this degree of acceptability, it becomes money, no matter what it is made of and no matter why people want it.

In the days of the first settlements the colonists carried on their trading by barter. They exchanged things; what they had for what they wanted. But neither article in an exchange could on that account alone be called money. To meet the necessary convenience of measuring quality in this exchanging, the colonists continued resort to the standards and denominations of their home countries. So in New Amsterdam the guilder and in the English Colonies the pound sterling were used for the verbal yardstick—so many guilders worth, so many pounds worth. As the production of a colony increased in some particular commodity, that article from continual use in exchange approached the status of money. In Virginia tobacco became money; and in New York beaver skins. In Rhode Island at one time wool was so recognized, and in South Carolina rice. But at best commodities were not adapted for use as money. As the supply of such a commodity varied, and the demand for it, its intrinsic or market value varied too, which tended to bring confusion into this produce money and to interfere with its usefulness. For example, tobacco in Virginia and Maryland was at one time valued at 3 shillings a pound with 1 shilling 6 pence for second quality; then it fell to 6 pence a pound; and in 1639 to 3 pence a pound. How could it be used as the measure of value? It had to be continually remeasured itself. Anything to be useful as money must be stable in its own value.

193

There was one article that for some years was quite practical for use as money in the Colonies themselves. This was the wampum of the Indians. Much of the small trading of the settlers was with the Indians, and the acceptance of their shell-bead money was sensible and practical. Wampum consisted of white and black or purple beads made from the shells of the periwinkle and of the clam. The black beads were the more valuable. The Indians always insisted in any payment on a certain proportion being in black beads. Wampum began to be used regularly by the colonists in Plymouth and in Massachusetts Bay in 1627. In 1637 wampum was made legal tender at the rate of 6 white or 3 black beads a penny for sums under 1 shilling. Connecticut about the same time received wampum in payment for taxes at the rate of 4 beads for a penny, in 1641 changing the rate for sums under £10. The beads were circulated as money in strings of eight; value: of white beads, 1 penny, 3 pence, 1 shilling, and 5 shillings; of black beads, 2 pence, 6 pence, 2 shillings 6 pence, and 10 shillings. Wampum continued to be legal tender in Massachusetts Bay for everything except taxes until 1661.

These home-made kinds of money did very well for the home trade, inside the Colonies, but they were useless in the foreign trade. Silver and gold were required for paying the balance in the export-import trade. The ocean commerce with the West Indies and with the Spanish Colonies took a great deal of the colonial forest products, and they paid for it in silver. This was more than fortunate while it lasted. But the policy of the British Government, based on the prevalent idea at that time that a colony existed for the commercial and political benefit of the home country, not for the benefit of its inhabitants, bore with disastrous effect on the commerce of the Americans. The English legislation in regard to navigation, beginning with the laws of 1651 and 1660, continuing through 1733 and accumulating up to the time of the Revolution, finally forbade any oceanic commerce to the Colonies except to or through English ports. These laws were however by no means strictly enforced. What might be called smuggling was more practised than mentioned. Accordingly Spanish and Portuguese silver still flowed in, carefully, and the Spanish milled dollar or "piece of eight" (precious to many generations of hay-loft small boys!) became almost a standard coin in all the English Colonies. (Therewith came also the habit of having the Spanish and Portuguese coins one received pretty promptly converted into silverware.)

In this state of things it was natural that Massachusetts Bay with its usual initiative should establish an official Mint for a coinage of its own in Boston with the silversmith, John Hull, in charge. The famous Pine Tree shilling and other coins of the series, rather arbitrarily designated as Willow Tree and Oak Tree coins, were the issues put forth in its thirty-five-year career, from 1652 to 1686, all alike dated the same, 1652. The idea of the single date was that the British Government might deem the coinage the violation of prerogative of a single year rather than as a continuous practice. First, however, coins were issued that are known as the New England shilling and sixpence. These had stamped on them only the initials N E on one side and XII or VI on the other. It was soon found that the large plain surfaces lent themselves readily to clipping and otherwise reducing the amount of silver in the coins. Therefore the New England coins were discontinued within a few months and new designs made that would cover the entire surface of the coin. These were the Pine Tree, Willow and Oak Tree coinages. As already stated, the dies were cast at the Saugus Iron Works and the design was made by the wife of Joseph Jenks, the master mechanic of the company. In 1686 Sir Edmund Andros came to Boston as Viceroy of New England and thereafter regulated the foreign coins for colonial business—that is, gave them a fiat value which might or might not be a true valuation.

But there was not in circulation even then an adequate amount of sound money to conduct the domestic business and foreign commerce of the American Colonies advantageously. There were different local conditions in the different colonies, but the conditions in all were at least similar or the same as in Massachusetts. That Colony had a way of letting itself be heard. The essential trouble, with regard to all alike, was the wrong colonial policy of the British Government. Again Massachusetts led off, with an issue of paper money in 1690. The other Colonies followed. The people generally liked it, accepted it; it was convenient, and it obviated return to barter. But paper money is only a promise. Like an ordinary check on a bank nowadays its value depends not on the name of the one who makes the promise, even though it be the head of the Government, but on the certainty of the promise being kept. In the case of this colonial paper money no provision was made for any proper redeeming of the paper, for any keeping of the promise. The paper money deteriorated in value. When the money was greatly discredited, the Colonial Governments with the consent or by the direction of the Royal Governors redeemed the notes at a small percentage of their face value, retired them, and put out a new issue, a very profitable procedure—for the Government.

Pennsylvania was the only Province in which restraint in the issuance of paper money was exercised. Accordingly the evils of depreciation were not as serious in the land of William Penn and Benjamin Franklin as elsewhere, and that Colony, building more nearly on a basis of sound business, grew up into something more like a real metropolitan prosperity.

For the rest of the Colonies and for the American Colonies as a whole it must be recognized that the results of the British Colonial policy would have been financial catastrophe, except for the unorthodox ways of a considerable and active body of the colonists on the fringe of the regular commerce with England, with their informal entry and clearance of ships, constituting a sort of freedom of the seaports, whereby a ship might clear for one port and arrive at another and yet land a fine cargo on the home wharf without getting into trouble; with their voyages to Madagascar, where one could always do great business—yes; and with their unofficial welcome to free-handed strangers in certain of the home ports.

Money bag and treasure chest

CHAPTER XV

Colonial Glass

ECHNICALLY, glass as made in the early days of the Colonies was a fusion of silica (sand) with two alkaline bases, either soda (found in salt water) or potash (leached from wood ashes) and lime (found in oyster shells). There was much and varied need for glass, in the form of beads, of window glass, and of bottles and other utensils for holding liquids and semiliquids. Steps were taken over and again for starting such factories. At Jamestown in 1621 and in Salem in 1639 glass beads were made for trading with the Indians. To the Indians these glass beads were a specially attractive kind of wampum. Accordingly, to the settlers they were good money, particularly for the fur trade. At New Amsterdam in 1654 a Hollander by the name of Jan Smeedes operated a glass factory, and in 1655 another, Evert Duyckingk, started a glass house in competition. Just what they made is not known, nor how they fared. But it would seem they made an impression, for the street on which they lived and worked was called Glass-Makers Street. It is now called William Street. But many as were the beginnings made by the early colonists, no substantial success attended their efforts until Caspar Wistar started his works near Philadelphia, on the Jersey side of the Delaware River, in 1739.

There was, however, no lack of popular interest in such enterprises. Everybody was glad to know about a new industry in town, and those in control were ready to take advantage even of the inconveniences of the situation, as is testified by at least one of the home-town newspapers:

The Boston Gazette, September 26, 1752—Tuesday last a ship arrived here from Holland, with about 300 Germans, Men, Women & Children, some of whom are going to settle at Germantown, and the others in the Eastern Parts of this Province. . . . Among the Artificers come over in this ship, there are Numbers of Men skilled in making Glass, of various sorts, and a House proper for carrying on that useful manufacture, will be erected at Germantown [now Braintree, Massachusetts] as soon as possible.

and a year later—(Manufacturing had its troubles!):

The Boston Gazette, September 4, 1753—Notice is hereby given, That for the future none will be admitted to see the new manufactory at Germantown, unless they pay at least one shilling lawfull money; and they are desired not to ask above three or four Questions, and not to be offended if they have not a satisfactory answer to all or any of them.

Note—The manufactory has received considerable Damage, and been very much retarded by the great Number of People which are constantly resorting to the House.

Well, people who live in glass houses should not—complain!

THE WISTAR GLASS WORKS

Caspar Wistar (1697–1752) came in 1717 from the Electorate of Heidelberg and settled in Philadelphia. He soon became a prosperous merchant. To his trading he added the manufacture of brass buttons, which, he advertised, he "warranted for seven years." Successful also in love, in 1726 he married well, taking as his bride Catherine Jansen, whose father owned "Wyck," one of the noted houses of Germantown, Philadelphia. In a year a son was born, Richard Wistar. A live man of business, Caspar Wistar recognized the opportunity for a good glass factory properly conducted. He acquired land on Alloways Creek down the river in West Jersey, where there was good sand, plenty of wood for fuel, and convenient access for transportation by water to his markets. Further he made a contract with a sea-captain to bring him from Rotterdam four expert glass-makers who should agree to teach him and his son, *and no one else,* how to make glass, he in turn meeting all expenses, including their support and giving them one third of the net profits.

Caspar Wistar was a good business man, and knew how to provide for his son. Building was increasing; there was a growing demand for window glass, and also for bottles of all kinds, or, as we might more inclusively say, for containers. Caspar Wistar died in 1752; Richard Wistar in 1781. Father and son, they conducted that industry with fine success in every way for forty-two years. Technically the product was of high order of quality. The Wistars were the first American glass manufacturers to make flint glass, substituting oxide of lead for the lime in their composition. Window glass and bottles of various sizes and kinds were their commercial mainstay, but many household and decorative articles were made by them in glass of which the artistic quality was a distinct achievement. As the making of medical concoctions from herbs and other ingredients was quite a household occupation in those days, phials, tubes, and other utensils for the purpose also were among the Wistar products. In 1769, when competition with Stiegel was on, Richard Wistar advertised that they made window glass in five regular sizes between 6x8 and 10x12, and that they would cut specially any sizes under 16x18 on short notice. Bottles from the gallon size down and including snuff and mustard bottles were mentioned as regular products. He also gave notice that "he continues to make the Philadelphia brass buttons noted for their strength and such as were made by his deceased father and warranted for seven years." Artistically considered, a rich green flint glass and a rich brown glass were among their most noted types. They also used two colors of glass, by skillful double-dipping, with excellent effect, and made an interesting cover for bowls and pitchers of glass to match in the form of a sphere that fitted perfectly and decoratively on the major article.

As a business the glass works of Wistarberg, as the place came to be called, were conducted in a prudent, businesslike way. They were a success commercially as well as artistically. The long depression attending the approach and duration of the Revolutionary War bore hard on the affairs of the Wistars as of all. In 1780, not long before the death of Richard Wistar, it was deemed best to discontinue the work and it definitely completed its fine career. The workmen scattered and started a number of glass-factories on similar lines in other localities.

A genius in glass—Heinrich Wilhelm Stiegel, Baron Stiegel of Manheim! Many historical students would doubtless feel safer if we put quotation marks on the baron. But it can never be known for certain whether he was a German baron in the Palatinate or not. Research in Germany has revealed no barony of that name. On the other hand, to himself and to his neighbors he certainly carried with him the atmosphere of a German baron, and carried it effectively, even though we do not accept every fine tale that enthusiastic legendry has produced. As to merit, if achievement in creative art were recognized in heraldry, he would unquestionably rank as at least a baron. His story may be to most of us a little absurd. But spend an hour in some museum looking at his glass with the light going through it, in this direction, in that direction, in sunshine and in shadow, and his story will seem tragic rather than absurd.

Heinrich Wilhelm Stiegel (1729–85) arrived in Philadelphia from Rotterdam in the *Nancy* on August 31, 1750, a young man of twenty-one, with his mother and brother. He came from the Rhine Valley near Cologne. His father had died in 1741. It may be he was of noble birth and that on coming of age he took advantage of his right to abandon his rank, liquidate his estates, and following the trail of so

Typical examples of Stiegel glass at the Metropolitan Museum of Art

1. Mug decorated in the style of the period. 2 and 3. Amethyst glass toilet bottles. 4. Sugar bowl in blue glass. 5. Decorated drinking glass. 6. Salt cellar in dark blue glass. 7. Creamer in clear glass with deep blue rim

many other Palatines, come to Pennsylvania, where he could freely pursue a creative business career in preference to a compulsory military career in European wars.

On November 7, 1752, Stiegel married Elizabeth, the daughter of Jacob Huber, an ironmaster of Lancaster County. She died on February 13, 1758, after giving birth to a second daughter, whom Stiegel named after the mother Elizabeth. A few months later he bought all of Jacob Huber's property there in Elizabeth Township and built a new furnace, which he named Elizabeth Furnace. This was the seat of a prosperous career as an ironmaster. He specialized in stoves. He cast fire backs with designs and inscriptions on them for use in fireplaces, and improved types of stoves, from the five-plate, common among the Pennsylvania-Germans, which had no opening into the room heated, to a noted Baron Stiegel ten-plate wood stove. He also made a variation on Benjamin Franklin's stove or open hearth. Stiegel's ironware was sent even to the West Indies to supply the needs of the sugar industry.

He did well, so well that he felt he could count on the iron business of the Elizabeth Furnace to support his interests and enable him to branch out into new enterprises. His business success proved that his dreams were entirely practicable. The glorious victories of England and of his new country, Pennsylvania, and the other Colonies, over the French at Fort Duquesne and at Quebec encouraged him. In 1760 he became a British citizen, and anglicized his name to Henry William Stiegel. There were possibilities in Glass, commercial possibilities and artistic possibilities, finer, more distinctive, more original than were being realized by any American glass factory (including that across the Delaware at Wistarberg). He could make a success of it. He had of iron. To be sure, at first the fine glass might not pay for itself. But he could afford it. Stiegel Glass! So unquestionably he dreamed. And a man of his temperament is quite apt not to give business considerations fair right of way before the demands of artistic achievement. And so it proved. And the old Barony in the Rhineland! There should be a new Barony equally great or greater on the Susquehanna!

In 1760 he also purchased another furnace, near Womelsdorf, to buttress his fortunes. He called it Charming Forge. There he made bar iron only. Then, as his dreams grew bolder, associating with himself two Philadelphia merchants, Charles and Alexander Stedman, and using his increasing properties as sureties, he went into mortgages and before he was through bought with borrowed money more than 11,000 acres of valuable but undeveloped mineral land, which in spite of the great success of his iron business was quite capable of making him land-poor. He built three baronial mansions. In one of these was a chapel where he expounded the Scriptures to his "retainers," and on the roof a platform for the performances of the band of musicians he gathered from among his workmen. He lived in state and enjoyed it, as William Penn had. When he went forth from his mansion, he drove with coachman and footmen in livery, drawn by eight white horses, and preceded by a pack of hounds. (Some doubt the number of horses, but why not? Four would be nothing special, quite usual.) A cannon reported to the countryside his departure and return. On one of his stove-plates he cast the couplet:

> *Baron Stiegel ist der Mann*
> *Der die Ofen machen kann.*

Der Mann der kann! That was his ambition. He would live in his new country as he might have as a baron in the old! —in spite of the predictions of—?.

And glass! All his success should lead up to what he could do with glass! In 1763 he began his experiments in glass-making at Elizabeth Furnace. At the same time he started building a large glass factory at Manheim. He went over to England and brought expert glassmakers from Bristol to Pennsylvania. On October 29, 1765, he began to produce fine glass at Manheim. It was successful, both artistically and financially, bringing him in an income of £5000. He built and opened another glass-house at Manheim on December 10, 1770. He was proud of his glass. He made window glass, sheet glass, bottles and flasks, yes, and glass tubes and retorts for physicians and chemists; and then drinking glasses of all kinds, decanters and pitchers; tableware, saltcellars, sugar bowls, finger bowls, vases, dishes of all kinds, snuff bottles for gentlemen, scent bottles for ladies of fashion, even toys—everything! He made flint glass too, colorless or "white" of an extraordinary brilliance, attained by the extraordinary purity of the ingredients. And colored glass of exquisite quality and responsiveness to the light—deep blue, amethyst, wine colored, and green. His

Glass-blowing

Adapted from a series of old engravings illustrating the craft

1. The mass of molten glass, taken from the crucible, on the end of the blowpipe is brought to a cylindrical form by rolling it on an iron plate. 2. Beginning the work with the blowpipe. 3. Continuing the blowing until the glass is swollen to a size approximating that of the intended object. 4. The swollen form is made to adhere, by the aid of a small portion of hot glass, to the end of an iron bar. 5. The glass having been detached from the blowpipe is now shaped to the desired form by the glass-worker as he rolls the iron bar on the two arms of his work-bench. 6. Re-heating the glass during the course of the work to have it retain its pliancy so that the glass-worker may shape it to the desired form

flint glass was of light weight and of such structure as to have a remarkably beautiful bell-like resonance to the touch. And he could weave opaque white spirals, "cotton stems," in the clear white stems of his wine glasses. He could engrave and paint in his flint glass—tulips and parrots!—as who had ever done before! Glass, his glass, was the crystallization of light!

But the British commercial policies that brought on the Revolution and destroyed business were having their grievous effect. As they bore hard on the Wistars, so too they bore hard on Stiegel: but Wistar was a better business man than Stiegel. In 1772 Stiegel adopted the name The American Flint Glass Company, and he had an American Flint Glass store in Philadelphia on Second Street, the fifth door above Race. He had a good market in Boston, New York, Philadelphia, and Baltimore, as well as in the near-by Lancaster and York, Pennsylvania. But the times and his affairs were getting worse. In 1773 he styled himself in a New York advertisement the "proprietor of the first American flint-glass manufactory in Pennsylvania," which was true (Wistarberg was in Jersey). But it was too bad; it showed the situation pinched. He needed money to maintain his solvency. His main assets were in land and he could not realize on it. He tried to raise money on lotteries, and failed. In February, 1774, he was sold out by the sheriff, and later in the year was even imprisoned for debt. When released, on Christmas Day—had predictions been fulfilled? He was bankrupt. He did what he could, a little here, a little there. He taught in a country school. He gave music lessons. He did anything, odds and ends. The dream had vanished, but the beauty of it was in the glass he had made during the ten creative years when he proved that he was indeed *Der Mann der kann!* And it is still there. He died at Charming Forge, January 10, 1785.

A beautiful custom perpetuates his memory. In his prosperous days he deeded a church he had built and the churchyard to its congregation, the Zion Lutheran Church. It was a gift, but in order to make the transfer legal it had to be in form of a sale. Accordingly Baron Stiegel required that the consideration be the payment at Manheim every year on the second Sunday in June of a red rose. It is most interesting that Caspar Wistar also gave land to a church in Pennsylvania on the same beautiful condition. The payments are kept up faithfully to the present day both in Richland and in Manheim. It is called the Feast of the Roses.

Diversity of shape and color in early American glass

CHAPTER XVI

New England Ships

IN TURNING to the subject of ships, we turn, both figuratively and literally speaking, to an ocean of interest. The ships as they went plying to and fro on the main road, the water—in the early years almost the only road— were the most important aspect of colonial life. There were two chief purposes for these ships as they sailed across the Atlantic or along its coasts: (1) to fish, and (2) to transport passengers. In both classes very good-sized ships were the first to lift their masts above the horizon of the American colonies. The first fishing boats came a long voyage across the Atlantic to the coast of Maine and to the Newfoundland banks, where a geological submerging of the Atlantic coast from Long Island to Newfoundland had left a shelf and shallow water ideal for fish, especially for cod, mackerel, and halibut. These boats were necessarily large enough and stout enough for the ocean trip. Similarly, passenger service was started with transatlantic voyages and with very substantial vessels for those days. The usual passenger list seems to have numbered about one hundred. Generally speaking, the fishing industry and all that grew out of it centered at Salem in Massachusetts; and the passenger transportation business and its developments at Philadelphia. No colonial seaport equalled either of these two. New York did not begin to equal them until about 1825. It was the Erie Canal that made New York.

The character of the New England shipbuilding and commerce was ordained by the fish long before there were any permanent settlements. The abundance of cod in the North Atlantic was noticed by John Cabot on his first voyage out of Bristol with his son Sebastian Cabot in 1497. He said that it would now no longer be necessary for England to go north to Iceland for its fish. By 1504 the French fishermen and soon afterward the English were already taking their lines and nets to Newfoundland. In 1602 Bartholomew Gosnold gave its significant name to Cape Cod. And when the Pilgrims landed and made the first permanent settlement on the coast of New England in 1620, they counted on the fisheries for their support. The Sacred Cod has for long been recognized as the true emblem of Massachusetts.

The shipbuilding of New England began with the shallop—an open boat fitted with both oars and a sail, that the Pilgrims built for themselves with which to do some exploring around the shores of Massachusetts Bay. It was, so to speak, a personal piece of work. In 1624 a ship carpenter came over from England to Plymouth. He was the first professional shipbuilder. He "quickely builte them 2 very good and strong shallops, and a great and strong lighter." He was going on to build them some larger boats when he fell sick of a fever and died. In 1629 six shipwrights were sent over to Salem by the "Governor and Company of Massachusetts Bay in New England." With them they brought a supply of pitch, tar, cordage, and sailcloth. They built a number of small fishing boats for immediate needs. Their first considerable ship, *The Blessing of the Bay,* a thirty-ton sloop, was built for Governor John Winthrop. It was launched in August, 1631, and was the first to engage in coastwise commerce, with the Dutch at New Amsterdam.

Boats of small size were built locally in numbers. They were usually co-operative ventures. Men of different trades went in together, each put in his kind of work; and when the fishing season came round, each went on the cruise as one of the crew, and had his share of the catch. Fishing and shipbuilding went on together and increased rapidly. From fishing near shore they soon advanced boldly out to sea. Outside the fishing season they brought cargoes of firewood down to Boston, developing a broad wood sloop for this purpose. Shipbuilding also fostered the lumber business, bringing the great white pine masts, many of them thirty-six inches in diameter, down from the Piscataqua River. From trading with near-by settlements they advanced to trading with more distant ports down the coast and steadily advanced to building still larger ships.

Nor was this any slow development. As early as 1634 one Marblehead merchant had eight fishing boats constantly in use, and in 1635 another at Portsmouth, New Hampshire, had six shallops, five other fishing boats with sails and anchors, and thirteen skiffs. This indicates the progress in the local fishing. In 1637 one Richard Hollingsworth had a shipyard at Salem, and following the increasing demand in 1641 built "a prodigious ship of 300 tons." The *May-*

The *Mayflower* of one hundred eighty tons. Twenty years later Hollingsworth's shipyard at Salem produced a ship of three hundred tons

flower was only 180 tons, and this was but twenty years later. Certainly Hollingsworth was justified in his adjective!

And still on! In 1645, according to Governor Winthrop's journal, the first ships went from Massachusetts to the Grand Banks for deep-sea fishing. In 1665 there were regularly 1300 boats fishing off Cape Sable. The increasing hauls of fish were salted and shipped to market. The best was sent to Spain and Portugal, the medium grade to the Canary and the Madeira Islands; the worst to Barbados and other West

Indies for the slaves. In 1665 also there were 300 New England ships trading with ports on the shores of the North Atlantic, from Virginia and the West Indies to Acadia (Nova Scotia) in the north, and across the ocean in Spain and Portugal and their islands. Of trading with England there was most of all, but that was regular; it did not indicate as much colonial initiative as did the trade with the other ports. The exports were fish, salt, lumber, furs and skins (especially beaver-skins), tobacco, horses, and rum.

The shipbuilding increased steadily, the ownership of the vessels also being mostly of New England. For example, in the six months from July to December, 1714, according to the clearance records, there sailed from the port of Boston 236 ships of various kinds, not including fishing boats and coasting craft. Of these 236 ships, 147 were owned in Boston, 61 in other American colonies, 24 in England, and 4 in the West Indies. All but 5 of these 236 were recorded as "plantation built," that is, built in the colonies. The largest was the *Sophia* of Boston, 310 tons, built in New Hampshire, armed with 18 guns, and carrying a crew of 20 men; she sailed for Barbados with a cargo of fish, corn, candles, and lumber. Again, in the 3 months of April, May and June, 1717, 27 ships of various kinds entered the port of Salem, of which 24 were "plantation built."

The attitude of the government of England—and of all governments in the seventeenth and eighteenth centuries— was that the possession of colonies gave a nation the right of absolute control of their productions and of their commerce.

This attitude was certain to make trouble as colonial empires developed for it meant the grave limitation of the growth of the colonies. From the beginning of legislation by the English Parliament along this line in 1645, smuggling also began, inevitably, and trade with privateers and with pirates. This makes the figures of New England shipbuilding and owning and trading, just cited, particularly significant, indeed no less than prophetic.

The slave trade became an important part of commerce in the eighteenth century. For many years the English slave trade was a monopoly of certain privileged corporations, but in 1697 the privilege was extended to all British subjects. Many American ships took part in this trade, most of them from New England. This grew up rapidly in connection with the manufacture of rum in the Triangular Trade. Rum was shipped to the west coast of Africa and exchanged for negroes. These were taken to the West Indies and exchanged for molasses. The molasses was taken home to New England and made into rum, and the triangular course continued. The profits were enormous.

Another fishing industry in which the New England fishermen and shipbuilders became famous was the whale fishing. Before the eighteenth century this was mostly incidental, consisting of catching and killing the whales that drifted into shallow water at low tide and could not get out to deep water again before the next high tide. Early in the eighteenth century, however, the adventurous sea captains and their crews, with their specially built whaling vessels, pursued the whales out to sea. In 1712 Christopher Hussey, cruising along the coast, was blown far out of sight of land. He ran across a sperm whale, which he killed and brought home to Nantucket. This was the first one of the kind known to be taken in those waters. The oil was much finer than of any other kind, and the whalers realized that it was much better worth while to go out into the deep after their prey. Toward the end of the century the whales left the New England coast for arctic waters and the intrepid whalers followed them up into Davis Strait and Baffin Bay, and in 1791 for the first time into the northern Pacific.

A large whale weighed about 90 tons, 30 times as much as an elephant. It often exceeded 100 feet in length. When struck by a harpoon a whale could go 25 miles an hour; the usual speed is about 12 miles an hour, developing something like 145 horse-power. A whale yields 80 barrels of oil, frequently more. There are at least seven kinds of whale. The Sperm Whale and the Right Whale are the most important. The latter was so called because in the early days it was considered the right kind of whale to hunt. Whalebone was obtained from the right whale. The sperm whale was the only one from which sperm oil was obtained. Candles were made of it and exported in large quantities from New England. Spermaceti was in Shakespeare's time considered a cure for almost any ailment, and was counted worth its weight in silver. In Henry IV, Hotspur quotes the dandy contemptuously, "The sovereign'st thing on earth was 'parmaceti [spermaceti] for an inward bruise."

Nantucket was the chief of all whaling ports. Whaling was their whole life, not only their livelihood; they cared

Cutting up the carcass of a whale at sea and hoisting the blubber aboard ship to be tried out into oil

for nothing else. It was regarded as a condescension for a Nantucketer to shake hands with an "off-islander." A young man who had not doubled Cape Horn or harpooned a whale could never win a Nantucket girl for his bride. One who did not live on the island was called a foreigner.

As the whaling vessels increased in size so as to carry greater cargoes, the voyages became longer and longer, until they lasted even four and five years; a two-year voyage was short. About 1730 try-works were built on the whalers instead of on the shore, and the oil was boiled and stowed away at sea, thus permtiting the ships to make still longer voyages. At this time Nantucket had as many whaleships as all the other ports of the American colonies together, and the island's prosperity increased until the Revolution. Then many of her ships were captured or lost, and over 1200 of her men were killed or made prisoners, but Nantucket carried on her whaling through the war, and after it was over started right in and built up her fleet again. The other leading whaling ports were New Bedford, Provincetown, and New London.

In such ways was the regular commerce of the merchantmen built up to the main current of intercolonial and international trade. It should be recognized that during these two centuries commerce was exposed to much regular and irregular danger. When a nation is at war its merchant ships could only expect to be attacked by the enemy. This was regular enough. But when war was declared, or begun without declaration, it was often some time before a merchant ship knew of it. This did not, however, exempt a ship from attack. Further, every nation had its privateers,—war vessels under private operation. The distinction between a government vessel and a privateer was often negligible, especially when the fighting began. Still further, there were many "privateers" that minimized and ignored the government authorization. These were called pirates and were a pretty ruthless type of seaman. It was a matter of fine judgment in those days for a sea captain to determine his attitude when he saw a sail lifting over the horizon. Was it a merchantman, a naval frigate, a privateer, or a pirate; and of what if any nation? He must be ready to maneuver or to fight at any time, and merchantmen were armed for that purpose. Nothing counted but a cool head and a bold front.

As the 1700s took command of the calendar there were all of 1000 vessels officially registered as built in New England, and Salem had the reputation of being the port of the most able and daring sea captains in the New World. That sums it up. As emphasis, for the sake of characterization and contrast, it might be said that the sea life of New England was a life of sailors who built their own ships in order that they might have just what they wanted on which to follow adventure on the seas and struggle for fortune. A few of these may be mentioned.

Philip English was the first of Salem's outstanding sea-captain merchants. In 1676 he owned and was himself sailing a ketch, the *Speedwell,* a fore and aft rigged vessel of no great tonnage with a small mizzenmast forward of the rudder. In only a few years he had twenty-one vessels and was trading down the coast with Virginia and straight out to sea with the West Indies and with Bilbao and French ports on the Bay of Biscay. These New England sea captains were Yankee traders as well as daring sailors!

William Phips (1651–94) came of able parents. Cotton Mather wrote:

His faithful mother had no less than twenty-six children, whereof twenty-one were sons; but equivalent to them all was William, one of the youngest, who, his father dying, was left young with his mother, and with her lived, keeping ye sheep in ye Wilderness until he was eighteen years old.

Then he became apprentice to a shipwright and learned to build sloops and such boats. He went to Boston. He heard and liked stories about Spanish galleons wrecked laden with treasure in the West Indies. He married a wealthy widow who or whose wealth enabled him to take these stories seriously. He failed. He went to London and persuaded the King to let him have a royal frigate for a second attempt. He failed again. A third time he tried, with a small merchantman. He found a galleon and brought up thirty-two tons of silver out of eight fathoms of water, besides other treasure. He played fair with those who fitted him out and with the King. James II made him Sir William Phips and appointed him the first Royal Governor of Massachusetts. He wore fine clothes and lace ruffles with great satisfaction, and with equal satisfaction he used his oaths and his fists. Rough and brave and honest, his troubles were not over, but he faced them like the man he was. He received his greatest honor at the hand of one Nathaniel Hawthorne of Salem.

Captain William Kidd died May 23, 1701, hanged on Execution Dock in London. The date of his birth is not known; he was probably a Scotchman. He was a bold and able seaman, most of his life of good reputation, it may be the same sort of man as Sir William Phips. As we have seen

From Bryant's "History of the United States"

Pirates cruised up and down the Atlantic coast both for trade and plunder

in the chapter about Silver, there had been considerable informal trading between the merchants of New York and not only the privateers but the pirates. Governor Fletcher had not been severe in his administration of the law and in turn had not suffered much at the hands of the merchants. Indeed they had Carol Van Brugh make that handsome silver cup for him as a token of their appreciation. Then William III sent over the Earl of Bellomont as Governor with the injunction to put an end to piracy. He equipped Captain William Kidd with a fine ship and a crew to hunt the pirates out of their ports on the coasts of Madagascar. The story goes that he turned pirate himself and outdid all the others. He returned and walked into a net the Earl of Bellomont laid for him. He was sent to London, tried for hitting a mutinous member of his crew over the head with a wooden bucket, from which he died; for that he was convicted and for that he was hanged. Ralph D. Paine, the marine historian, believes that Captain Kidd was made a scapegoat for disappointed politicians who had expected to gain great riches from his cruise. It is no less a mystery than ever and one that will reward sincere research into the historical material available.

During the Revolutionary War the longest dimension of the American Colonies, almost the only dimension, the coast, was exposed to the depredations of the British Navy. But Lord North proposed in 1775 to forbid the American Colonies to export fish and also to carry on their fisheries off Newfoundland. What would happen to the Americans if they submitted was clear. Submission was unthinkable. We have noticed what happened to Nantucket and its whale fleet. The Colonies had no navy, nor any united authority to create one. Accordingly they authorized merchantmen to arm and to fight at their own expense with the blessing of the Congress. Separate Colonies did the same. These fighting merchantmen were called Privateers. The question of fish made them zealous. One of the finest, most invincible of the privateers of the Revolution was Captain Jonathan Harraden of Salem (1744–1803). He commanded the *General Pickering,* 180 tons, fitted out with 14 six-pounders and 45 men with a letter of marque in the spring of 1780. Harraden sailed for Bilbao with a cargo of sugar, beating off a British privateer of 20 guns on the way. In the Bay of Biscay he found another hostile privateer, the *Golden Eagle.* Sailing up to it after nightfall he roared through his trumpet, "Strike, or I'll sink you with a broadside!" Surprised, the *Golden Eagle* obeyed. As Harraden led his prize into Bilbao, another privateer appeared, the *Achilles* of London, 40 guns and 150 men, which quickly recaptured the *Golden Eagle.* Harraden prepared his ship for battle and then waited for morning. As the *Achilles* bore down on him, every man on the *General Pickering* was ready at his post. For two hours Harraden handled his ship with perfect skill so as to avoid the fire of the *Achilles* while he poured his broadsides into her. Then the *Achilles* put to sea in flight, and Harraden went on with the *Golden Eagle* into Bilbao. Such was Captain Jonathan Harraden out of Salem, and many others.

Another of the same kind was Silas Talbot (1751–1813), who took to the sea at twelve and was a prosperous shipmaster of Providence at twenty-one. He was Colonel of

Infantry under Washington, but took sixty men who knew salt water and cleared Long Island Sound of Tory privateers. This, however, was only a beginning. Talbot accomplished remarkable feats in a little sloop, the *Argo*. In one engagement, well out to sea, with the British privateer, the *Dragon,* more than twice his size in tonnage, in guns, and in men, Talbot had two men lowered over the side to plug the holes in his ship while the fight went on, as the *Argo* was sinking. Soon after the *Dragon's* mainmast came crashing down, which gave him the victory. But while he was patching up the *Argo* and pumping water from her hold another British privateer, the armed brig *Hannah,* bore down on him. Another Yankee, however, came to the help of the *Argo*. The result was that together they took the *Dragon* and the *Hannah* as prizes into New Bedford. Later, in 1799, Silas Talbot as a captain in the American Navy commanded the famous frigate *Constitution*.

Richard Derby, John Derby, Elias Hasket Derby, Elias Hasket Derby, Jr., all four in three generations of one Salem family, did their part to make Salem famous as a seaport. But there were others! Richard Derby was the son of an earlier Richard Derby of Salem; and there was a third Elias Hasket Derby, who was associated with the development of the railroads, those land roads that followed these water roads of his forebears in the transportation of American products. Such families as this make good argument in favor of heredity. But also they bear witness to the effective power of the apprentice system in education. Nowadays engineers, physicians, lawyers gain their special training in professional schools. In the colonial days the sons gained their special training from their fathers in the schools of actual experience. In the chapter on Silver the succession was noted of Paul Revere, Sr. and Jr., in Boston, of Bartholomew LeRoux and Charles LeRoux in New York, and of Philip Syng, Sr. and Jr., of Philadelphia, to cite instances in only one industry. There are advantages to be recognized in both systems. After all there are only two elements in education: the teacher and the student.

Richard Derby (1712–83) went to sea as a youngster. At twenty-four he was commanding a sloop of his own, the *Ranger*. He traded down the coast and doubled on his profits until at forty-five he personally retired from the sea and became a Salem merchant with a fleet of ships trading New England fish, lumber, and farm produce with Spain and the West Indies. As Spain and France were much of the time during the eighteenth century at war with England, Derby's ships were subject to attack from the ships and privateers of these nations as belonging to English colonies, and also to attack by English ships and privateers as they were trading with enemy nations. But Richard Derby accepted these conditions as matters of fact and went ahead, mounting eight to twelve guns on each ship, "with four cannon below decks," as he said, "for close quarters," in case a ship should be boarded. In February, 1775, General Gage sent British regulars out to Salem to seize nineteen cannon stored there,—of which eight belonged to Richard

Derby. On demand that they be surrendered, Captain Derby, at the head of the citizens who met the soldiers at the North River Bridge, replied, "Find them if you can. Take them if you can. But they will never be surrendered." The British commander turned and marched for Boston without more ado. Perhaps there was something in the old sea captain's manner suggestive of the "four cannon below decks for close quarters." This was two months before Lexington and Concord.

It was Captain John Derby, Richard Derby's oldest son, that took to England the news of the fighting at Lexington and Concord, in his swift schooner, the *Quero*. The Royal messenger had started four days before, but Captain John, probably at his father's orders and certainly with his specific approval, put on all sail and arrived in twenty-nine days, a record time in those days. Even in delivering news Salem men had a way of going direct to the enemy and giving it quickly at close range.

Elias Hasket Derby (1739–99), second son of Captain Richard and brother of Captain John, was brought up by his father in the right way and at about the outbreak of the Revolution succeeded to the management of his father's business and built up the family fortune. As the Derby fleet was seriously reduced by the war, he took an active interest in privateering, subscribing regularly for all such shares as were not taken by his fellow citizens. It has been said he owned shares in eighty privateers out of Salem during the Revolution. Soon realizing that many of these ships were not suited for that kind of service, he established shipyards of his own, made a thorough study of the subject, and was in a short time turning out ships of larger size, better design, and greater speed than New England had previously known. Captain Richard Derby was probably the greatest sailor of the family; Captain Elias Hasket Derby was the greatest Salem shipbuilder. There is more to his story and to the story of the family, much more. And to the story of Salem shipbuilders and sea captains. It went on long after the Revolution and after the period of this book.

Now Gloucester has become by general consent the center and symbol of the New England fishermen. Ever since 1623 when the town was first settled this has been one of the chief harbors out of which fishermen have sailed to the Banks and returned with their great hauls of cod and mackerel and halibut. Here at Gloucester stands the bronze statue of the Gloucester Fisherman. Here the tribute is paid to Those Who Have Gone Down to the Sea in Ships and have not returned, their families and fellow fishermen strewing the out-running tide with flowers that shall be carried out to the sea whither have gone the men of this town, of this coast, of this country, in life and in death, for more than 300 years.

CHAPTER XVII

Shipbuilding at Philadelphia

WILLIAM WEST was the first one to build a ship at Philadelphia and was therefore the first shipbuilder at that port. He came over with William Penn in the *Welcome,* arriving on October 24 (Old Style), 1682. He built a ship of some kind for Penn, and Penn paid West for building it in whole or in part with land on the water front, at the foot of Vine Street. There West built him a shipyard and no doubt built other ships, and prospered. In 1762 on a map of Philadelphia there is a wharf or shipyard marked West's at the foot of Vine Street. In the following eighteen or twenty years others also built ships along the Delaware River water front. Of this period William Penn himself said: "Some vessels have been here built and many boats; and by that means [we have] a ready convenience for the passage of people and goods." And Richard Norris, writing in 1690, said of the commerce of Philadelphia, "We have wharfs that a ship of 100 tons may lay her side to." Where there were facilities such as this asserts shipyards would soon appear.

But the most important of the early shipyards of Philadelphia was clearly that of Bartholomew Penrose (1674–

1711). A substantial shipyard was in the field of William Penn's vision for the benefit of his colony. The New England shipbuilding was carried on for the purpose of founding or advancing fortunes by fishing or trading. William Penn was not interested in making a fortune; he had one, a considerable fortune. At his father's death in 1670 he inherited an income equivalent to about $30,000 in money of our time. What William Penn wanted was to populate a large territory. He wanted to transport colonists to Pennsylvania wholesale and fill up the region that Charles II had given him extending far back up into the mountains. As one writer has stated it, Penn's dream was to found a great peaceful Quaker continent. Several shipyards turning out a number of ships would not be enough. The first year after his arrival sixty ships had come into port; that was more than one a week. And yet that was only a mere beginning. For his purpose Penn needed to provide for an increasing supply of ships, establish shipbuilding as a large industry. He must not let the coming of his population be slowed up by any lack of ships for its transportation. His motive and his problem were entirely different from those in New England.

Accordingly it seems probable that he himself took measures for the establishing of the industry on the right lines by inducing Bartholomew Penrose, that exceptionally able young shipwright of Bristol, England, to come over to Pennsylvania for the purpose. The families knew each other. Young Bartholomew's grandfather was a captain in the

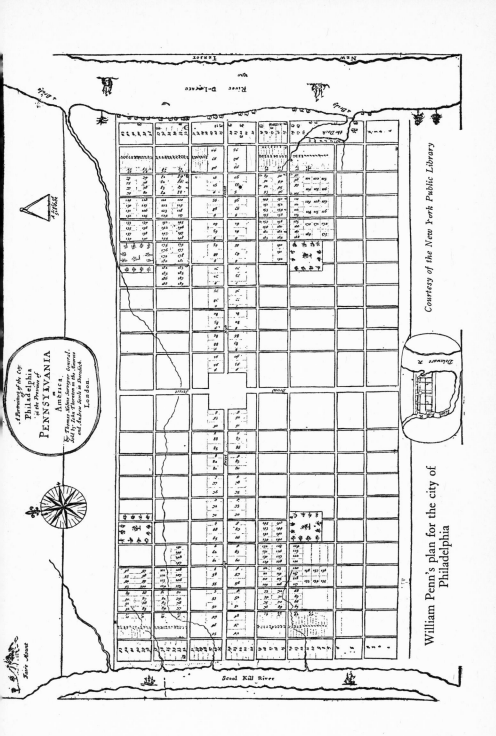

William Penn's plan for the city of
Philadelphia

Royal Navy. He and William Penn's father, Admiral William Penn, knew each other. The captain's son, Bartholomew Penrose, Sr., our Bartholomew's father, was a prominent shipbuilder of Bristol and a member of St. Stephen's Church, where he was married in 1666. There were four children of whom the oldest, Thomas, born in 1669, and the youngest, Bartholomew, Jr., born in 1674, followed their father and became shipbuilders. William Penn knew young Bartholomew and knew his antecedents. He was quite able to judge his quality and his ability.

Young Bartholomew in turn knew all about Pennsylvania from his small boyhood. He was eight years old in 1682 when William Penn sailed in the *Welcome* from Deal in Kent for Pennsylvania; and now he was twenty-four. The idea appealed to him of going to Philadelphia and starting his own shipyard. As Penn had the man for it he wanted, he put money into the plan himself. William Penn, Jr., twenty years old, also put money into it, no doubt with his father's approval if not at his father's suggestion. James Logan, who came to Pennsylvania with William Penn as his secretary in 1699, and William Trent, the Philadelphia merchant and founder of Trenton, also invested in the plan. Young Penrose was starting out under exceptional auspices. Indeed, there were indications of everything being done in accordance with colonial policy. It has been said that these eminent men were partners of Penrose in the shipyard. To the extent of investing money, yes, but it is not at all likely that they took any part in the management or in the work.

This was attended to entirely by Penrose; he was capable. On the other hand it seems that James Logan kept the accounts for some time at least. So Bartholomew Penrose sailed for Philadelphia and arrived in 1700.

Penrose was accepted in good standing in the community as soon as he arrived. He soon acquired land on the water front of excellent location. In 1703 he married Hestor Leech, the daughter of a prominent Quaker. In 1705 he sold a plot of land which was described as bounded by other land of his, and in 1706 he bought from one Edward Smout for £250 a plot of 108 feet on King Street (now Market Street) and 250 feet on Delaware Avenue. What otherwise he was doing these first five years we do not know definitely. Maybe he was building small vessels; maybe he was giving attention to preliminary work, like accumulating a stock of oak and other lumber, so that he could go to work on large ships. The first ship of which we have specific information was the *Diligence,* 150 tons. Construction was begun on this in 1706 at his shipyard at King Street and Delaware Avenue, and it was launched on May 4, 1707.

That day news arrived in Philadelphia of the union of the Kingdoms of England and Scotland. The ship was therefore given the name of the *Happy Union,* but she was nonetheless registered under her original name, the *Diligence,* given her by her builder for the quality that he believed produced results. Bartholomew Penrose himself as captain took her on her first voyage—to Virginia, thence on April 5, 1708, to England, with a convoy consisting of the

London Merchant and two other vessels for mutual protection, then back to Virginia and to Philadelphia. The *London Merchant* was captured by a French privateer, but the *Diligence* made a successful voyage. On this voyage Captain Penrose carried £500 to deliver for James Logan to William Penn in England, and £300 to William Penn, Jr. Little more is known about Bartholomew Penrose. He died when still young, only thirty-six years of age, and was buried in the graveyard of Christ Church, Philadelphia, on November 17, 1711.

Historical material is lamentably lacking in the detail we would wish. But two notable facts have come down to us in regard to the Penrose Shipyards which tend to assure us of William Penn's satisfaction with the plan and with its realization, so far as dreams are ever realized. On Nicholas Scull's map of the Delaware River water front dated November 1, 1762, to which reference has already been made, no less than four wharves or shipyards are marked "Penrose," between Margharetta Street and Wicaco Lane. They are at the following locations, in order from north to south and are designated in the following ways:

1. Between Walnut and Spruce Streets,—Penrose;
2. To the north of the foot of Almond Street,—T. Penrose;
3. To the south of the foot of Almond Street,—Penrose;
4. To the north of the foot of Queen Street,—Penrose.

This would indicate that the Penrose Shipyards, in which William Penn himself was so much interested, were not, especially for those times, any little single business, but attained something of the magnitude required by Penn's plan. It may also be mentioned in confirmation of this that Thomas Penrose (1733–1815) built a British warship in 1762 in his yard at the foot of Almond Street, which was engaged in the attack of some of Spain's colonies in the West Indies.

The other fact is that the Penrose Shipyards continued in Philadelphia for four generations in succession. They were:

1. Bartholomew Penrose (1674–1711);
2. Thomas Penrose (1709–1757);
3. Thomas Penrose (1733–1815);
4. Charles Penrose (1776–1849).

The four generations covered one hundred and fifty years. But there was also Bartholomew Penrose of Bristol, who added at least thirty-five more years to the family's service in the industry. And there were other Penroses that should not be forgotten, beginning with Thomas, the son of Bartholomew of Bristol and older brother of Bartholomew of Philadelphia. Heredity and the apprentice system accounted here for nearly two hundred years of continuity and integrity in the shipbuilding profession. Almost it might seem a fair question to ask what right has a Penrose to go into any other occupation!

This glimpse of the Penrose Shipyards is about as concrete an illustration of Philadelphia shipbuilding as can be shown in the paucity of detailed information. Meager as it is, the story of the Penrose yards is characteristic of the whole both in general conditions and in significance. The situation in the industry was that the best wood for ships was getting scarce in England; it was abundant and of more than special excellence in America. Living conditions were much less expensive here. The great economic opportunity of the time was the opportunity for any one and every one in the colonies across the Atlantic. So to speak, a great draught was drawing the peoples of Europe to America. England had the best territory for colonies and accordingly had the lead in the race. Ships, ships, ships! The ship was the means and the emblem of British prosperity. Every one was interested in ships; every one believed in ships.

It is inevitably of interest to us that just as fifty or sixty years later, as we have seen, there were books on architecture spreading interest in well-built houses, so now there were books on shipbuilding. Edmund Bushnell's *Complete Shipwright* was published in London in 1678, and James Lightbody's *Mariner's Jewel,* also in London in 1695. But England had not come through the days of great Elizabeth without producing a fine body of expert shipbuilders! There was still and always a good and growing market for ships, and William Penn thoroughly understood the importance of the industry. When he went back to England in 1684, he instructed his two sons to learn shipbuilding.

There was a market, there were many markets crying aloud for all the products American ships could bring them. The conditions of commerce at Philadelphia were exactly the same as at the other American colonial ports, except sometimes in varying degree. Whether advantages or difficulties, they were essentially the same. They had troubles with privateers; and they sent out their own privateers. The Quakers very early drew away from the lucrative slave trade and soon forbade it. Penn and his government took active measures to suppress piracy, which was condoned in Philadelphia as much as anywhere. One very frank and amusing instance of this leniency occurred on February 22, 1717, when five pirates acknowledged themselves to be guilty before the Provincial Council, but were acquitted nonetheless by the jury, who were of course under the English law the absolute judges of the facts in the case.

That America had great advantages over England in shipbuilding has been noted. A vessel could be built of superior oak in America for $24 a ton, whereas nowhere in Europe could such a vessel be built for less than $60 a ton. It was a natural result of such conditions that one third of the total tonnage of Great Britain was colonial built. Ships were being built, of some kind, of some tonnage, all the way from Maine south, at Salem, and most of all, thanks to Penn's genius for planning, at Philadelphia. From the coming of Penn to the Revolution, from 1682 to 1775, more than 900 ships of size (not mere boats) were built in the Delaware River yards. Of these many were owned in England and other foreign countries, either absolutely or in partnership. In regard to size, Charles Lyon Chandler says that one of the largest ships built in Philadelphia up to its time was the *Westmoreland,* 200 tons, built in 1743, and owned in London; and that the largest vessel built in Philadelphia before the outbreak of the Revolution was the *Delaware,* 300 tons, listed in 1773 as belonging in part in London and in part in Philadelphia.

During this prosperous period it became quite customary, as has been said, to send from England in advance the goods and mercantile credits to pay for the buying of lumber and for the building of ships which were to be owned in England. This was good business and promoted the interests of both parties, quite contrary to the British theory of the time that only one side could benefit from a business bargain, and that in a colonial empire that side should be the empire. But the Mercantile Theory, as it was called, went to extremes, beyond all hope or possibility of evasion or retraction and brought on the Revolutionary War. England was passing laws that even to England colonial, *i.e.* American, goods could be brought only in British-built ships.

The climax of her eighteenth-century shipbuilding came for Philadelphia just before war broke out, in a time of special prosperity in the industry, from 1775 to 1777, when Joshua Humphreys built on the Delaware the *General Washington* and others of the first ships for the Navy of the Continental Congress. And in December, 1775, the Committee appointed "To devise ways and means for furnishing these Colonies with a naval armament" reported in favor of building 13 ships, of which 4 should be constructed in Pennsylvania, 2 each in Massachusetts, Rhode Island, and

New York, and 1 each in New Hampshire, Connecticut, and Maryland.

In summing up the progress of shipbuilding in Philadelphia before the Revolution, it will be interesting and pertinent to quote Tench Coxe (1755–1824), the eminent economist and a director of the first three censuses of the United States. The passage, written in 1790, is taken from *A View of the United States of America,* a series of papers, which was published in 1794. This is somewhat later than our proper period, but it is for that reason the better inasmuch as it testifies to the result of William Penn's plans in this field and the developments that followed, even after endurance of the strain and pressure of the war.

Shipbuilding is a business in which the port of Philadelphia exceeds most parts of the world. Masts, spars, timber and plank, not only from our own State and the other states on the Delaware, are constantly for sale in our markets; but the mulberry of the Chesapeake and the evergreen or live oak, and the red cedar of the Carolinas and Georgia, are so abundantly imported that nine tenths of our vessels are built with them. No vessels are better than these; and in proof of it, English writers of rank might be quoted who have published for and against us [*i.e.,* in regard to other matters]. A live oak and cedar ship of 200 tons carpenter's measurement, can be fitted to take in a cargo for fourteen pounds currency a ton, and there is not a port in Europe in which (A.D. 1790) an oak ship can be equally well built and fitted for twenty pounds per ton in our money, or twelve pounds sterling. This fact may appear doubtful or extraordinary; but it is certainly true; and it is greatly in favor of our ship carpenters and other tradesmen employed in fitting ships; as well as our merchants and farmers, whose interests are so much connected with navigation. . . .

We find that our trade increases. The crop of 1789 and other exports from the harvest of that year to that of 1790, it is supposed will load 120,000 tons of shipping. We have a very extensive back country; and many large bodies of new land, which must send their produce to the Philadelphia market, are settling fast. The population of Pennsylvania, by the last account taken, was three hundred and sixty thousand men, women and children; but as some years have elapsed, it is supposed it will not fall much short of four hundred thousand when the present enumeration shall be completed.[1]

[1] It proved to be 434,000 by the census of 1791, T. C.

Old Philadelphia water front

CHAPTER XVIII

Trails and Roads

FROM the standpoint of travel there was at first practically only one way to go, by water. From the standpoint of communication also there was only one way,
to send a messenger by water. There were no land roads.
The natural water system, with its many sounds along the
Atlantic coast, with the many estuaries and rivers giving
access for miles up into the continent, and many tributary
streams opening up the fertile tracts, fortunately made land
travel for a long time unnecessary. Even as late as 1735
when Andrew Hamilton of Philadelphia was sent for to
come to New York to defend John Peter Zenger in the
famous trial that established the freedom of the press, he did
not come by land on horseback. He came by water around
Cape May, and he went back the same way.

In the early 1600's the only people who travelled regularly by land were the Indians. They travelled single file,
and one foot straight in line in front of the other. Accordingly the width of the foot, about four inches, was all they
needed for their trails, which were seldom more than eighteen inches wide. These trails were excellent for the Indians.

They went by the shortest distances, usually following streams, and by the easiest grades over hills and mountains. They wound in among the rocks and fallen trees, which were usually of great size. Occasionally in the large growth of the forests, where the crowns shut out the sunlight from the shrubbery beneath, there was easy going for short distances, but except as narrow footpaths the trails were rough in the extreme. It would be exaggeration indeed to speak of them as roads in the white man's sense of the term.

To realize the difference between an Indian's trail and a white man's road one should consider that to make a road only one mile long and only one rod (16½ feet) wide, the settler would have to clear of rocks and trees and brush as much space as a field 90 by 100 feet, more than 10 times the size of the patch covered by a mile of the Indian trail, counted at its widest of 18 inches. It is pertinent also that the Indian did not clear his trail at all; he found it and kept going over it, until it became a good trail. To make a good road in the pioneer days required long hard work.

Much information in regard to road development is available in Connecticut. As this account can only be suggestive and in no way complete we will accept information from that colony as more or less typical of all with gratitude as well as interest.

The first roads were made in the vicinity of the settlements, and went where the settlers had to go habitually, from their homes to the meadows, the pastures, the woods, the mill, and the meeting house. Wherever possible they went along the edge of fields that had already been cleared for raising crops, in other words, through private land. There was a good deal of feeling that a road was still really private land. A road was made by order of the Town, but there were two kinds of town roads, public town roads and private town roads, and the respect for a road as such was closely related to its connection with the settler's own daily life. In the case of a private town road the expense of laying out and maintenance was borne by those who benefited by it. If a road went through a man's land, as it was not fenced, it made an easy way for his cattle to go astray. Neither was a man's farm all fenced, as would seem right and proper to us. Accordingly many of the private town roads or private ways were "pent," or closed at either end by swinging gates, which were paid for by the owner of the land, but had to be opened and closed by the traveller, even if the gates were out of repair.

The inconvenience to the traveller is shown in some of the petitions for public town roads to the meeting houses. The settlers were required by law to attend and were taxed to support particular meeting houses. One petition of people in Lebanon in 1732 said they were four miles from public worship, and had to go through "particular men's proprieties [properties] as trespassers and through thirteen or fourteen fences and many miry places as well as over bad hills and be troublesome to our neighbors."

Again, taking an illustration from trade instead of from religion, the people of the town of Preston petitioned for a road to Stonington harbor, some fifteen miles or more. They carted much lumber down to market, but under present conditions on every journey they had to pull down and replace forty or fifty pairs of bars, and when the owners of the land refused them passage, they often had to go

Many Southern planters located on banks or bays to insure easy transportation for their crops

several miles out of their way over hills and through swamps, and had to take an extra yoke of oxen and an extra man for every load. One can understand their point of view! But one can also understand the point of view of the land-owner whose cleared fields were treated simply as a convenience by people who lived far off somewhere and did not pay for passage. Nor is it a matter for great surprise, in case he wanted a load of gravel, if he took it out of the road that passed his place or passed through his place; nor if he built a fence across a public road and brought suit against those who pulled it down. There were not a few such lawsuits. Many claimed that it was the road that was encroaching on their private property, not they with their fence on the public road.

One John Rall made the issue with the town authorities distinctly personal. Rall built a fence across a public road running from the shore. The authorities evidently called upon him and protested with him for so doing, which was reasonable of them, from their point of view. But according to the record John Rall "did in a violent manner with his hands and attempts with an ax and calling for his sword and gun threatened by force to oppose their passage." Rall was evidently in earnest, and it is fortunate that no one was cut or shot.

The earliest history of roads can therefore be summarized as follows: The local town streets came from the paths through the settlers' cleared fields. These were legalized a little later as rights of way. The legal status of the path between Fulton and Vesey Streets across the churchyard of St. Paul's Chapel in New York City is preserved to this day by the church's formally closing the gates at either end for a day every year.

The highways or country roads between towns, sometimes over great distances, came originally from following the Indian trails, appropriating them by use and widening them by hatchet and axe. The settlers could then go faster and more easily on foot; they could go on horseback; and as long as there were still Indians in the region, they were more free from ambush at close quarters. Even after such improvement there would still be long distances, and those the most difficult, that could only be called Settlers' Trails. Through the eighteenth century these country roads were usually called the King's Highways. The oldest one was laid out in 1638 and connected Hartford with Windsor. There was also a Path, frankly so called, connecting Hartford and New Haven. One road leading in the direction of Providence was in 1691 still a mere bridle path, and it was not until about 1720 that it was widened so that carts could be hauled along it. There was a great deal of indifference to the laws requiring the colonists to work on these roads and keep them in repair. Consequently their condition was usually very bad. The going was tolerably good only near towns. Only one of the King's Highways connected with other colonies. It followed the old Pequot Path and was called the Lower Post Road. It is now called the Boston Post Road.

Even after the roads were most of them wide enough to permit the use of carts or stage coaches, even then ruts and roots and rocks and fallen trees and mudholes and washouts in the bed of the road frequently overturned vehicles and broke cart-wheels and axles, and often stopped progress absolutely by sheer obstruction. Every driver carried an axe with him. It was only the expert traveller who would not better take a guide with him on a journey over the highway. Rivers were crossed at fords, or by ferries propelled by ropes or oars, or sometimes by a sail. There were a few wooden or stone bridges. But bridges were washed away sometimes and it took a long time to build another; and ferries were not all very dependable, though they were often better than the bridges. In such circumstances a long detour upstream to a fordable place was by no means unknown.

Madam Sarah Kemble Knight, the daughter of a Boston merchant and a woman of initiative and courage, made the journey from Boston to New York, under necessity of business, with guides, in the fall of 1704. She wrote a journal of her experiences, which were vivid, as is her account of them. A few extracts will give us equally vivid associations with the Boston Post Road whenever we drive over it. It may well be noted that in case a horse stumbles over a stone in fording a stream the side-saddle did not give as firm a seat as riding astraddle.

About Three afternoon went on with my Third Guide, who Rode very hard: and having crossed Providence Ferry, we came to a River wch they Generally Ride thro'. But I dare not venture; so the Post got a Ladd and Cannoo to carry me to tother side, and hee rid thro' and Led my horse. The Cannoo was very small and shallow, so that when we were in she seem'd redy to take in water, which greatly terrified mee, and caused me to be very circumspect, sitting with my hands fast on each side, my eyes stedy, not daring so much as to lodg my tongue a hair's breadth more on one side of my mouth then tother, nor so much as think on Lott's wife, for a wry thought would have oversett our wherey: But soon put out of this pain, by feeling the Cannoo on shore, wch I as soon almost saluted with my feet; and Rewarding my sculler, again mounted and made the best of our way forwards. . . .

The Post told mee we had neer 14 miles to the next Stage, (where we were to Lodg.) I askt him of the rest of the Rode, foreseeing we must travail in the night. Hee told mee there was a bad River we were to Ride thro', wch was so very firce a hors could sometimes hardly stem it; But it was but narrow, and wee should soon be over. I cannot express The concern of mind this relation sett me in; . . . Thus, absolutely lost in Thought, and dying with the very thoughts of drowning, I come up wth the post, who I did not see till even with his hors: he told mee he stopt for mee; and wee Rode on Very deliberatly a few paces, when we entred a Thickett of Trees and Shrubbs, and I perceived by the Hors's going we were on the descent of a Hill, wch, as wee come neerer the bottom, 'twas totally dark wth the Trees that surrounded it. But I knew by the Going of the Hors wee had entred the water, wch my Guide told mee was the hazzardos River he told me off; and hee, Riding up close to my Side, Bid me not fear—we should be over Imediatly. I now ralyed all the Courage I was mistree of, Know that I must either Venture my fate of drowning, or be left like ye Children in the wood. So, as the Post bid me, I gave Reins to my Nagg; and sitting as Stedy as Just before in the Cannoo, in a few minutes got safe to the other side, which hee told me was the Narragansett country.

Here wee found great difficulty in travailing, the way being very narrow, and on each side the Trees and bushes gave us very unpleasant welcome wth their Branches and bow's, wch wee could not avoid, it being so exceedingly dark. My Guide, as before so now, putt on harder than I, wth my weary bones, could follow; so left mee and the way beehind him. Now Returned my distressed aprehensions of the place where I was: the dolesome woods, my Company next to none, Going I know not whither, and encompased wth Terrifying darkness; The least of which was enough to startle a more Masculine courage.

Madam Knight did not enjoy fording rivers in the night, but neither did she prefer bridges that had been strained by the storms and floods, if not washed away, such as one at Norwalk where she "crept over a timber of broken Bridge about 30 foot long and perhaps 50 foot to the water"; nor another at Stamford which was "exceeding high and very tottering and of vast length."

It does not appear that Madam Knight's fears were the result of "feminine timidity," for in 1773 Josiah Quincy travelled from Boston to New York over this more or less same Post Road and returned by water to Newport and so to Boston, as he doubted whether his horses could stand the journey again. And in 1788 Brissot de Warville travelled over the same Norwalk and Stamford section of the Post Road and wrote of it:

I knew not which to admire most in the driver, his intrepidity or dexterity. I cannot conceive how he avoided dashing the carriage to pieces and how his horses could retain themselves in descending the staircase of rocks.

In comparison with these actual experiences, consider how smoothly a boat would go through the water, whether it were a ship in deep water, or a shallop or a canoe in a running stream, and whether in fair or stormy weather. In the 1700s many a journey took two days or more by land, but only one by water. Even in short distances the preference was habitual. When St. Paul's Chapel in New York City was built in 1764, the main entrance faced the

Hudson River and the parishioners came to church in boats on Sunday mornings, beached at the foot of the church-yard and walked up the green slope to the church.

The roads of the colonial times were built quite as much or more for trade as for travel, for the transportation of goods as for the passage of people. For this work horses were inadequate. Horses were used for riding and later when the roads were passable for drawing carriages and stage coaches. But for hauling loads of lumber or of farm produce through such rough country horses were almost useless. The slow but irresistible power of oxen was better. Horses though strong were too nervous, and their superior speed had no chance over such twisted rocky roads. A horse would give all his strength in vain. It would simply kill him. The eighteenth century was the supreme day of the unhurried ox.

Nonetheless a network of roads gradually spread over the state and their condition was gradually but steadily improved. One of these went from Hartford through the northwest hills to Albany and the Hudson River. It was regularly used in hauling the iron pigs from the furnaces of the Salisbury mines to Hartford and to the Hudson, but the frequent impassability of the road, comparatively good as it was, as frequently interfered with the industry.

There is a delightful incident that should not be omitted in any historical account of colonial roads, just so the technical distinction between what is true and what is truthful be not forgotten. A young Negro belonging to one J.

Danielson of Killingly in the northeast corner of the state was sent to Boston with a load of farm produce. But on account of the exceptionally bad condition of the road, he made so little progress that he went back home again to spend the first night.

Now we leave Connecticut and her bad roads, with regret and with the assurance that every reader will find the colonial roads of the state where he lives or from which he came as bad originally and as interesting as those of Connecticut herself.

But colonial roads inevitably suggest stage-coaches and hotels and roadside inns, though the suggestion almost consists of exaggeration to the point of creation. The development of roads and the development of wheeled vehicles naturally went together. Roads over which it was practicable to drive carriages extended out gradually from the towns and were really extensions of the town streets. In the South they also consisted of the plantation roads of the private estates and the extensions of them. It would be a mistake to think of what roads there were in the eighteenth century as constituting any complete system practicable for carriage use. The farther from towns these "roads" went the worse they became and the more rapidly they lapsed toward being mere broad paths passable only on horseback. During the eight years of the Revolution there was no money nor were there men to spare for road-building. Accordingly while there were carriages and coaches, also chaises (chairs on wheels), they were only such as were adaptable to the existing roads and were used only within those limits. The stage-coach got its name from the limited distance to which it went.

So too a correct understanding will be reached by considering how much business there would be for hotels or inns very far out on roads such as existed in the colonies before the Revolution. Travellers stopped at such houses as there were, expected to be put up, and expected to express their appreciation of hospitality. But also the householder felt free to refer the traveller arriving in the night or even in a storm to another house five miles farther on.

The Reverend Grant Powers tells of such an incident in the upper Connecticut Valley in 1765 or soon thereafter. His father, the Reverend Peter Powers, was returning on horseback one dark rainy night to his home in Newbury. He came to the house of a Deacon Howard near the river in Thetford, and asked to put up. Howard never dreamed that Mr. Powers was anywhere near, nor within many miles. Somewhat abbreviated, the story continues:

"No," said the deacon, "I cannot keep you. Folks have come here until they have eaten me out of house and home. There is a house for entertainment three miles ahead, and you must go there." But at the urgent suggestion of his wife the deacon said, "Where are you from, sir?" "Newbury," replied Mr. Powers. "From *Newbury?*" "Yes, sir." "Well, you know the Reverend Mr. Powers, then, don't you?" "Yes, very well." "And he is a very good man, ain't he?" "Some have a good opinion of him," said Mr. Powers, "much better than I have." "Well, you may go along." But the wife said, "Husband, I *verily* believe that is Mr. Powers." So, making rapid strides after the stranger, the deacon cried out, "Sir, what is your name?" "My name is Powers," was the reply. *"You rascal!"* exclaimed the deacon; and seizing him by one leg, drew him from his horse, held him fast until he got him into the house, and there he made all concessions to the man he loved above all others.

Our ideas of hotels and inns in the eighteenth century should be reconciled with Madam Knight's actual experience, if possible:

When we had Ridd about an how'r, wee come into a thick swamp, wch. by Reason of a great fogg, very much startled mee, it being now very Dark. . . . In about an how'r, or something more, after we left the Swamp, we come to Billinges, where I was to Lodg. My Guide dismounted and very Complasantly help't me down and shewd the door, signing to me wth his hand to Go in; wch. I gladly did—But had not gone many steps into the Room, ere I was Interogated by a young Lady I understood afterwards was the Eldest daughter of the family, with these, or words to this purpose, (viz.) Law for mee—what in the world brings You here at this time a night?—I never see a woman on the Rode so Dreadful late, in all the days of my versall life. Who are You? Where are You going? I'me scared out of my wits—with much more of the same Kind. I stood aghast, Preparing to reply, when in comes my Guide—to him Madam turn'd Roreing out: Lawfull heart, John, is it You?—how de do! Where in the world are you going with this woman? Who is she?

Famous taverns of the better kind were Fraunces' Tavern in New York and the Raleigh Tavern in Williamsburgh, Virginia. The semi-official nature of these taverns is shown by their use on well-known public occasions. The *Virginia*

Gazette reported at one time, not long after the Raleigh Tavern was built in or about 1742:

> Last Friday being the Anniversary of our Most gracious Sovereign's Accession to the Throne, his Excellency the Governor gave a Ball and an elegant Entertainment at the Palace, to a numerous and splendid Company of Ladies and Gentlemen. The Raleigh Tavern likewise, by direction of his Excellency, was opened for the Entertainment of such as might incline to spend the Evening there; Plenty of Liquor was given to the Populace; and the City was handsomely illuminated

Thither also in May, 1769, the members of the House of Burgesses, having been dissolved by the Governor, repaired and organizing as a Convention drew up Articles of Association in a Non-Importation Agreement.

Fraunces' Tavern was the place chosen by Washington to say farewell to his officers on December 4, 1783, at the close of the Revolutionary War. Raising a glass of wine he said simply, "With a heart full of love and gratitude I now take my leave of you, most devoutly wishing that your latter days may be as prosperous and happy as your former ones have been glorious and honorable." The toast was drunk in silence. Then Washington said, "I cannot come to each of you and take my leave, but shall be obliged if you will come and take me by the hand." One by one they came up to him. Not trusting himself to speak and with his eyes full of tears, he grasped the hand of each man and embraced him.

CHAPTER XIX

The Provincial Post

I
T MAY be that people have faults and shortcomings so that other people may have a chance to accomplish something. Water travel was excellent in many respects, but "the wind bloweth where it listeth," and that gave land travel its chance, if only it could develop sufficiently to justify itself and, quite literally, to deliver the goods. This creative necessity came at last with all the dignity and flowing wigs of the Royal Governors. Could land travel develop greater certainty and speed than water for their communications? That was the question. Communication gives unity to endeavor. So it is that the development of the Colonial Posts gave important impetus to the development of land roads, to the opening up of interior territory, and to the creation of intercolonial unity.

There was certainly quite as much advantage to be gained by private citizens through an improved system of communication for them. All progress leads to the welfare of the people as a whole. That is what government is for, for the benefit of all. But people who are engaged in the work that is for all, *i.e.,* in government, are apt and always have been apt to forget that it is not a privilege they confer on the governed but a privilege they receive in the opportunity to share in so great and so important a work. The best standpoint is that work is work and must be done, and he who has the understanding to enjoy his work is the gainer. It is a fact that the first development of the Colonial Posts to amount to anything came for the benefit of the Royal Governors, and then rapidly grew and spread for the benefit of all the people of the American Colonies.

At first any one who had a message to send, be he Governor or private person, sent it by a friend or by a servant, and either by word of mouth or written by hand. There was no regular way. Letters coming from over seas were left at some coffee house or inn, and people came there to get what there might be for them and took what they thought they should have opportunity to deliver. It was some years before any one in the Government thought of establishing any rule or regulation about the matter.

Massachusetts had a way of going ahead simply on call of necessity for action of some kind, without waiting to pay respect to the Royal or other Authorities in such case made and provided. Massachusetts therefore was quite naturally the first to do something about the sending and receiving of letters from over seas. In 1639 the General Court of Massachusetts Resolved: For the Preventing the Miscarriage of Letters:

It is ordered that notice be given that Richard Fairbanks his house in Boston is the place appointed for all letters, which are brought from beyond the seas or are to be sent thither, are to bee

A post rider.—In the beginning (January, 1673) each first Monday in the month one set out from New York, to return within the month

brought to him and he is to take care, that they be delivered, or sent according to their directions, and hee is allowed for every such letter 1d. and must answer all miscarriages through his owne neglect in this kind; provided that no man shall bee compelled to bring his letters thither except hee please.

This applied only to letters from England and made sure they were left at one and the same place on arrival in Boston Harbor.

In 1647 the Dutch Government for New Netherland passed a law to regulate the transmission of letters, which provided that no one might visit an incoming ship until the representative of the Governor had boarded her and had received any and all letters she carried, under penalty of heavy fine. This law also applied only to foreign letters.

With regard to domestic letters it was evidently still presumed that the sender could use his own judgment in selecting the messenger to whom he entrusted his letter and was responsible for the results of his selection. There were nonetheless many expressions of opinion that conditions might be bettered, like the reason given by an Ipswich man to Governor John Winthrop, Jr., in 1652, for his not writing sooner, "the uncertainty when and how to convey letters."

Virginia was the first to provide for delivery of letters in America. It was also the first formal provision in favor of official letters. In 1661 the Virginia Assembly voted into law what had become a custom by 1658, that the planters must forward official letters from plantation to plantation until they reached the ones to whom they were addressed. The penaly for failure so to forward an official communication was 350 pounds of tobacco.

But the best plan and the first to establish an intercolonial post or mail was that of Governor Francis Lovelace of New York in 1673. In just appreciation of this plan it should be remembered that there was no through road at this time between New York and Boston. The relations between the English and the Dutch were not such as to require facilities for communication or indeed to make them desirable. Until New Amsterdam became New York a good defensible barrier was better. A good route for such a post road had to be determined. The first post rider took on his first trip the news of the plan proposed by Governor Lovelace, and he embodied it in himself.

On December 10, 1672, Governor Lovelace issued a proclamation for his own people, and wrote a letter to Governor John Winthrop, Jr., of Connecticut, which the post rider was to deliver. With it went "a pacquett of the latest intelligence I could meet withal" from England, as a demonstration of the practical advantages of his plan. Some extracts from this letter will show how well it had been thought out.

This person that has undertaken the imployment I conceaved most proper, being both active, stout and indefatigable. He is sworne as to his fidelity. I have affixt an annuall sallery on him, which, together with the advantage of his letters and other small portable packes, may afford him a handsome livelyhood. Hartford is the first stage I have designed him to change his horse, where constantly I expect he should have a fresh one lye. All letters outward (from New York) shall be delivered gratis, with a signification of *Post Payd* on the superscription; and reciprocally, we expect all to us free. Each first Monday of the month he sets out from New York, and is to return within the month to us againe. . . . Thus you see the scheme I have drawne to promote a happy correspondence.

I shall only beg of you your furtherance to so universall a good work; that is to afford him direction where and to whom to make his application to upon his arrival at Boston; as likewise to afford him what letters you can to establish him in that imployment there. It would be much advantageous to our designe, if in the intervall you discoursed with some of the most able woodmen, to make out the best and most facile way for a Post, which in process of tyme would be the King's best highway; as likewise passages and accommodation at Rivers, fords, or other necessary places.

Governor Lovelace further expressed his hopes for the plan as follows:

If it receive but the same ardent inclinations from you as at first it hath from myself, by our monthly advisoes all publique occurrences may be transmitted between us, together with severall other great conveniencys of publique importance, consonant to the commands laid upon us by His sacred Majestie, who strictly injoins all his American subjects to enter into a close correspondency with each other. This I look upon as the most compendious means to beget a mutual understanding.

His hopes were justified. The plan was statesmanlike.

It was Governor Lovelace's intention that his post rider

should start from New York on his first trip on January 1, 1673. He decided to defer the date however and the rider did start on January 22, 1673. He was sworn to behave civilly, to inquire the best route for the post to follow, and to blaze a path for the guidance of future travellers. The plan started out auspiciously, but failed after only a few trips on account of stupid and fatal policies on the part of the Royal Government in England. A Dutch fleet, of twenty-three warships under Admiral Cornelis Evertsen, with 1600 troops in addition to the crews, sailed up from the West Indies and in a few days changed New York back to Nieuw Nederlandt again. The plan was not revived when Nieuw Nederlandt was returned to England in 1674, as the foreign motive was now lacking, to unite the colonies against the attacks of a European enemy. There was no further need appreciated by the home government, and that government never dreamed there would ever be need to strengthen the ties that united the colonies to England. A wise development of Lovelace's plan would have been an excellent step in such a statesmanlike policy.

Massachusetts was first again in appointing a letter carrier for the domestic mail, when the merchants urged and the General Court passed a law "to depute some mete person to take in and convey letters according to direction"; and also "to sett the prices on letters." John Hayward was appointed to this office on December 27, 1677, and held it until his death in 1687, when his son was appointed to continue the work.

About twelve years later, in 1684, Governor Dongan in New York had a plan for a chain of post houses and riders from Nova Scotia to the Carolinas, but there was much that was impracticable about it and there were no substantial results. In Pennsylvania, William Penn's government sent their official communications at first through justices of the peace, sheriffs, and constables, as these officers had authority to press horse or man into service at any time. In 1685 Penn ordered a post office to be established with authority to Henry Waldy of Tekonay to carry letters and to supply passengers with horses to New Castle or to the Falls of the Delaware (Bethlehem), once a week, with prices for single letters from 3d to 9d according to size.

The affairs of the post, such as they were, were troubled during the brief reign of James II, formerly Duke of York. He sent Edward Randolph over with authority as Deputy Postmaster General, but in the vigorous little revolution in Massachusetts in 1689 he went into prison in Boston along with Sir Edmund Andros, King James's devoted Governor of New York and New England. So ended the first period of the development of the postal system of the American Colonies.

Under William III a new system for the Posts in the Colonies was inaugurated, as a monopoly under royal patent on February 17, 1692, to one Thomas Neale, for a period of twenty-one years. Neale was simply a court favorite, whose personal loyalty to the King would ensure attention to the interests of the Government, and who would give the Colonial Posts sufficient attention to ensure a profit, from which he was to pay six shillings a year into the Royal Treasury. In other words, whatever he could make was to be his. He was not expected to go to America, and he did not. He sent as his deputy a Scotchman named Andrew Hamilton, who had been in the Jerseys in 1685 as the Agent of the Proprietors and had also been Governor there. Hamilton was an excellent appointment, and secured co-operation from some of the colonial governments, notably from New York, Massachusetts, Pennsylvania, and Virginia. Hamilton established a line of posts from Portsmouth, New Hampshire, to Philadelphia, with a weekly service each way.

But the inaction of some of the Colonies and the impracticability of a post service at that time in others made the development of the system uneven and expensive. The best business showing was from the offices of the "Boston, Road Island, Connecticut and Piscataway Posts." But from Neale's standpoint of a profitable monopoly, there were no profits. To May, 1697, Neale's expenses were £3817, and his receipts £1457, leaving him a deficit from the royal generosity of £2360, which he had to make good. He naturally felt he had had enough and offered to give up his rights in the American posts for £5000, or for £1000 a year for the life of his patent. But the Government declined to agree to this proposal. The next year Thomas Neale died, heavily in debt. His interests in the American Posts were assigned to two creditors, Hamilton and an

Englishman by the name of West. These two continued the administration until 1703, when Andrew Hamilton died. His widow inherited his rights and authority until 1706. In 1707 the British Government bought all the rights in the American Post Office for £1664.

An Act of Parliament in 1710 centralized the postal systems of all England's possessions. The Post Master of London became the Post Master General and under him there were four Deputy Post Masters General, at Edinburgh, Dublin, New York, and in the West Indies. It was evident that a service showing such steady development and such increasing public importance as the postal service in the American Colonies should not be subject to the changes of private fortune. On the other hand the success of private management under Andrew Hamilton and since his death under his son was recognized, and accordingly John Hamilton, Andrew Hamilton's son, was appointed Deputy Post Master General at New York with charge of all postal business in the continental Colonies; and he so continued until 1730.

Steady improvement was made in the American post under John Hamilton. Improvement is usually the result of attention to details based on a practical knowledge of the work. Some of the difficulties to be overcome were of a natural character, such as the bad roads or the absence of any roads at all. Without through roads there can be no through interests. In other words there can be no common interests in the absence of adequate communication. As long as New York was Dutch there could be no through road to Boston or into Connecticut. As long as there were only occasional common interests a monthly or a weekly post would be sufficient and that was all there was. It was a matter of natural growth. The population of all the colonies at this time amounted to about 275,000, of which 100,000 were in New England, and 20,000 more in New York. The more people the more common interests, and the more posts.

In 1707 there was a regular weekly post from Boston into New Hampshire, into Maine, into Rhode Island and Connecticut and into the middle colonies, but beyond Philadelphia there was no regularity in the transportation of letters. Lord Cornbury, Governor of New York, writing to the Lords of Trade said that "sometimes a letter is six weeks coming from Virginia, sometimes longer."

But the weather often made trouble and delay enough. For example, *The Boston News-Letter* reported in its issue for February 5, 1705:

> The East post came in Saturday, . . . who says there is no Travailing with horses, especially beyond Newbury, but with snowshoes, which our people do much use now that never did before. The West post likewise says 'tis very bad Travailing.

No doubt Madam Knight would have confirmed their report. This was only three or four months after her journey. The weather had its effect farther south also. In 1717 Jonathan Dickinson of Pennsylvania wrote that advices from Boston unto Williamsburg in Virginia is completed in four weeks from March to December and in double that time in the other months of the year.

The regular schedule of the post in 1715 was creditable. The post left Philadelphia for New York every Friday by way of Burlington and Perth Amboy. Arriving at New York on Saturday night, he left for Boston on the following Monday morning by way of the shore of Long Island Sound to New Haven and to Saybrook, where he met the rider from Boston and exchanged bags. He also had left Boston on Monday and had served Bristol, Rhode Island, Stonington and New London, Connecticut, on his way. North of Boston there were offices at Salem, Marblehead, Newbury and Portsmouth. The rates of charge, fixed by law, were according to the distance of the destination—4d. up to 60 miles; 6d. from 60 to 100 miles; and so forth.

Politics entered into the difficult situation of the post in the days of its development, as was inevitable. There was a fundamental disagreement between the British Government and the American Colonists, whether the Colonies existed simply for the benefit of England or whether the Colonists were simply Englishmen in America and had the same rights as Englishmen in England. The Post had before 1710 been mainly a concern of the Colonies. Accordingly the Colonial Legislatures continued to pass acts whenever they thought it good and right to establish new post routes and to encourage the use of them, even though the posts were now all under the management of the British

Post Office. It was practically an informal joint control that was now in charge of the American posts.

But serious opposition developed in Virginia against the postal system when it was noticed that the rates charged for the transmission of letters were greater than those charged before. The House of Burgesses charged that the establishment of postal rates by Act of Parliament without submission to the Colonial legislatures constituted taxation without representation. The House declared the Act of 1710 void, refused to grant supplies of money, and passed other obstructive acts. They maintained a quarrel with Governor Alexander Spotswood for a number of years. Finally in 1730, Governor Spotswood was appointed Deputy Post Master General for America, a good and wise appointment, and the situation improved. The weekly mail from Portsmouth to Philadelphia was the same year extended to Virginia.

There was now a distinction between the postmasters who collected and delivered the letters in the various towns and the post riders who carried them between the towns on their regular routes. The postmasters did not yet have the right to refuse delivery without payment of postage. The prepayment provided by Governor Lovelace in his plan was a wise measure. The postmaster at Perth Amboy decided to give fair warning in *The American Weekly Mercury,* in October, 1735, as follows:

This is to give notice to all persons in Town and Country that are indebted to Andrew Hay, Postmaster at Perth Amboy for the postage of letters to pay the same or they may expect T[r]ouble; some having been due near four years. Signed   And. Hay.

Governor Spotswood undertook to manage and extend all the American posts for a salary of £300 a year plus 10 per cent of the clear profits, for a period of ten years. He served however only nine years. He appointed Benjamin Franklin to be Deputy Postmaster at Philadelphia in 1737, one of the best things he did in itself, and one of the most fruitful in the experience it gave Franklin. In 1739 Spotswood was succeeded by Head Lynch, and he in turn in 1743 by Elliott Benger of Virginia. In 1753 Benger died and Benjamin Franklin and William Hunter of Virginia were appointed joint Postmasters General for America. Each of them was allowed a salary of £300 a year out of the profits of the office. It was for them to see that there were profits. Franklin had very much wanted the appointment. In those days it was quite customary for a man or his friends to contribute to the campaign expenses when the vacancy was to be filled by appointment as well as when by election. Friends of Benjamin Franklin did contribute generously, £300, among them Judge Allen of Philadelphia. Franklin said in a letter that £200 had been raised to help the appointment of both Lynch and Benger, but he hoped that he would not lose because of too small a contribution. With his inimitable humor he closed a postscript to the letter,

However, the less it costs the better, as 'tis an office for Life only, which is a very uncertain tenure.

£300 it was. And whether we have better ideas on the general question now or not, no better appointment could possibly have been made.

From his experience in the post office at Philadelphia Franklin knew just where improvements needed to be made and could be made and from his practical sense how they could be made. He made a tour of inspection of all the post offices in the north and as far south as Virginia very soon after his appointment. In consequence he effected a saving of half the time in the transmission of letters by requiring the post riders to ride at night as well as by day. In 1763, when William Hunter had been succeeded in 1761 by John Foxcroft of New York as Franklin's associate, Franklin made another tour of inspection to the north, while Foxcroft went to the south. Of the almost insuperable difficulties before the posts in the south it was found that in one district it was necessary to ride one horse 200 miles before a fresh one could be obtained. Further, the distance from Williamsburg, Virginia, to Charleston, South Carolina, was 480 miles. Water travel still had the advantage over land!

The law did not provide for the carriage of newspapers by the post, and specified no rates for them. Accordingly the post did not carry newspapers, officially. But unofficially, they did. Lovelace had something very much like a newspaper in mind in his "pacquett of the latest intelligence he could meet withal," of which the post would bring a monthly fresh supply. Most of the postmasters published newspapers. *The Boston News-Letter,* the first American newspaper, was published by William Campbell, the postmaster at Boston, and he gave his sheet a specially significant, indeed a literal, name. So the postmaster gathered his news through the post to a great extent, and had the post rider carry and distribute it—and he saw to it that the post rider carried no other newspaper but his. Franklin did the same. Telling of his appointment to be postmaster at Philadelphia, the candid Benjamin wrote in his autobiography:

I accepted it readily and found it of great advantage; for though the salary was small, it facilitated the correspondence that improved my newspaper, increased the number demanded, as well as the advertisements to be inserted, so that it came to afford me a considerable income.

But when Franklin became Postmaster General he put an end to his own monopoly and to that of all postmaster-newspaper publishers. He ordered post riders to carry all newspapers, and established rates for them: not over 50 miles 9d.; between 50 and 100 miles 1s. 6d., and so on. He asserted that "newspapers which are on many occasions useful to Government and advantageous to Publique" should be admitted to the mail.

As the postmasters enjoyed natural perquisites, so also did the post riders. As he was going to such and such a town anyway, certainly he would do an errand for a friend, glad to, and the friend would in turn give proof of his grateful appreciation, and both parties benefited, even if that were not in accordance with the theory of the British Government. If such courtesies do not go to extremes, there is usually no great harm done. And if they do go to extremes, they may not always become really serious, but they do become distinctly humorous. One particular rider was reported as habitually carrying only four or five letters in his bag, officially, but a whole "tableful" unofficially for his own profit. In another instance, a high government official met a post rider driving some oxen along the road which he had undertaken to deliver for a customer in another town!

But these were extremes. One person can go to an extreme; it takes many to improve a service and to maintain it. This fine service of most of the post riders was summed up in the remittance that Franklin sent to the Royal Treasury in 1761 as the total surplus for the first eight years, £494, 4s. 8d. the appreciative acknowledgment of which was that it was "the first remittance ever made of the kind."

Franklin himself however got into trouble. He accepted the position of Agent for Massachusetts in London to secure the repeal of the Stamp Act. Foxcroft meantime stayed in America attending to their joint responsibilities as Postmasters General. No man can serve two masters, even if there be not a growing difference between them. His absence from America gave his enemies opportunity to criticize him. Franklin came into possession of some letters of Governor Thomas Hutchinson tending to rouse the hostility of the British Government against Massachusetts, and he felt it his duty to send the letters to the Massachusetts Assembly. The matter came to the attention of the Privy Council and a few days later Franklin was dismissed from his position as Postmaster General. This was in 1774.

Meantime feeling was rising high in the American Colonies. Under the lead of the Sons of Liberty the observance of the postal regulations was not at all particular, any more than was the observance of other British regulations. Franklin would have been in a difficult position if he had still been obliged to enforce those regulations. The Colonial leaders fully appreciated the importance of the post, and developed their own Committees of Correspondence. On April 28, 1775, the Committee of Safety at Boston recommended the formation of an independent postal service, and on May 29, 1775, the Continental Congress appointed a committee with Benjamin Franklin at its head to perfect the organization of such an independent postal service. But the competition of this Colonial service had already killed the British postal service. On May 4, 1775, it became known that the British Post Master General, John Foxcroft, had discharged his post riders for lack of funds.

Before the days of envelopes letters were folded and sealed

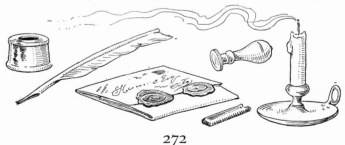

CHAPTER XX

Agriculture in the Colonies

THE Colonial Posts with their official importance insisted on roads, and the Colonial Roads as they came into being led out from the towns to the country, to the newly opened regions, and toward the as yet unopened wilderness. To the towns the roads meant a plentiful supply of food and other farm products. To the individual family the roads meant freedom and independent opportunity, quiet, and a chance to become self-reliant. Roads might also lead to other towns, but insofar they continued town functions and were really streets rather than roads.

Towns as well as people need to keep in touch with the country, with the soil. The old Greek fable of the giant Antæus, who drew his strength from the soil, who was a giant because he kept in touch with the earth—that fable was so literally true that almost it was not a fable. So the individual has always gone for re-creation to the country, and always will, though for rec-reation he may go to the town. So too the towns themselves go necessarily for rejuvenation to the country, even for their water supply.

Then too in the country the roads lead to the new.

Normally progress comes from the country, the source of strength. The large number of leaders in public affairs of all kinds have been country-born and country-bred. The strength of Virginia in colonial days lay in its leading

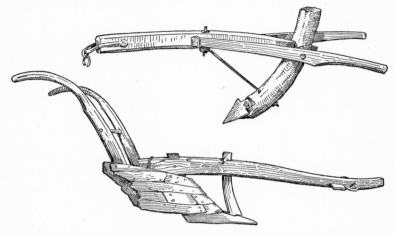

Above: An early Pennsylvania plow of simple construction
Below: One of the first forms of a plow with mould-board

entirely a country life, not in the pleasant aristocratic quality of that life. Essentially it was the same strength as that of New England, of the Middle Colonies, of the Scotch-Irish in the Alleghenies, looking out toward the West, and of the other colonies of the South.

As different as were the aristocratic Virginians and the Puritan New Englanders and the rough-and-ready Scotch-Irish, so different also was their farming, inevitably different, for the earth gives freedom to be independent and to be as different as one wills. A little may be told of colonial farming, but it should not be forgotten that general statements are made at the risk of becoming thereby untrue. Only in the particular instance is there entire safety of statement. In that lies its interest, its fascination.

Until the year 1763 the English Colonies, their settlers and their farms were shut down by the French and their allied Indians to a strip along the Atlantic coast seldom more than 100 miles wide. Of the farming they did in this strip, Jared Eliot of Killingworth, Connecticut, wrote in 1747:

When our forefathers settled here, they entered a Land which probably never had been Ploughed since the Creation; the Land being new they depended upon the natural Fertility of the Ground, which served their purpose very well, and when they had worn out one piece they cleared another, without any concern to amend their Land, except a little helped by the Fold and Cartdung. . . . Our Lands being thus worn out, I suppose to be one reason why so many are inclined to Remove to new Places that they may raise Wheat: As also that they may have more Room, thinking that we live too thick.

Of the rotation of crops little had been found out then, nor that it was a better and a quicker way to restore the land than letting it lie fallow. Incidentally, Jared Eliot refers to those who valued the quiet of the country, those who even in those days thought they lived too thick and wanted more room.

The chief natural grain crop was Indian corn or maize. So far as the English settlers knew, this was indigenous to North America. They learned about it and learned how to cultivate it from the Indians. Maize had so many advantages as a crop for pioneers that it immediately took precedence over the grains of which the settlers brought seed with them from Europe. For example, in a considerable

From the old "Scribner's Monthly"

An old farm-yard, Long Island

group of farms in Massachusetts that raised altogether 666 bushels of maize, wheat, barley, peas, oats and rye, 275 bushels were of maize; wheat came next with 152 bushels.

One of the advantages in maize from the pioneer's standpoint was that beans and pumpkins could be planted in the same ground at the same time. The maize matured first, and when that crop was in the cornstalk still served as poles for the beans and the pumpkin vines spread among

276

the hills of maize with their golden food crop in the autumn.

Wheat was a failure at Plymouth in 1621. The particular adaptation in the cultivating of the wheat in that soil, or in any of the New England soils, had not yet been worked out. Twenty years afterward, in 1641, at Hartford, wheat was a success. The whole Connecticut Valley became a wheat and cereal raising and exporting region. After the harvest of 1652 John Pynchon of Springfield made ship-ments of 1500 bushels of wheat alone.

Throwing light on both the richness of the virgin soil and on the bold intelligence of much of the colonial farm-ing, a Doctor More wrote of his own experiences in Penn-sylvania. This was in 1686, quite early for Pennsylvania.

The last year I did plant about twelve Acres of Indian corn, and when it came off the Ground, I did only cause the Ground to be Harrowed, and upon that I did sow both Wheat and Rye, at which many Laughed, saying, That I could not expect any corn [grain] from what I had sowed, the Land wanting more Labour; yet I had this Year as good Wheat and Rye upon it, as was to be found in any other place, and that very Bright Corn [grain of good color].

Doctor More got the benefit to some extent of the rotation of crops as well as of a native rich soil, did he not?

The cultivation of garden vegetables, except pumpkins, beans and other squashes with the maize was lacking in the earliest days down through all the colonies. When they were introduced some can be credited to distinct re-

277

gions. Cabbages, turnips, onions, carrots and parsnips came through New England. Beets, spinach, endive, leeks, and some of the herbs such as parsley, dill and chervil were brought by the Dutch. Muskmelons and watermelons also

From the old "Scribner's Monthly"

An old farm-house on Newport Island

came through the port of New Netherland. Asparagus and cauliflower are of Pennsylvania German local origin. Sweet potatoes, which belong to the morning glory family, were indigenous in Virginia and the eastern shore of Maryland. White potatoes, no relative of the sweet potato, came from farther south, but mostly by a roundabout way, through the West Indies and Ireland, some say by way of Virginia. They did not reach New England until about 1718, when they came along with the Scotch-Irish. These Scotch-Irish had a bit of special independence in them, and while they no doubt should be credited to William Penn and his advertisement for settlers, they wished to go somewhere else than their cousins in Pennsylvania. But for some time the potato was a special dish everywhere in America, not to say a rarity, eaten only with roast meat. Three bushels was a large quantity to raise for a farmer's family, to last them through the year. In the latter part of the eighteenth century they were a great crop in the South. One planter in Georgia raised 300 bushels on a quarter of an acre, by contemporary testimony.

Our fruit-Trees prosper abundantly, Apple-trees, Pear-trees, Quince-trees, Cherry-trees, Plum-trees, Barberry-trees. I have observed with admiration, that the Kernels sown or the Succors planted produce as fair & good fruit, without graffing, as the Tree from whence they were taken: the Countrey's replenished with fair [beautiful] and large Orchards.

Thus testified another contemporary, named Josselyn, an English traveller, of the fruit in the Colonies in the 1700s. Of the apples near Bergen in New Jersey more specific information was available:

One kind was very large, fair, and of good taste, fifty-six of which only could be put in a heaped up bushel, that is, half a bag.

Peaches arrived on the Delaware River before William Penn did, probably with the Swedes. And grapes were raised, of a kind right for the making of wine in the early days of the Jerseys. The peaches were used for making peach brandy too, for which copper stills were used. But both for eating and for drinking the apple was the supreme fruit. Before 1700 cider attained a popularity as a farm beverage that was unequalled for many years, though it did not displace beer for some time after the turn of the century.

Of live stock the colonist had neat cattle, sheep, goats, swine, and horses—but at first none. The Indians had no domestic animals, not in the hundred-mile strip east of the Allegheny Mountains. One reason doubtless was a reason that continued as a difficulty for the white man, there was not adequate forage for such animals. North America was deficient in forage plants such as timothy, blue grass, and the red and the white clovers. The colonists had to import from Europe both the domestic animals and the forage plants for their sustenance. The only source was Europe.

The first pastures were the clearings in the woods which the Indians had burned open, and the natural clearings along the banks of the streams. Here grew two kinds of forage plants. One was the wild rye, the common grass along the Atlantic coast from Virginia north; the other was broom straw, which was the more abundant grass in the Middle Colonies. In the summer these were all right, but the proportion of roughage to nutriment in them was so great that cattle did not thrive on them in the winter. The ever-practical Captain John Smith gave warning on them.

From the old "Scribner's Monthly"

Pitching off a load of hay

Haying in the old days of hand mowing was a thirty or forty day war in which the farmer and his "hands" were pitted against the heat and rain and the legions of timothy and clover

There is grasse plenty, though very long and thicke stalked, which being neither mowne nor eaten, (when it is young) is very ranke, yet all their cattell like and prosper well therewith, but indeed it is weeds, herbs, and grasse growing together, which

From the old "Scribner's Monthly"

One of several types of old hay-wagon

although they be good and sweet in the Summer, they will deceive your cattell in winter; therefore be carefull in the Spring to mow the swamps, and the lowlands . . .

English forage plants were introduced into America as early as 1663 or 1665, probably by accident, in the fodder for cattle on shipboard. They were blue grass and white clover. These soon were commonly known as "English grass." In a work written in 1685 entitled *Good Order Established in Pennsylvania and New Jersey,* it was stated that mutton throve well on the natural grass, but if we sprinkle a little *English* Hay-Seed on the Land without Plowing, and then feed Sheep on it, in a little time it will so encrease, that it will cover the Land with *English* Grass, like unto our Pastures in *England,* provided the Land be good.

The farm of the settler or pioneer is of necessity self-sufficing; he must practise mixed husbandry. To protect his growing crops from his live stock each settler would have to fence all his fields. It would be easier to fence his live stock in than to fence them out. Still easier and better was it to get together with the other settlers of the town or of the neighborhood and to pasture all their live stock in one common field, which soon was called for short the common. This was an old Dutch as well as English custom. In the Duke of York's Laws for his new Province of New York, 1664, it was provided:

The feed of Cattell is free in commonage to all Townships. The Lots of Meadow [cleared field] or Corne Ground are peculiar to each Planter.

The working oxen, the horses and the milch cows were pastured fairly near the village, so they could be driven back and forth daily. The swine as the most troublesome were kept farthest away. In 1641 New Haven ordered that they be kept five miles from the town, and that each hog or pig have a ring in its nose and a wooden yoke around its neck to keep it from rooting. The swine, it is evident, were allowed only surface feeding.

The town of Ipswich, Massachusetts, had an agreement

with its herdsmen which was entered on the records. It read in part, omitting many of the details:

Haniel Bosworth is to keep the herd of cows on the north side of the river, from the 1st of May to the 20th of October. He is to go out with them half an hour after sunrise and to bring them home a little before sun-set at 13s. a week, a peck of corn a head at their going out, one pound of butter or half peck of wheat in June, and the rest of his pay at the end of his time, whereof half to be paid in wheat or malt; the pay to be brought to his house within six days after demanded, or else to forfeit 6d. a head more. Agreed with Henry Osborn to join Bosworth to keep the cows on the same terms. One of them to take the cows in Scott's Lane and to blow a horn at the meeting house green in the morning.

After the crops were harvested an occasion came which was almost a festival. It was the Opening of the Meadows. The meadows were the fields on which crops had been raised. Each settler had the right to turn in to feed so many animals, according to his ownership, his right being strictly counted out by a committee on the basis of one ox as a unit. Brands and ear-marks were used on cattle of a half year of age, but not on horses.

Every farmer raised swine, which were fed in summer on the dairy and kitchen waste. He fattened four or five of these, which supplied salt pork for the family use during the year and also probably some which he could export in a joint shipment with his neighbors. This export of salt pork in barrels became a considerable item during the eighteenth century. In the winter the swine were turned out into the forest.

From a drawing by Darley in the old "Scribner's Monthly"

Threshing grain on the barn floor with flails—this method obtained in colonial days and is still practiced on some small farms in Connecticut and elsewhere

As soon as the acorns, beech-nuts &c begin to fall, they are driven to the woods, in large herds, to feed on them. The delicacy, taste and nutrition of these nuts are particularly suited to the palate of the animals, so that in a short time they grow to a great size. The hog prefers the beech-nut to any other, and the effect of that preference is visible in growth and fat, hence a good beech nut year may be called a good swine year.

Before 1750 there were few wheel vehicles of any kind light enough for horses to draw. Horses were used chiefly for riding. The ox was the working animal, as has been said. In Massachusetts Bay the Devonshire was the breed of cattle mostly imported. Upon the Piscataqua River the Danish cattle were found, large yellow draft animals suited to the lumber work. There were red cattle imported from Holland, and black cattle from the Spanish West Indies. New England imported much live stock from England and also from the Southern Colonies, especially from Virginia. To meet the hard surface and the unevenness of the rocky ground both oxen and horses had to be shod. This made a steady task for the blacksmith of the neighborhood. For shoeing the oxen there had to be used a strong scaffold with a wide belly-band by which the ox was swung up off his feet. The ox with his great bulk and his small feet cannot stand up on three feet while the fourth is being shod; he would fall down. And his hoof is divided, so that shoeing an ox meant making and fastening to the hooves eight small iron half-shoes. But bringing the full strength of his great bulk to focus on the four small feet, the ox could move almost anything.

Every farm had its dairy where milk was kept in pans and butter was made
with a hand churn. This branch of the work usually fell to the women on
the farm

In the latter part of the century the use of horses increased. For light work, like cultivating corn in a well-worked field, or for harrowing, a horse was sometimes used alone. In heavier work sometimes in team with an ox or with oxen, the horse was used, usually as the leader, as he was so much more intelligent. But still the horse was used mostly with people, for riding or for carriage work or with stage coaches. The first horses in New England were imported from Old England, but in 1635 these were supplemented by twenty-seven Flanders mares and three stallions from Holland. William Penn brought three brood mares with him in 1682, and, with the special purpose of improving his breed, in 1699 he imported into Pennsylvania "the magnificent colt, Tamerlane, of the best strain in England."

Horses were raised for racing in the Narragansett Country and in Virginia. The Narragansett horses were pacers, that came originally from Andalusia in Spain. They were a small hardy breed, with a comfortable gait over the rough roads of the time, and very fleet. Of them a Rhode Island clergyman wrote,

I have seen some of them pace a Mile in little more than *two* Minutes, a good deal less than *three*.

It was unquestionably one of these that helped Samuel Casey, the silversmith, to life and liberty. But the breed was practically extinct by 1800. They were exported to the West Indies on a steady demand all through the middle of

From the old "Scribner's Monthly"

Tenants of the old barn on a small farm

the century that left comparatively few in the American Colonies, and the Revolution cut off the possibility of continuing the export. They had been bred and trained exclusively for the saddle, never for harness. So with the improvement of the roads and the need for harness horses for teaming during the Revolution, the raising of trotting horses became more profitable. And even for staff officers in the Army, the trotter was better, more correct—though this one could go when handled right. So by the end of the century, by 1800, the Narragansett Pacer was a memory. He was of his time, the great time of the American Colonies.

There was another horse. (Some of my readers will approve the statement that great times in human affairs are typified by their horses.) This was the Conestoga Horse, "the finest draft animal on the continent in the colonial age," some one said of him. He was a strong large breed developed by the Pennsylvania-German farmers out of English stock, and named from a stream there in Lancaster County. The day of the Oxen was passing. The Ox had had his day, and no animal that God ever made could have taken his place in his day. But his day was passing and the Horse, always more intelligent, more nervous, had become equally strong for all practical purposes, had become "the finest draft animal on the continent." Drawing a wagon of the same name, a wagon that could travel any kind of road, the water road or the land road, the horse would open up the continent and the West, and incidentally pay the debt that the road owed to the Colonial Posts. As yet, however, this is only the mention of a new breed, to come later, after a horse by the name of Messenger has been imported from England to Philadelphia in 1788, and a stallion named Justin Morgan has been foaled in 1793 at West Springfield, Massachusetts.

Much has been said about the houses and mansions in which the American colonists lived, but little or nothing about the buildings in which their horses and cattle found shelter. Naturally, these were like the houses of their owners, and were different according to the various regions. In New England the lean-to kitchen often connected with the barn through a long woodshed in which were kept under cover and at hand the piles of wood, large and small, for the fireplaces during the winter. The barn itself was often at right angles with the house and woodshed, so as to make a sheltered barnyard protected from the storms. In Pennsylvania and the other Middle Colonies, the barns were often great high structures suggesting that the farm and the farm work were the whole interest of the people, which was to a considerable degree true, especially among the Pennsylvania Germans. In Virginia and the South the barn was one of the detached buildings, or it would be better to say the barns were among the detached buildings of the plantation and were adapted in their structure and arrangement to the purpose of protecting the live stock from the heat of summer instead of from the snow and storms of winter. With all alike a common feature was the floor in the center of the main barn, into which the largest load of hay could drive and which could be used also as the threshing floor, when the grain was beaten out from the chaff with the hand flail or trodden out with the horses, as was usual in the Middle Colonies, beginning at about Thanksgiving time.

For the grinding of the grain, whether it was the maize into corn meal or wheat into white flour, the grist mill came with the miller. It was one of the specialized occupations, one mill serving an entire neighborhood rather than one of the home industries. The power was usually water power, as all along the Atlantic coast most of the streams had plenty of falls or grades amply sufficient for the mill-race. In some locations, however, like Long Island and Cape Cod the windmill gave as steady and as effective power for the grinding as the streams of the more hilly regions.

In the self-supporting and self-sufficing farms of the colonial agriculture the clothes of all the household were made right there, just as the food was produced right there. Flax and wool were the two great clothing staples, flax being made into linen, and the wool of the sheep being made into woollen cloth, and the two being combined into that distinctly colonial material, linsey-woolsey. The manufacture of linen from the flax was a complicated and difficult process. It was not until the clothes the settlers brought with them were worn out, and until the fur trade with the Indians began to fail, that the settlers took up the raising of flax and the making of it into linen with much energy. The same amount of work put into other lines would produce greater and for the time more important results. But when the situation made it practical, the English colonists took up flax raising and linen making in earnest, and the beautiful little flax spinning wheel, at which the spinner sat, multiplied in the land and soon most women and girls could use it very skillfully. The Dutch women did not spin much,

The Conestoga wagon of early Pennsylvania days, ancestor of the "covered wagon" or "prairie schooner" of later times. A feature of the Conestoga wagon was the box on the side, having ornamental wrought iron hinges and fastenings

and so little flax was raised in New Netherland, but after about 1670 when English people began to settle in New York, flax and the flax spinning wheel came in too.

During all of the eighteenth century the making of woollen cloth from the raising of the sheep and the shearing to the weaving on the loom was one of the home industries. Some of the work in both the linen and the woollen making required the physical strength of the men, but the physical strength and agility of the women was nonetheless fully brought into play. With the large woollen spinning wheel the spinner stood,—or rather walked. With the hum of the wheel she stepped backward quickly one, two, three steps, holding high the long yarn as it twisted and quivered, as Alice Morse Earle has described the operation, then suddenly she glided forward and let the yarn wind onto the spindle. Six skeins of yarn a day was counted a good day's work, in spinning which she walked with her backward and forward steps over twenty miles.

The dyeing of the wool should be mentioned even in the briefest reference. Blues were the favorite color, and indigo was the most common of the blue dyes. Indigo was imported from the West Indies until it was introduced into South Carolina through the perspicacity and energy of Eliza Lucas, the daughter of the Governor of Antigua, who married Chief Justice Pinckney of South Carolina and was the mother of Charles Cotesworth Pinckney. Indigo by 1747 had become a successful crop in South Carolina and was exported thence to England and to the north. It was in such demand as a dye that it was peddled around through the country. Various flowers, such as the iris and goldenrod, were used in the making of beautiful dyes, as well as berries and barks of red oak and hickory.

The making of woollen cloth continued as a home industry until after the Revolution in every respect but one. The fulling mill was, like the grist mill, one of the comparatively early instances of industrial co-operation. The home woollen cloth was uneven in texture, and in some parts quite thin. The fulling mill, by pounding the cloth with a large oaken mallet while it was kept thoroughly wet in warm soapy water, shrunk the fibers of the woollen cloth together and after drying made of it a much better and more practical article. One such fulling mill was sufficient for a whole neighborhood. To it the home weavers brought their cloth, just as they brought their grain to the grist mill to be ground.

There was in the farming of the colonial period a great deal of working together, of co-operation, not only of the whole family, of the grown-ups and the children, but of different families. Among the English people the men worked in the fields and the women in the houses or around the door-yards. Among the German people the women often worked in the fields with the men. Then, too, there were the indentured whites, who paid for their passage across the ocean by contracting their labor for a certain period to successful employers. And there were the Negro slaves in the North as well as in the South. The abandonment of slavery in the North and its continuance in the South were due to economic reasons rather than to moral or religious motives. The change of attitude on the question by the Quakers was due to their religious ideas in large measure. But, for instance, slavery was well established in the Narragansett Country in Rhode Island, where it may be the gay life of the prosperous stock-raisers called for many house servants. In 1730 in the town of South Kingston from a third to a half of the population were of negro or Indian blood. What might be called economic co-operation was common in colonial America in both the seventeenth and the eighteenth centuries, from the experimental communism of the first settlements at Jamestown and Plymouth to the political co-operation of the American Colonies in the Revolution. Co-operation was a practical necessity and was characteristic of all colonial life in its time.

The lack in colonial agriculture was not in the people or in their instinctive readiness for co-operation, whether that be in the field of individual activity or of community enterprise. The deficiency lay in their farm implements. And yet this was no fault of theirs. Until there were roads on which horses could be driven at something like their possible speed, which was only in or near the towns, they could not be expected to build vehicles or wagons except of a primitive type. If the farmers had had them, they could not have used them. Until fields of considerable acreage were cleared and well cleared of stumps and roots, the long-bladed sickle was the most practical tool for reaping. Agriculture had to wait upon invention, and invention could not come until it was proved to be justified. As there would be no grist mills until there was grain to be ground, and enough grain; as there would be no fulling mills until there was cloth being woven in the neighborhood to be shrunken and pressed; so there would be no improvement of farming tools by invention until there was certain possibility of their use in a new farm life.

In the making of the farm implements the wooden parts

of the plows and carts, the yokes, and the handles of the tools were made at home. The iron parts—the chains and plowshares, the axeheads, the scythe blades, the hoes and pitchforks and sickles—were made by the village blacksmith. The first carts had for wheels simple cross-sections of hardwood logs. For hauling, a heavy clumsy two-wheeled cart was in general use in summer, and in New England at least before the Revolution a four-wheeled wagon was practically unknown.

Plows were scarce. Indeed, the Pilgrims at Plymouth had none for twelve years. What would they have done with a good plow, if they had had one? In 1636 there were only thirty plows in all Massachusetts Bay. As they came into use, often a man who had a plow would take it around and do the plowing for all his neighbors. With their small fields it was not worth while for every farmer to have a plow of his own. These early plows had a wooden mold-board, which was often roughly plated with pieces of sheet iron; it had a clumsy wrought-iron share and the handles were upright. It took a strong man to hold it, and only the ox could draw it. This implement was not to replow a well-cultivated field; it was to go through a field that still had in it many large stones and tough roots. The harrow, with teeth sometimes of wood, sometimes of iron, was the only implement for which animals were used. For harvesting the long thin-bladed sickle was used most, sometimes in the latter part of the period also the scythe. In the Middle Colonies where the grain fields were so much larger and more even, they had a grain cradle, with four long slender wooden fingers to catch the grain as it fell from the blade.

But they had the men who could hold the plows. And they developed horses that were "the finest draft animals on the continent." And it was the sons and the grandsons of these colonial farmers who invented and manufactured the finer tools of the new American agriculture.

An ox-yoke

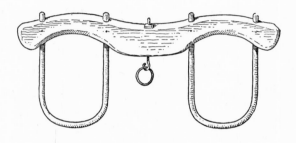

CHAPTER XXI

The Colonial Town

THE Colonial Posts, with their official importance, also insisted on the inception and development of newspapers. Indeed, as we have seen, the posts insisted on them unofficially by grace of the side interests of the postmasters even before, by order of the Postmaster General, Benjamin Franklin, the newspapers gained official recognition. The newspaper is distinctly of the nature of the town. Its significance is communication and co-operation. It is the sign of people getting together. That is in fact what a town is—people getting together. The newspaper consists of information and advertising, and offers people an important means for co-operation in each other's affairs, whether of business or of pleasure. The development of the colonial newspapers therefore parallels the development of the colonial towns, and contributes to and reflects the development of colonial union into a National Union.

The first newspaper in the Colonies was *The Boston News-Letter,* started by William Campbell in 1704. William Campbell was the postmaster at Boston. Being thus the clearing house for whatever people were telling each other and for whatever news was being received with the ships arriving from England, he learned a great deal, and he wrote letters to friends along the post routes. These found the news worth paying for. Postmaster William Campbell made some very useful money, all told, writing his letters. It got to be a long and tiresome task to write out by hand all the copies he needed to send with his post riders. So he printed them. Then the more promises to pay (subscriptions) for copies he had the better instead of the worse. It was the story of the printing press repeated and applied to the colonial situation. Whether or not William Campbell dreamed he was starting a great institution did not matter, certainly not to him. He was saving a great deal of very fatiguing manual labor and making money at it besides. The story of other postmasters was the same. To make good as a postmaster with the people along the route, he had to send the news. In 1730 an exceptionally able printer named William Parks arrived in Williamsburg in Virginia and opened up a shop. In 1736 he started a newspaper, *The Virginia Gazette,* and therewith did something to establish the newspaper on its own independent basis, as he was not the postmaster. Certainly he did much to help in Virginia's contribution to the colonial union and American nationality. Meantime, Benjamin Franklin, printer and newspaper publisher and postmaster, became Postmaster General in 1753, and played fair with his rivals and competitors by opening the posts to all newspapers, thereby making another important contribution to the aforesaid American union.

The great principle that it is well to hear both sides of

every story is emphasized by the famous case of John Peter Zenger of *The Weekly Journal* of New York. One William Bradford, a printer, had come from Philadelphia to New York in 1693. In 1725 he started a newspaper, *The New York Gazette,* which was practically a government organ. Zenger was an apprentice of Bradford's. In 1733 Zenger started an opposition newspaper, *The Weekly Journal,* to represent the other side, the side of the people. Zenger denounced in his paper certain arbitrary and tyrannical acts of the Royal Governor, which were undeniably true. Four numbers of *The Weekly Journal* were declared seditious and ordered burned by the hangman; Zenger was imprisoned and his two attorneys were disbarred. The people of New York engaged the services of Andrew Hamilton of Philadelphia to defend Zenger and he offered to serve without a fee. The position of the Government was "the greater truth the greater libel." The position of the defense was that the truth is a valid defense against the charge of libel.

It was an important trial, vital to the success of all people in their efforts to get together for their welfare. Andrew Hamilton closed his address to the jury as follows:

The question before the court, and you, gentlemen of the jury, is not of small or private concern; it is not the cause of a poor printer, nor of New York alone, which you are trying. No! it may in its consequences affect every freeman that lives under a British government on the main of America! It is the best cause, it is the cause of liberty, and I make no doubt but your upright conduct this day will not only entitle you to the love and esteem of your fellow-citizens, but every man who prefers freedom to a life of slavery will bless and honour you, as men who have baffled the attempt of tyranny, and by an impartial and uncorrupt verdict have laid a noble foundation for securing to ourselves, our posterity, and our neighbors, that to which nature and the laws of our country have given us a right,—the liberty both of exposing and opposing arbitrary power—by speaking *truth!*

Although the Chief Justice charged the jury that the only point for them to consider was whether the seditious statements had been printed and published, the jury returned immediately with the verdict of Not Guilty. Thus was established the freedom of the press in America, and therewith also the freedom of the people to co-operate in their public development.

Actually the first newspaper printed in America was entitled *Public Occurrences, both Foreign and Domestic,* but only one number was printed, on September 25, 1690, in Boston. It can hardly be spoken of as more than an attempt to start a newspaper. The first twelve permanent newspapers were:

The Boston News-Letter, Boston, April 17, 1704;
The Boston Gazette, Boston, December 21, 1719;
The American, Philadelphia, December 22, 1719;
The New York Gazette, New York, October 16, 1725;
The Maryland Gazette, Annapolis, June, 1728;
The South Carolina Gazette, Charleston, January 8, 1732;
The Rhode Island Gazette, Newport, September 27, 1732;
The Weekly Journal, New York, November 15, 1733;
The Virginia Gazette, Williamsburg, 1736;
The Connecticut Gazette, New Haven, January 1, 1755;

THE
New-York Weekly JOURNAL.

Numb. I.

Containing the freſheſt Advices, Foreign, and Domeſtick.

MUNDAY November 5, 1733.

Mr. *Zenger,*

UNDERSTANDING you intend ſhortly to publiſh a Weekly Paper, I recommend to your diſpoſal the incloſed Verſes upon Wiſdom ; which is ſo noble a Theme, that whoever takes the Pains ſeriouſly to reflect thereon, will find himſelf happily loſt in the boundleſs Ocean of Benefits and Satisfaction attending it. It is without Diſpute the chief Wood of Mankind ; the firm Bank that conſtantly ſecures us again the impetuous Raging of that turbulent Sea of Paſſions, which inceſſantly daſh againſt the Frame of human Nature. It is a Fort impregnable by all Aſſaults of Vice, Folly, and Misfortunes, and a ſecure Rock againſt all the Caſualties of Miſery. It is a Guide and Security to Youth, Health, and Vigour in Old Age ; and a Remedy and Eaſe in Sickneſs and Infirmity. It is Comfort in Adverſity, it is Plenty in Poverty, and a conſtant Source of true Joy and Delight. It is infinitely beyond all that the feigned *Fortunatus* ever could wiſh, or *Gyges's* Treaſures purchaſe ; *For her Ways are Ways of Pleaſantneſs, and all her Paths are Peace.* She is of eaſy acceſs to all that diligently ſeek her ; and refuſes none that with Sincerity apply to her, and is always a ready Help in Time of Need : Therefore pray continue to recommend the earneſt Purſuit of Her to all Mankind ; and you will particularly oblige.

PHILO-SOPHIA.

On WISDOM.

VIctorious Wiſdom whoſe ſupreme Command
Extends beyond the Bounds of Sea and Land ;
'Tis thou alone that doſt reward our Pains,
With Pleaſures that endure, and ſolid Gains.

But Oh ! What art thou, and where doſt thou dwell ?
Not with the Hermit in his lonely Cell ;
The ſullen Fumes of whoſe diſtemper'd Brain,
Make the dull Wretch torment himſelf in vain :
Whilſt of the World affectedly afraid,
He ſhuns the End for which Mankind was made.

Not with the Epicure in all his Pleaſures,
Nor with the Miſer in his Bank of Treaſures,
The one's a Slave bound faſt in golden Chains,
The other buys ſhort Joys with laſting Pains.

Not in the vain Purſuit of partial Fame,
The gaudy Outſide of an empty Name ;
When moved by Chance, not Merit common Breath,
Gives the falſe Shadow ſudden Life or Death.

Honour, when meritoriouſly aſſigned,
The noble Actions of a God like Mind,
Is then indeed a Bleſſing ſent from Heaven,
A bright Reward for human Labour given.

But when 'tis Fame's miſtaken Flattery,
A popular Applauſe of Vanity,
The worthleſs Idol ought to be abhor'd;
And is by none but Knaves and Fools ador'd.

Thus as I'm ſearching with the feeble Light
Of human Reaſon, in dark error's Night,
For what has oft eſcap'd the curious Eye,
Of lofty Wit, and deep Philoſophy,
From the bright Regions of eternal Day,
Methinks I ſee a ſmall but glorious Ray,
Dart ſwift as Lightning throug the yielding Air.
To an unſpotted Breaſt, and enter there.

This is the Wiſdom I ſo much adore ;
Grant me but this, kind Heaven, I ask no more,
This once obtain'd, how happy ſhall I be ?
Kings will be little Men, compar'd to me :
They in their own Dominions only great,
I Conquer of the World, my ſelf and Fate.

Thus arm'd, let Fortune uſe me as ſhe will,
I ſtand prepar'd to meet with Good or Ill,
If I am born for Happineſs and Eaſe,
And proſp'rous Gales ſalute the ſmiling Seas ;
This Path I'll tread, (the Bleſſings to repay)
Where Virtue calls and Honour leads the Way,

But if the Weather of my Life prove foul,
Though Storms ariſe that makes whole Kingdoms rowle.

Yet—

The North Carolina Gazette, New Berne, December, 1755;
The New Hampshire Gazette, Portsmouth, August, 1756.

It may be noticed that nine of the twelve were called Ga-
zettes, reflecting the connection of the news-sheet with the
official post.

The interests for which it is necessary that people get
together are those which are broadly classed as public affairs.
First among these is Government. Insofar as government is
democratic it is co-operative, both between the individual
citizens with each other, and between the dominant individual body with the governed. The history of England and
of America consists to an important degree in the development of such co-operative government, its advance, its
retrogression, and the resumption of its advance. Here it
will simply be pointed out that all political activities of the
people center in the town. This was conspicuous in Williamsburg. It was the capital of Virginia and the Governor
resided there the year round. But when the House of Burgesses, the legislative assembly, convened at Williamsburg,
the people flocked thither from all over Virginia, and the
population increased, filling every house, from say 2000 to
5000 or 6000. Considerable business was carried on. The
opportunity was availed of for military training and parades.
There were horse races. There were balls and dinners. There
were plays in the theatres. Many other social activities were
engaged in at these times.

The official governmental activities centered naturally
in the capital; and the official social activities in the Gov-

ernor's Palace. But there were also the informal activities, quite as important, those of the citizens themselves in their discussions of public questions, and their social activities. These in Williamsburg often centered in the Raleigh Tavern and other inns; in Boston at Faneuil Hall and the Old South Meeting House; in New York at Fraunces' Tavern.

Williamsburg was distinctively the gathering place of Virginia, and Virginia gathered usually twice a year, in the spring and in the fall. It was not devoid of all gaiety at other times by any means, as seemed to be the first impression of a young English clergyman, the Reverend Andrew Burnaby, who travelled through the American Colonies in 1759 and 1760:

Upon the whole, it is an agreeable residence. There are ten or twelve gentlemen's families constantly residing in it, besides merchants and tradesmen: and at the time of the assemblies, and general courts, it is crowded with the gentry of the country. On those occasions there are balls and other amusements; but as soon as the business is finished they return to their plantations, and the town is in a manner deserted.

Later Mr. Burnaby seemed to have found more than ten or twelve sociable families in the town, and enjoyed his sojourn among the Virginians very much indeed, whether he met them at the capital or on their plantations. He travelled many miles through the colony, as far as Winchester on one trip, and twice at least spent several days with a Colonel Washington at his place called Mount Vernon, on the Potomac, a noted young officer, whose exploit in going through the wilderness to Fort Duquesne with only one companion Mr. Burnaby recounted in his book.

The same young traveller gave an interesting glimpse of the streets of Philadelphia, which shows the difference in physical appearance of the two towns.

The streets are laid out with great regularity in parallel lines, intersected by others at right angles, and are handsomely built. On each side there is a pavement of broad stones for foot passengers and in most of them a causeway in the middle for carriages. Upon dark nights it is well lighted, and watched by a patrol. There are many fair houses, and public edifices in it.

Compare with this praise his few words about the streets of Williamsburg.

The streets are not paved and are consequently very dusty, the soil hereabouts consisting chiefly of sand.

Nevertheless he did record one fact which in the opinions of young people might qualify the town for evening strolls between dances through the beautiful gardens or down the wide Duke of Gloucester Street toward the Bruton Parish Church.

However, the situation of Williamsburg has one advantage which few or no places in these lower parts have, that of being free from mosquitoes.

A practical point from the social standpoint!

The peculiar interest of Williamsburg was that it distinguished the town and the country functions of colonial

College of William and Mary and the Botetourt Statue, Williamsburg,
Virginia

A pen and ink adaptation after a photograph by F. S. Lincoln

life as did no other of the towns and cities of the time. The
mistake is sometimes made of taking for granted that the

The Raleigh Tavern
A pen and ink adaptation after a photograph by F. S. Lincoln

people of the eighteenth century were incipient Americans,
certainly, but still quite crude. The fact is rather that the
men and women who produced the political masterpieces
of the United States were equally able in other lines. There

were beginnings that had to be begun. There were problems —in agriculture, in industry, in culture—that had to be solved before the extraordinary developments of the nineteenth century could come. They solved them. And they brought to them a personal attention that was experienced and that was thorough.

Virginia was a country colony. So were all the colonies. Every town in the colonies was a country town, differing essentially from the towns of our day. Those towns were the centers of widespread agricultural regions; our towns are centers of compact industrial regions. The capital of Virginia was a typical town of the 1700s and was the capital of an important colony, in spite of its unpaved streets and its intermittent population. When John Adams urged Thomas Jefferson to undertake the writing of the Declaration of Independence, he said to him, "You are a Virginian, and a Virginian ought to appear at the Head of this Business."

Washington was a farmer. Others may have thought of him as a soldier and as a statesman, but not he. It was his pride to be thought of as the first farmer of America. He said specifically:

My whole life long I have yearned to escape from it all, [from the army and from public life] and at length, dressed in the gray coat of a Virginia farmer to become a private citizen on the banks of the Potomac.

And again,

Agriculture has always been the most favorite amusement of

my life. The more I am acquainted with agricultural affairs the better I am pleased with them. To see plants rise from the earth and flourish by the superior skill and bounty of the laborer fills the contemplative mind with ideas which are more easy to be conceived than expressed.

In the management of his farms he gave details his personal attention. He maintained a correspondence with Arthur Young and Sir John Sinclair, two of the great agriculturists of England. Having secured some special seed through Arthur Young, Washington wrote to his agent in London from Mount Vernon on August 5, 1786:

Let me entreat your particular attention to them, with a request that the captain of the vessel on board of which they are shipped may be solicited to keep the seeds in the cabin, or out of the ship's hold, at any rate, as they never fail to heat and spoil when put there.

As an agricultural colony the characteristic crop and the crop determining the nature of its business affairs was Tobacco. Virginia had many other fine crops, and every plantation could raise practically all that was needed for food. But the land of Virginia and its neighboring colonies, Maryland and North Carolina, was adapted to the raising of exceptional tobacco, so that there was a greater return in value from tobacco than from corn or other grains. Tobacco was also the most economical cargo to ship, a matter of the space it required compared with its value. Tobacco could be conveniently transported to the wharves and loaded on the ships. While the leaves were still soft they were packed into hogsheads, an iron bar was thrust through the middle of the hogshead and it was rolled by oxen or horses to the wharf. Finally a more valuable cargo of tobacco could be

A Virginia tobacco wharf

The drawing is based upon an engraving which is a part of Albert and Lotter's map of North America published 1784

stowed in a ship than of anything else. Tobacco constituted at times from a quarter to a half in value of all the exports of the American colonies.

When one considers how little gold and silver there was in the Colonies during the eighteenth century and how much tobacco, it is easy to understand how business trans-

Tobacco ships in the James River, Virginia

actions in Virginia, Maryland, and North Carolina were based on tobacco rather than on gold and silver, and how tobacco was made the legal money in those Colonies. Similarly, beaver skins were at one time the legal money in New York, wheat in Pennsylvania, and rice in South Carolina and Georgia. The way this commodity money worked was that in Virginia, for example, after about 1734 there were public warehouses to which planters could send tobacco and receive in return therefor certificates, usually called

crop-notes, in various amounts large and small. These certificates stated the value not in money but in pounds of
tobacco. These could be passed as money and were accepted
as such. The trouble with all these certificates of commodity
money was that the tobacco, or the wheat or the rice changed
in value so frequently as often seriously to disturb the regular
transaction of business and cause general discontent and
misfortune.

In 1679 the tobacco crop was very large, so large it could
not all of it be sold that year. In 1680 the tobacco crop was
still larger. In consequence the price of tobacco went down.
There was so much tobacco on hand that the English market could be supplied for two years without a single pound
more being raised. The government proposed to order that
no planting of tobacco be permitted during the year 1681.
There was serious trouble, riots and general disturbance,
and at a time when it was most important that the value of
services and of goods in trade should be steady and reliable,
it was very unsteady and not at all reliable.

In 1758 after several bad years for tobacco, there was a
general failure of the crop. The price of tobacco went from
about 2d a pound up to 6d. Accordingly the Assembly
passed a law providing that the clergy, of whom there were
about sixty-five in Virginia, and public officers, must accept
their salaries in money instead of in tobacco. To us this may
sound amusing, but to them it meant practically accepting
for their salaries one third of the sum they might regularly
receive through the advantage (to them) of the rise in the

price of tobacco. They took their legal appeal to England, and the Royal Government repealed the act of the Virginia Assembly. This exasperated the people, and made more trouble. In both instances the results were inherent in the commodity money.

It is all very well to say that they ought not to have had commodity money. But we have commodity money now; it is based on a commodity—silver. Massachusetts had a double silver money at one time: the full silver money of John Hull, mintmaster, and the part money, practically commodity money of John Hull, silversmith, and others, including our lost friend, Samuel Casey. Nowadays only some silver is used as a basis of money, that which has been coined in the mints of the United States Government; not all silver, not silverware. The Colonies were fortunate in having able men, men like John Hancock, the merchant, Robert Morris, the financier, George Wythe, the lawyer, and many others, working out the confused problem, to be followed by others like the young Alexander Hamilton.

It was usually confusion that made trouble in the American Colonies in the eighteenth century. In clarifying the confusion and solving the problems there were necessarily two results to be achieved: to ascertain the right and practical solution; and to establish it in popular practice. To know what is best is not sufficient. What is best must be adopted into general practice. A Virginia merchant of reputation wished to borrow a sum of money for a reasonable time. There were no banks at the time. The lender wanted more than the legal 5 per cent interest; he wanted 10 per cent. To meet the requirements of the law, he proposed that the borrower give him a bill of exchange on some merchant in London with whom the borrower had no account. The bill of exchange would then be returned within about the term of the loan, and the law would require the borrower to pay the lender the 10 per cent on the protested note. The borrower agreed, and gave him a bill of exchange on a London merchant with whom he had never had any dealings whatsoever. But the London merchant knew of the American by reputation and thought this note meant that the American intended to start an account with him. Therefore he honored the note and paid it. The lender therefore received only the legal 5 per cent instead of the 10 per cent agreed upon, and considered that he had been outrageously tricked by the borrower in giving him a good instead of a false bill of exchange. The practice was common enough and in his mind there could be no objection to his course provided he were frank in his dealings.

Such commercial problems as these could be solved only by being worked out with ability, honesty, and patience. The result of the work begun by the Colonial Americans has been the science and practice of finance and banking, a wonderful achievement. These business activities are all distinctly town affairs. Progress is made in them only by people getting together and co-operating with each other.

Intellectual life does not thrive in entire isolation. It needs some isolation for reflection and meditation, to "consolidate its returns." But essentially the intellectual life is a social affair. We are apt to think the primary and the secondary schools the most important agents of education, those in which the main body of the public is prepared for its work

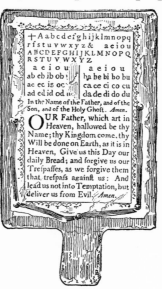

The horn-book

while the colleges and the universities lead the more able elect on into training for service as specialists and as leaders in life. The eighteenth century in its recognition of the growing colleges of the time emphasized the standards of mature thought and familiarity with the best experience of the world; to this, other education led up, for this, earlier education prepared. Each course used for its purpose the material available in its time, and that material was different; and each philosophy of education was better for its time.

In the seventeenth and eighteenth centuries Massachusetts was ahead in the establishment of schools, because schools

The New England primer

are town affairs, and Massachusetts was built on a town system. In 1642 the General Court passed a law requiring all parents to teach their children to read as well as to ply a trade; and in 1647 a law requiring every township of fifty families to support a school in which children should be taught reading and writing, and every township of one hundred families to support a grammar school that could prepare for college. Thus began the public school system as an ideal.

In these primary schools the subjects taught were reading, writing, arithmetic, and religion—a forward-looking program. There were also some more elementary private schools, frequently called Dame Schools, which taught the alphabet, the catechism, and sometimes a little reading and writing. Most prominent among the textbooks were the horn-book and the New England Primer. The horn-book was a wooden paddle, on which was pasted a sheet of paper with the alphabet, the Lord's Prayer, verses from the Bible, and religious poetry printed on it. All was covered by a sheet of transparent horn, whence the name. The handle made it convenient for the teacher to use in inducing scholarship at one end of the pupil when all effort failed at the other.

The New England Primer was a compendium of all that would be needed for the schooling of children. It was used in all the colonies and was, Moses Coit Tyler says, "the most widely used book in America." For those pupils who went beyond the New England Primer the Bible was used as a reader. It had quality as a curriculum. A familiarity or even a glimpse of the history and literature of the Hebrew people and somewhat of the earlier Christians was no mean introduction to life, especially as the material available in the new country was not extensive.

Passing directly to the colleges of the colonial period, all such higher education concentrated on the study of the classics. The education of the ministry was the chief purpose of the colleges, but nonetheless the secular classics were given veneration if not reverence equal to the religious classics. The classics as a whole constituted the standards of mature thought and the best experience of the world—the world back there whence they had come into this wilderness.

The first nine colleges in America, with their present locations, established as such in the colonial period, before the outbreak of the Revolution, were:

Harvard College at Cambridge, Massachusetts, 1636;
The College of William and Mary at Williamsburg, Virginia, 1693;
Yale College at New Haven, Connecticut, 1700;
The College of New Jersey at Princeton, 1746;
King's College (now Columbia), New York, 1754;
Philadelphia College (now University of Pennsylvania), 1755;
Rhode Island College (now Brown University), Providence, 1764;
Queen's College (now Rutgers University), New Brunswick, New Jersey, 1766;
Dartmouth College, Hanover, New Hampshire, 1769.

The requirements for entrance to Harvard were stated in these unmistakable terms as early as 1643:

When any scholar is able to understand Tully or such like classical Latin author extempore, and make and speak true Latin in verse and prose; . . . and decline perfectly the paradigms of nouns and verbs in the Greek tongue, let him then, and not before, be capable of admission into the college.

The curriculum of a colonial college was quite apt to include Latin, Greek, and Hebrew; also elementary Chaldee and Syriac; arithmetic and geometry; history, politics, logic, and ethics; the Bible; rhetoric, composition and oratory; astronomy, elementary physics and elementary botany. These subjects were of course varied somewhat in the different colleges and at different periods. With such a college program it will be seen that those who planned the subjects for the teaching of the primary schools were entirely consistent and simply provided for an early start in the course that led to the highest education to be obtained in the Colonies. There was further a liberal spirit active in these institutions, progressive enough to be continuously practical and conservative enough to be strong and steady in that progress. Some connections may nowadays seem curious if not questionable. The Reverend James Blair was sent to England in the interest of establishing a college in Virginia. He secured the charter for the College of William and Mary and a good endowment for it from the King and Queen. He also secured considerable contributions of money from certain pirates in jail who were glad at once to encourage education and ensure their own freedom. The first instance of the elective system was also in this same College of William and Mary.

In 1749 Benjamin Franklin proposed an institution of higher learning for Philadelphia, free from sectarian control, in which instruction of a practical nature should be given, in which history, economics and politics should be made prominent, modern languages should be taught, and English put on a par with Latin. This plan was modified before he succeeded in establishing it in 1751 as the Academy and soon after as Philadelphia College. It is now the University of Pennsylvania. Naturally science had an early welcome there.

King Charles II has not a good reputation among many good people, but the world is better for two things he did—his befriending of William Penn, and his befriending of science. The formation of the Royal Society gave an incomparable impetus not only to the study of physical science but to the development of the modern standpoint in the entire intellectual and spiritual fields throughout the world. The naïve popular attitude in matters of scientific nature during this period is reflected in a contemporary statement about lightning rods about 1759.

I believe no country has more certainly proved the efficacy of electrical rods than this. Before the discovery of them, these gusts [thunder-storms] were frequently productive of melancholy consequences; but now it is rare to hear of such instances. It is observable that no house was ever struck, where they were fixed. . . . These circumstances, one would imagine, should induce every person to get over those prejudices which many have entertained, and to consider the neglect rather than the use of them as criminal, since they seem to be means put into our hands by Providence for our safety and protection.

But though such was the popular timidity in practical matters of applied science, consider the eminent list of the scientific leaders of that century: Governor John Winthrop of Connecticut (1606–76), the great John Winthrop of Harvard (1715–79), Doctor John Clarke, the physician, of Newport (1609–76), John Bartram, the botanist of Philadelphia (1699–1777), and his son, William Bartram (1739–1823), David Rittenhouse, the astronomer (1732–96), also of Philadelphia, the universal-minded Thomas Jefferson (1743–1826), and the incomparable Benjamin Franklin (1706–90), to whom in 1754 the greatest physicists of France—Buffon, Marty, Dubourg, Fonferriers, and Dalibard, such was their respect for him, sent the message, "We are all waiting with the greatest eagerness to hear from you."

But that branch of science which affects all men and women, and all children most directly may also claim the right to represent science by way of illustration in a book like this—Medicine and Surgery, which from being the science of the cure of disease has become the science of Health.

The seventeenth and eighteenth centuries were unquestionably times of abundant good health, and also of terrible epidemics and of great mortality, especially among children. The good health was due chiefly to the strong constitutions of the settlers and to the healthful outdoor life they led. Further, sensible rules of hygiene were sometimes made and quite well enforced. William Strachey, writing in 1612, reported a regulation at Jamestown which (somewhat abbreviated) declared:

> There shall no man or woman dare to wash any unclean linnen within the Pallizadoes, nor rench, and make clean, any kettle, pot, or pan within twenty foote of the olde well, upon pain of whipping.

This might lead us to expect an early and rapid development of sanitation in the colonies. But like intensive agriculture and forest conservation anything like scientific sanitation was still far ahead in the future.

When there was sickness, the minor aches and pains and colds with which most sickness begins, the mother of the family attended to it, administering the home remedies with which she was familiar, as mothers do still. In the South the wife of the planter was the doctor for all on the estate, those of the family, the indentured white servants, and the negro slaves. No doubt a little cheering encouragement was the most effective medicine in these cases. Every house had its little herb garden and every housewife had her own home-grown, home-made remedies. In the earlier days the Indians also contributed some suggestions from their native pharmacœpia, such as the use of tobacco as an astringent for a cut. Thus was cared for the larger part of the sickness, or deviation from working health.

When the sickness persisted and became serious enough to suggest awful possibilities, and when therefore extraordinary attention was needed, then theology was apt to come in with ideas for treatment, and remnants of old-time magic and plain gratuitous imaginings flocked into the terrified home and harassed community. Preparations of crushed toads and other unpleasant formulæ were recommended and used. But there was honorable precedent for all this. King James I, "the most learned fool in Christendom" but nonetheless king, and handsome King Charles I both touched the sick to cure scrofula, which was therefore called the King's evil. This was before King Charles II had come forward as the champion of clear thinking and science. But not even in this field of bad taste and superstition was everything as doubtful as it might seem. Governor John Winthrop of Massachusetts Bay (1587–1649) wrote to his wife in 1630 in regard to the voyage when she came to join him:

> . . . & for the physick you shall need no other but a pound of Doctor Wright's Electuaria lentivii, & his direction to use it, a gallon of scurvy grease to drink a little 5 or 6 mornings togither, wth some salt peter dissolved in it, & a little grated or sliced nutmete.

This would sound like some patent medicine of the day, but an electuary was only medicine made up with sugar or honey as a confection, so it may not have been too bad to take. In another letter he said:

> Remember to bringe juice of lemons to sea with thee, for thee and thy company to eate with your meate as sauce.

Good advice, out of the way only in its spelling. On the other hand, Governor Winthrop had in 1656 a remedy for ulcers of his own devising which he highly recommended. It consisted principally of "1 oz. of crabbe's eyes and 4 oz. of strong wine vinegar"!

One of the remarkable therapeutic discoveries of that time, the time of the "crabbe's eyes," continues in use to the present day, cinchona bark, named after the Spanish grandee whose wife was cured of an intermittent fever with it in South America, or Peruvian bark from the country of its origin, or quinine for short, the permanent specific for malaria. It was brought to Spain in 1640, and to England in 1655, whence it was soon introduced into the tobacco colonies. Governor Berkeley said in 1671 that formerly not one servant in five but died of the fever in his first year in Virginia, but now almost all escaped. And recently in some low-lying regions quinine is served at every meal in a vegetable dish and taken with a large spoon.

There were physicians of excellent reputation in the colonies. Doctor Lambert Watson was engaged by the Massachusetts Company to come over to New England. Doctor William Avery was skillful in his practice, invented several surgical instruments, and conducted chemical experiments. Doctor John Pott was eminent in Virginia as a physician, though also for other proclivities of a more unscientific character. Of Doctor Benjamin Bullivant John Dunton in his *Letters Written from New England* in 1686 said:

To the Poor he always prescribes cheap, but wholesome medicines, not curing them of a consumption in their Bodies, and sending it into their Purses; nor yet directing them to the East-Indies to look for Drugs, when they may have far better out of their Gardens.

The local apothecaries sold their drugs either to the physician or to the patient, but most doctors made their own medicines. Some drugs were imported from London, the most important being mithridate, which was much used for poison, the plague, madness, leprosy, cancer, gout or dysentery. Indeed at first medicine, surgery and pharmacy were considered all one profession. The first to distinguish these from each other was Doctor John Morgan of Philadelphia who returned from the University of Edinburgh with a license also from the College of Physicians of London in 1765, and brought with him David Leighton, a qualified apothecary and surgeon, to whom he turned over all his work which was not strictly medical. He also made it his custom to collect his fee at the end of each visit—for the first visit 1 pistole, a Spanish gold coin of value about 16 shillings, and 1 dollar for other visits, but not for more than one visit a day.

It may seem curious to speak of an apothecary as a surgeon. A large part of the surgery was undoubtedly bleeding, almost a superstitious practice, as bleeding was resorted to in nearly all cases, in a state of weakness as well as of high fever, with infants as well as with robust adults. George Washington died, it is now recognized, from unnecessary bleeding as much as from the serious case of quinsy or laryngitis from which he was suffering. Barbers were considered surgeons as well as doctors. "Barber and Chirurgeon" was the familiar sign, and the red stripe on the barber's pole represented the blood he spilt and the white the bandage, while the pole itself the patient held as the operation proceeded. These were all surgical symbols, but may not have been entirely inappropriate for the barber, if we accept the testimony of a grave old Puritan preacher who declared in a sermon that God imposed the duty of shaving

The Barber-Surgeon

Redrawn from an early seventeenth-century print in the collection of Charles DeZemler
Rockefeller Center

upon men to even up for the pains of childbirth imposed upon women. A wise preacher and a conscientious thinker! A comment on the early iron industry also. Steel has since been invented for the benefit of the men!

Then as always, the family physician was the great friend in time of trouble, whether his knowledge and skill were comparatively great as judged by our standards or not.

Doctor Griffith Owen (1647–1717), a Welshman, of Philadelphia, was one of the outstanding physicans of his time. He came over in the *Welcome* with William Penn. Of him it was recorded:

His practice as a physician, in which he was very knowing and eminent, rendered him of still greater value and importance in the place where he lived.

He was also characterized by a contemporary as "tender Griffith Owen, who both sees and feels." He performed the first amputation in the Colonies, a young man whose arm was severely lacerated in the firing of a salute in honor of William Penn's second visit to Pennsylvania.

Epidemics were not infrequent. Heroic service was rendered in attendance on the sick and steady progress was made in the fight against them and against the panic that always attended them. Yellow fever, diphtheria, smallpox, scarlet fever, and influenza! No wonder so many people believed that the devil was personally active in them and must be dealt with! There was not enough cessation in the prevalence of the "decline" (consumption, or tuberculosis) to class it as an epidemic, but it was quite as hopelessly serious.

On the ships coming to Virginia in 1610 yellow fever broke out, and a number of the infected were forthwith thrown overboard. Hard treatment for the sick but it can be understood. Progress may be recognized in smallpox. Lady Mary Wortley Montagu, the wife of the English Ambassa-

328

dor to Turkey, brought knowledge of inoculation to England in April, 1721. The Turks, heirs of the Arabs in such matters, long had availed themselves of it. The Reverend Doctor Cotton Mather was the first to suggest its use in America, telling his friend, Doctor Zabdiel Boylston, about it. He inoculated his only son, a boy of thirteen, and two Negro servants with complete success on June 27, 1721. This was the beginning of the triumphant fight against the smallpox. Benjamin Franklin in his *Autobiography* gave his feeling about the treatment, referring to the death of a child of his.

A fine boy of four years old, by the smallpox, taken in the common way. I long regretted him, and still regret that I had not given it to him by inoculation. This I mention for the sake of parents who omit that operation, on the supposition that they should never forgive themselves if a child died under it, my example showing that the regret may be the same either way, and therefore that the safer should be chosen.

Benjamin Franklin contributed also to the fight against yellow fever. Doctor John Mitchell came to Virginia in 1700. He had a large practice on the Rappahannock, though his chief fame was for his botanical work and for an *Essay on the Causes of the Different Colors of People of Different Climates,* published in 1743. He wrote a paper on yellow fever in Virginia, based on his experiences in the epidemics of 1737, 1741, and 1742. This paper later fell into the hands of Benjamin Franklin. He communicated it to Doctor Benjamin Rush, who acknowledged his indebtedness to it for information enabling him to detect and combat the yellow fever epidemic of 1793 in Philadelphia. So is the torch handed on!

Nowadays it might be said that some, if not a great deal, of the sickness of the colonial days was caused by an excessive meat diet. However that may be, it is pleasant to read of the tempting table of which our young English friend did not approve:

> In several parts of Virginia the ancient custom of eating meat at breakfast still continues. At the top of the table where the lady of the house presides, there is constantly tea and coffee; but the rest of the table is garnished with roasted fowls, ham, venison, game, and other dainties. Even at Williamsburg it is the custom to have a plate of cold ham upon the table; and there is scarcely a Virginian lady who breakfasts without it.

But that was Smithfield ham! One cannot help wondering what was set on the table at the other meals.

All the colonial people were great hosts and they had a good time. In Philadelphia it was reported:

> Their amusements are chiefly dancing in the winter; and in the summer forming parties of pleasure upon the Schuylkill and in the country. There is a society of sixteen ladies and as many gentlemen called the Fishing Company, who meet once a fortnight upon the Schuylkill.

They had "a room" there. May it not have been an early country club! The dancing in all the Colonies consisted of the minuet, the Sir Roger de Coverley, and the like, no doubt. Since the Revolution the last dance has forgotten its English name, whipped up its tempo, and come down to us as the Virginia Reel. One account of a dance in the 1700s is specially interesting in these days. It refers to the jigs danced at the end of the evening:

These dances are without method or regularity. A gentleman and lady stand up, and dance about the room one of them retiring, the other pursuing, then perhaps meeting, in an irregular fantastical manner. After some time another lady gets up, and then the first lady must sit down, she being, as they term it, cut out. The second lady acts the same part which the first did, till somebody cuts her out. The gentlemen perform in the same manner.

But in all good sport in colonial America who does not think of horses,—riding to hounds, and horse races! It is nearly forgotten that to hunt horses used to be a great sport. In the early days the Indians stole the white men's horses sometimes or horses were often turned out in the woods to graze and strayed away. They got to be quite wild, some of them. That was one theory of the origin of the Narragansett pacers; an imported Spanish stallion was turned out by a Rhode Island planter in the woodlot on his 2000-acre estate and was never found again. But his descendants were. The first regular race course was the New Market on Hempstead Plains, on Long Island. Daniel Denton told about it in his Description of New York, 1670:

Toward the middle of Long Island lyeth a plain sixteen miles long and four broad, upon which plain grows very fine grass, that makes exceedingly good Hay, and is very good pasture for sheep and other Cattel; where you shall find neither stick nor stone to hinder the Horse heels, or endanger them on their Races, and once a year the best Horses in the Island are brought hither to try their swiftness, and the swiftest rewarded with a silver Cup, two being Annually procured for that purpose.

And down the dusty Duke of Gloucester Street in Williamsburg every spring and every autumn, at least, there were horse races, and good ones! The Virginia horses were great runners. And often the Narragansett Planters would bring their pacers down to Williamsburg—and there were some good races!

But in all sociability, when people get together, the chief thing is the people themselves. They do not need great banquets or breakfasts of marvellous viands, not even of Smithfield ham. They do not need theatres, or dances, or horses. They only need themselves. Here is a delightful evening of which Miss Anne Blair of Williamsburg told in a letter to her sister in August, 1769. The letter was found quoted in a history of Williamsburg written recently quite as the book might have been written one hundred and seventy years ago. It happened in the days of the Right Honorable Norborne Berkeley, Baron de Botetourt, His British Majesty's Lieutenant, Governor-General and Commander-in-Chief:

Mrs. Dawson's Family stayed ye Evening with us, and ye Coach was at ye Door to carry them Home, by ten o'clock; but everyone appearing in great Spirits it was proposed to set at ye Steps and Sing a few Songs wch was no sooner said than done; while thus we were employ'd, a Candle or Lanthorn was observed to be coming up Street; (except Polly Clayton censuring their ill Taste for having a Candle such a fine Night) no one took any Notice of it—till we saw, who ever it was, stop to listen to our enchanting Notes—each Warbler was immediately silenced; whereupon the Invader to our Melody, call'd out in a most rapturous Voice, Charming! Charming! proceed for God Sake, or I go Home directly—no sooner were those Words uttered, than all as with one Consent sprung from their Seats, and ye Air echo'd with "pray, Walk in my Lord"; No—indeed he would not, he would set on the Step's too; so after a few ha, ha's, and being told what all knew —that it was a delightful Evening, at his desire we strewed the way over with Flowers [repeated some of the songs] &c &c till a full half Hour was elaps'd when all retir'd to their respective Homes.

Philadelphia, the metropolis of its province; Boston, the chief town meeting of New England, the region of the towns; New York and Charleston, the focus, each of them, of its region; Williamsburg, the intermittent town of the combined estates of Virginia—all of them were the concentrated embodiments of their colonies, characteristic of them and different from each other. Truly Boston was the most a town and Philadelphia was the most a city in the eighteenth century. New York was to become, but it had not yet reached its splendid importance. Even during the Revolutionary War it was the Hudson River dividing the Colonies and possibly forestalling their union that was fought for. And now—the colonial Boston is gone; the colonial Philadelphia is gone. Every colonial town is gone. But Williamsburg in Virginia, which had its day from 1699 to 1779, has been brought back by historical appreciation. Every reader can see it as it was, by driving thither in his automobile and spending a few days there. There he can actually see for himself a Colonial Town of the 1700s.

Tobacco the wealth of early Virginia

Bibliography

For readers who ask where they can find more material in this same field, the following books are suggested as covering the field generally or as covering the fields of several chapters. These are by no means all nor a considerable part of the titles that would be found valuable or interesting, but enough to give a start in further reading.

Oliver Perry Chitwood, *History of Colonial America*. (A recent and good work covering the general field of this period.)

John Fiske, *Old Virginia and Her Neighbors*. (John Fiske was a sound scholar and a human one.)

John Fiske, *The Beginnings of New England*.

John Fiske, *The Dutch and Quaker Colonies*.

Herbert L. Osgood, *The American Colonies in the Seventeenth Century*.

Herbert L. Osgood, *The American Colonies in the Eighteenth Century*.

Fiske Kimball, *American Architecture*. (A small book.)

Fiske Kimball, *Domestic Architecture in the American Colonies*. (A large and standard work.)

Thomas H. Ormsbee, *The Story of American Furniture*.

R. T. H. Halsey and Elizabeth Tower, *The Homes of Our Ancestors*. (A valuable work about the American Wing of the Metropolitan Museum.)

Harold D. Eberlein and Abbot McClure, *The Practical Book of American Antiques*.

Harold D. Eberlein, *The Architecture of Colonial America*.

Charles M. Andrews, *Colonial Folkways*. (Chronicles of America.)

Edward Warwick and Henry C. Pitz, *Early American Costume*.

Alice Morse Earle, *Two Centuries of Costume in America*.

Alice Morse Earle, *Home Life in Colonial Days*.

Alice Morse Earle, *Margaret Winthrop* (1591–1647). (A biography of the wife of Governor John Winthrop.)

Katharine Stanley-Brown, *The Young Architects*. (For children.)

Much interest will be found in the old original sources, from some of which quotations have been made in this book. There is nothing to

BIBLIOGRAPHY

equal the accounts of what they did as told by Captain John Smith, Governor William Bradford, Governor John Wentworth, and William Penn themselves. These accounts have been made available in the following series:

Original Narratives of Early American History: Reproduced under the Auspices of the American Historical Association; General Editor, J. Franklin Jameson.

Narratives of Early Virginia, 1606–1625. Editor, Lyon Gardiner Tyler. (Includes Captain John Smith's A True Relation.)

Bradford's History of Plymouth Plantation, 1606–1646. Editor, William T. Davis. (Governor Bradford's Of Plimouth Plantation.)

Winthrop's Journal, 1630–1649. Editor, James K. Hosmer. 2 volumes. (Governor John Winthrop's History of Massachusetts Bay.)

Narratives of New Netherland, 1609–1664. Editor, J. Franklin Jameson.

Narratives of Early Pennsylvania, West New Jersey, and Delaware, 1630–1707. Editor, Albert Cook Myers. (Including several papers by William Penn.)

There are also other volumes of similar character.

Benjamin Franklin, Autobiography.

Sarah Kemble Knight, The Private Journal of a Journey from Boston to New York in 1704.

Rev. Alfred Burnaby, Travels through North American, 1759 and 1760.

Hugh Finlay, Journal of the Surveyor of the Post Roads on the Continent of North America, 1773.

Rev. Joseph Doddridge, Notes of Setlements and Indian Wars in Virginia and Pennsylvania.

Rev. Grant Powers, Historical Sketches of the Coos Country.

Albert Bushnell Hart, American History Told by Contemporaries, 3 volumes. (An excellent selection of excerpts.)

With special reference to the particular chapters the following books may be of interest.

CHAPTER I

SHELTERS AND FIRST HOUSES

Captain John Smith, A True Relation; and the General History of Virginia. (Original Narratives.)

BIBLIOGRAPHY

Governor William Bradford, *Of Plimouth Plantation*. (Original Narratives.)

CHAPTER II

THE FIREPLACE CENTER OF THE HOME

George F. Dow, *Every Day Life in the Massachusetts Bay Colony.*
Jane de Forest Shelton, *The Salt-Box House.*

CHAPTER III

IN DUTCH NEW YORK

Harold D. Eberlein, *Manors and Historic Homes of the Hudson Valley.*
Harold D. Eberlein, *Manor Houses and Historic Homes of Long Island and Staten Island.*
Helen Wilkinson Reynolds, *Dutch Houses in the Hudson Valley before 1776.* (Auspices of the Holland Society of New York.)
Rosalie Fellows Bailey, *Pre-Revolutionary Dutch Houses and Families in Northern New Jersey and Southern New York.* (Auspices of the Holland Society of New York.)

CHAPTER IV

PENN'S QUAKER CITY

Sydney G. Fisher, *The Quaker Colonies.* (Chronicles of America.)
Arthur Pound, *The Penn Family in Pennsylvania and England.*
Benjamin Franklin, *Autobiography.*

CHAPTER V

PENNSYLVANIA GERMAN FARMS

G. Edwin Brumbaugh, "Colonial Architecture of the Pennsylvania Germans," *Proceedings of the Pennsylvania German Society,* Volume XLI, 1930.

CHAPTER VI

HANDWORK AT EPHRATA

Julius F. Sachse, *The German Sectarians of Pennsylvania.* 2 volumes.

BIBLIOGRAPHY

CHAPTER VII

AT MORAVIAN BETHLEHEM

J. M. Levering, *History of Bethlehem, Pennsylvania*.
W. J. Heller, "The Gun Makers of Old Northampton," (County) *Proceedings of the Pennsylvania German Society*, Volume XVII, 1908.

CHAPTER VIII

SCOTCH-IRISH IN THE MOUNTAINS

Joseph Doddridge, *Notes of Settlements and Indian Wars in Virginia and Pennsylvania*.
William Maclay Hall, *Reminiscences and Sketches, Historical and Biographical*.
Charles M. Stotz, *Early Architecture of Western Pennsylvania*.

CHAPTER IX

GEORGIAN MANSIONS

Fiske Kimball, *Domestic Architecture in the American Colonies*.
William Lawrence Bottomley, Chairman of Achitects' Emergency Committee, *The Great Georgian Houses of America*.

CHAPTER X

EIGHTEENTH-CENTURY FURNITURE

Thomas Hamilton Ormsbee, *The Story of American Furniture*.
Luke Vincent Lockwood, *Colonial Furniture in America*.
Wallace Nutting, *Furniture of the Pilgrim Century*.
Wallace Nutting, *Furniture Treasury* (3 volumes).

CHAPTER XI

IRON MINED AND WROUGHT

Herbert C. Keith and Charles Rufus Harte, *The Early Iron Industry in Connecticut*. (Conn. Soc. Civil Engineers, Proc., 1935.)
Albert H. Sonn, *Early American Wrought Iron*. (3 volumes with 320 plates.)

BIBLIOGRAPHY

CHAPTER XII

PEWTER IN THE COLONIAL HOME

Harold D. Eberlein and Abbot McClure, *The Practical Book of American Antiques.*
John Barrett Kerfoot, *American Pewter.*
N. Hudson Moore, *Old Pewter, Brass, Copper, and Sheffield Plate.*

CHAPTER XIII

SILVERSMITHS AND SILVERWARE

Harold D. Eberlein and Abbot McClure, *The Practical Book of American Antiques.*
C. Louise Avery, *Early American Silver.*
William Davis Miller, *Six Silversmiths of Little Rest.*

CHAPTER XIV

MEASURES OF VALUE

Agnes F. Dodds, *History of Money in the British Empire and the United States.*

CHAPTER XV

COLONIAL GLASS

Harold D. Eberlein and Abbot McClure, *The Practical Book of American Antiques.*
F. W. Hunter, *Stiegel Glass.*

CHAPTER XVI

NEW ENGLAND SHIPS

Ralph D. Paine, *The Old Merchant Marine.* (Chronicles of America.)
Howard M. Chapin, *Rhode Island Privateers in King George's War, 1739–1748.*
State Street Trust Company, Boston, *Whale Fishery of New England, 1915.*

CHAPTER XVII

SHIPBUILDING AT PHILADELPHIA

Charles Lyon Chandler, *Early Shipbuilding in Pennsylvania.* (The Cyrus Fogg Brackett Lecture at Princeton University, 1932.)

339

BIBLIOGRAPHY

Howard M. Chapin, *Privateer Ships and Sailors: The First Century of American Colonial Privateering, 1625–1725.*
Howard M. Chapin, *Privateering in King George's War, 1739–1748.*

CHAPTER XVIII

TRAILS AND ROADS

Isabel S. Mitchell, *Roads and Road-Making in Connecticut.* (Tercentenary Commission of Connecticut.)
Sarah Kemble Knight, *The Private Journal of a Journey from Boston to New York in 1704.*

CHAPTER XIX

THE PROVINCIAL POST

Wesley Everett Rich, *History of the United States Post Office to 1829.*
Mary E. Woolley, *The Early History of the Colonial Post Office.*
Hugh Finlay, *Journal of the Surveyor of the Post Roads on the Continent of North America, 1773.*

CHAPTER XX

AGRICULTURE IN THE COLONIES

Lyman Carrier, *History of the Beginnings of Agriculture in the United States.*
Percy W. Bidwell and J. I. Falconer, *History of Agriculture in the Northern United States.*

CHAPTER XXI

THE COLONIAL TOWN

Architectural Record, December, 1935, *The Restoration of Williamsburg.*
Rev. Alfred Burnaby, *Travels through North America, 1759 and 1760.*
Benjamin Franklin, *Autobiography.*
R. G. Gent., *Williamsburg in Virginia* (1936).
Gertrude Selwyn Kimball, *Providence in Colonial Times.*
Francis J. Packard, *History of Medicine in the United States.*

340

Index

Academy of Philadelphia, 320
Acadia (Nova Scotia), 215
Achilles, The (ship), 224
Adam, Robert, 149
Adams Houses, Quincy, Mass., 25
Adams, John, 18, 309
Advertising, 299
Africa, 216
Agent for Massachusetts in London, 271
Agriculture, 64, 125, 296; Cooperation in, 96
Albany, N. Y., 38, 142, 250
Alden, John, 28, 32, 148
Allegheny Mountains, 53, 112, 113, 123, 169, 274, 280
Allen, Ethan, 164
Allen, Judge, of Philadelphia, 268
Allentown, Pa., 106
Alloways Creek, 201
Alpine Race, 110
Alsace, Upper, 69
Altoona, Pa., 124
Alum, 122
American Civilization, 1, 65, 113
American Colonies, 10, 125, 126, 129, 130, 177, 181, 188, 215, 223, 256, 262, 264, 266, 272, 290, 296, 305
American Flint Glass Company, 209
American Philosophical Society, 187
American, The, Philadelphia, 302
American Weekly Mercury, The, 267
Amsterdam, Holland, 181
Andalusia, Spain, 288
Andros, Governor Sir Edmund, 182, 196, 262
Annapolis, Md., 142
Anne, Queen of England, 56, 152, 154, 156
Antes, Henry, 96
Anthony, Joseph, 187
Antiqua, 294
Apothecaries, 325, 326
Apples, 279, 280
Applied Science, 321
Apprenticeship, 179, 188, 221, 225, 235
Arabs, 329
Architects, 127, 130
Architectural Books, 129
Architecture, 1, 60, 76
Arctic Ocean, 217
Argo, The (ship), 225
Armstrong, Major George, 119
Armstrong, John, 119
Army, American, 164

Army, British, 104
Army, Continental, 104, 164
Ashlar, 132
Asparagus, 278
Atlantic Ocean, 211, 212
Autobiography of Benjamin Franklin, 329
Avery, Dr. William, 325
Axe, 113, 245
Axeheads, 297

Baffin Bay, 217
Bakehouse, 82
Bake-kettle, 21
Balls, 304
Baltimore, Md., 113, 209
Banking, 315
Barbados, 214, 215
Barbers, 326
Barber's Pole, The, 326
Barge, Penn's six-oared, 56
Barley, 276
Barns, 73, 97, 291
Barnyard, 291
Baron Stiegel in the Rhineland, 206
Barter, 122, 177, 193
Bartram, John, 321
Bartram, William, 322
Beads, 199
Beans, 276
Beaver Skins, 193, 215, 312
Bedford, Pa., 114, 118, 119, 123, 124
Beds, 25, 26, 34; Folding, 34; Four-poster, 36; Trundle, 35
Beer, 280
Beeswax Candles, 23
Beets, 278
Beissel, Johann Conrad, 74–86, 88
Bell House, 90–93, 99, 100
Bellomont, Earl of, 223
Bellringer, 92
Benches, 7, 24
Benger, Elliott, P.M.G., 268
Bergen, N. J., 279
Berkeley, Rt. Hon. Norborne, 332
Berkeley, Governor William, 325
Berries, 294
Bethlehem, Pa., 64, 69, 87, 106, 109, 166, 262; Naming of, 89–90
Bethlehem Water Works, 109
Bible, 24, 113, 318
Bible-Box, 152
Bilbao, Spain, 224
Biscay, Bay of, 220, 224

341

INDEX

Blacksmith, 165–166, 286, 297
Blair, Miss Anne, 332
Blair, Rev. James, 320
Bleeding, 326
Blessing of the Bay, The (ship), 213
Blue, 294
Blue Grass, 280, 282
Blue Mountains, 64
Blum, Ludwig, 84
Boardman House, Saugus, Mass., 3, 11
Boehner, John, 109
Bond, English, 16
Bond, Flemish, 16, 57
Bookbindery, 81
Books: Furniture, 148–9; Architectural, 129; Shipbuilding, 236
Bookstore, 100
Boone, Daniel, 114
Boston, Mass., 106, 133, 170, 175, 179, 180, 181, 209, 215, 226, 227, 247, 259, 263, 265, 270, 272, 299, 305, 333
Boston Gazette (quoted), 200
Boston Gazette, The, 302
Boston News-Letter, The, 265, 270, 299, 302
Boston Post Road, 246, 247–49
Botetourt, Baron de, 332
Bottles, 199, 201, 202
Bouquet, Lieut.-Col. Henry, 119
Boylston, Dr. Zabdiel, 329
Braddock's Trail, 114
Bradford, Governor William, 14, 42; (quoted), 13
Bradford, William (Printer), 301
Brands, 284
Brass Buttons, 201, 202, 210
Bremer, Martin, 78
Brewster, Elder William, 32
Brewton, Miles, Charleston, S. C., House, 135, 136
Brick, 15, 16, 17; building material, 132
Brick Houses, 72
Brick Oven, 22, 23
Bridges, 102, 247
Brief Account of the Province of Pennsylvania, A, 50
Bristol, England, 212, 230, 232
Bristol, R. I., 266
British Government, 194, 264, 271
Bronze, Composition of, 172
Brooklyn, N. Y., 11
Broom Straw, 280
Brown sandstone, 133, 140
Bruton Parish Church, Williamsburg, 306
Buffon, George Louis Leclerc Comte de, 322
Buildings, Types of, 3–4, 10–11, 15, 44–45, 54, 57, 58–61, 66–67, 71–73, 76, 90, 115–17, 127–42, 291
Bullivant, Dr. Benjamin, 325
Bureau, 30, 151
Burlington, N. J., 266
Burnaby, Rev. Andrew (quoted), 305, 306
Bushnell, Edmund, 236

Byrd, William, 166
Byzantine Empire, 32

Cabbages, 278
Cabinetmakers, 28, 95, 147–48
Cabot, John, 212
Cabot, Sebastian, 212
Cabriole leg, 152, 154, 155
Callowhill, Hannah, 56
Cambridge, Mass., 135, 136, 142
Cammerhoff, Bishop, 93
Campbell, William, 270, 299, 300
Campfire, 23
Canary Islands, 214
Candles, 23, 24, 215, 217
Cape Cod, 212
Cape Horn, 217
Cape May, 241
Cape Sable, 214
Capen, Parson, of Topsfield, Mass., 144
Carlisle, Pa., 118
Carolinas, the (North and South), 262
Carpenter, Samuel, 54
Carriages, 250, 288
Carrots, 278
Carts, 246, 297
Carver, Governor John, 32
Carving, 26, 28, 34, 36, 132, 133, 146, 149, 152, 154, 156
Casey, Samuel, 178, 185, 288, 314
Casks, 28
Cattle, 39, 64, 121, 122, 280, 284, 286; (Black) from Spanish West Indies, 286; (Red) from Holland, 286
Cauliflower, 278
Cavaliers, 36, 37
Certificates, 312
Chains, 297
Chairs, 24, 26, 28, 156, 157; Banister-back, 33, 34, 156; Bishop's, 30; Brewster, 32, 33, 156; Carver, 32, 33, 156; Dutch, 45; Fiddle-back, 33, 34, 156; Great, 30, 34; Hitchcock, 32; Ladder-back, 156; Lady, 34; Leather-back, 34; Side, 34; Slat-back, 34; Wainscot, 30, 34; Windsor, 30; Wing, 156
Chairman, 32
Chair-table, 25, 26
Chaises, 252
Chandler, Charles Lyon, 237
Chapel, 92, 128
Charcoal, 160
Charles I, King of England, 323
Charles II, King of England, 41, 42, 50, 230, 321, 324
Charleston, S. C., 135, 136, 181, 269, 333
Charming Forge, 206
Charter for Iron Works, 160
Chase House, Annapolis, 142
Chesapeake Bay, 110
Chest of Drawers, 152, 154
Chest-on-Chest, 152
Chester, Pa., 64
Chests, 26, 71, 151

342

INDEX

Children's mortality, 322
Chimneys, 10, 11, 13, 18, 20, 22, 24, 25, 116
Chinaware, 122, 169, 175
Chinese Chippendale, 155
Chippendale, Thomas, 148–157
Christ Church, Philadelphia, 234
Christiansen, Hans, 109
Church, 128, 161, 250
Church of England, 60
Church Pewter, 175
Cider, 280
City Planning, 57
Clam, 194
Clark, George Rogers, 114
Clarke, Dr. John, 321
Classics, 318
Claw-and-ball Foot, 154
Cliveden, Germantown, Pa., 136, 142, 144
Clock, Town, 92
Clothes, 44, 47, 119–20, 292
Clover, Red, 280; White, 280, 282
Coastwise Commerce, 147, 213
Cod, The Sacred, 212
Coffee, 122
Coffee-houses, 256
Coinage, 177, 179
College of New Jersey at Princeton, The, 319
College of Philadelphia, 187
College of Physicians of London, 326
Colleges, 316, 318
Cologne, Germany, 203
Colonial Village, 9
Colonies, 3, 5; English, 38, 48; Middle, 38
Colors, Dutch, 47
Comenius, Johann Amos, 88
Commercial Practice, 179
Committee of Safety, 106, 272
Committees of Correspondence, 272
Commodities as Money, 177, 313–14
Common Room, 10, 18, 19, 23, 25, 26, 35
Communication, 130, 241, 255, 264, 299
Communion Silver, 175
Community House, 102
Complete Shipwright, The (Book), 236
Concord, Battle of, 227
Conestoga Horse, 290
Conestoga Manor, 111
Congress, the Continental, 224, 238, 272
Connecticut, 4, 11, 34, 161, 162, 194, 239, 242, 251, 259, 263, 265, 321
Connecticut Gazette, The, New Haven, 302
Connecticut Valley, 277
Constitution, The, (Ship), 225
Constitution of the United States, 187
Consumption, 328
Conversion of Coins, 195
Cooking, 19, 20; boiling, 20; roasting, 22; baking, 22
Cooperation in Farming, 295, 296, 299
Cooperative Shipbuilding, 213

Copley, John Singleton, 133
Copper, 172
Copperware, 26
Corn, 215
Cornbury, Lord, Governor of New York, 265
Cornwall, 52
Costume, 36, 37, 47, 50, 60, 61–62, 77–78, 86, 119–20, 221
Cotton wicks, 23
Counterfeiting, 192
Country, 273
Cowell, William, 188
Cowpens, Battle of the, 108
Cows, 283
Coxe, Tench (quoted), 239
"Crabbe's eyes," 324
Cradle, 34
Cradle, Grain, 297
Crane, 20
Crib, 34
Crop-notes, 313
Crown Inn, Bethlehem, 100, 102
Cumberland Valley, 110, 118
Curriculum of a Colonial College, 319

Dairy, 68, 96
Dale, Sir Thomas, 14
Dame Schools, 318
Dances, 117
Dancing, 330
Danielson, J., 251
Danish Cattle, 286
Dartmouth College, Hanover, N. H., 319
Davis Strait, 217
Dayton, Robert, House, 11
Deal, Kent, England, 232
Declaration of Independence, 187, 309
"Decline," 328
Decoration, 66, 71, 78
Delaware, State of, 4
Delaware Avenue, Philadelphia, 233
Delaware River, 9, 55, 60, 62, 64, 67, 138, 199, 229, 234, 279
Delaware, The (Ship), 238
Denton, Daniel (quoted), 331
Deputy Postmaster General, 262, 264, 267
Derby, Elias Hasket, 225, 227–28
Derby, Elias Hasket, Jr., 225
Derby, Elias Hasket III, 225
Derby, John, 225, 227
Derby, Richard (Jr.), 225, 226–28
Derby, Richard (Sr.), 225
Description of New York (Book), 331
Detached Buildings, 291
De Tirck Johan, 69, 71, 72
Devonshire Cattle, 286
Dickinson, Jonathan, 265
Diet for singers, 86
Diligence, The (Ship), 233, 234
Dinners, 304
Diphtheria, 328
Disbrowe, Nicholas, 148
Dishes, 71, 121, 169

343

INDEX

Dishes, Penna.-Germ., 66
Dispensary, 102
Dockyards, 126
Doddridge, Rev. Joseph, 114
Dongan, Governor Thomas, 262
Door, Dutch, 45
Dormer Windows, 66, 142, 176
Draft, Commercial, A, 315
Dragon, The (Ship), 225
Dress, 36, 44, 47, 86, 119–120
Dresser, 26
Dripping Pan, 22
Drippings, 20
Drugs, 325, 326
Dublin, at, D.P.M.G., 264
Dudley, Thomas (quoted), 13
Duke of Gloucester Street, Williamsburg, 306, 332
Dummer, Jeremiah, 179
Dunbar, Battle of, 3
Dunkers, 69
Dunton, John (quoted), 325
Durham, Pa., 106
Dutch, 36, 38, 39, 41, 42, 43, 44, 133, 188, 213, 259, 265, 278, 283
Dutch East India Company, 38, 181
Dutch Government, 42, 258
Dutch heritage, 47
Dutch New York, 38–47
Dutch period, 4
Dutch West India Company, 42
Dutch Women, 293
Duyckingk, Evert, 199
Dyeing, 294
Dye-peddler, 294

Earle, Alice Morse, 294
Ear-marks, 284
East Hampton, Long Island, 12
East River, 39
Easton, Pa., 102, 106
Eberbach, on the Necker, 75
Edict of Nantes, Revocation of, 63
Edinburgh, at, D.P.M.G., 264
Education, 98, 316
Edward I, King, 43
Edward III, King, 43
Eliot, Jared, 275
Elizabeth, Queen of England, 18, 181, 236
Elizabeth Furnace, 205, 207
Elizabeth Township, Lancaster County, Pa., 205
Endive, 278
England, 5, 24, 36, 63, 177, 215, 226, 227, 233, 300, 310, 325
English Cattle, 286; Customs, 18
"English Grass," 282
English Horses, 288, 291
English People, 42, 259
English, Philip, 220
English Tradition, The, 188
Entrance, 128, 133
Entrance Requirements, 319
Ephrata, Pa., 64, 69, 74–86, 87, 88, 176

Epidemics, 322, 328
Essay on Causes of Color in People, 329
Evertsen, Admiral Cornelis, 261
Exchange, Bill of, 315
Execution Dock, London, 221
Exports, 9, 125, 182, 226, 284, 288

Factories or Shops, 187
Fairmount Park, Philadelphia, 54
Falling Creek, Virginia, 158
Faneuil Hall, Boston, 305
Fanmaker, 95
Farm Produce, 226, 250, 251, 273
Farming, 96, 97, 117, 158, 273–98, 309
Farms, Pennsylvania-German, 63–73
Fastening (in building), 12, 15
Feast of the Roses, 210
Federal City, The, 57
Fees, Doctors', 326
Fencing, 283
Ferry, 100, 102, 246
Finance, 315
"Finery" (Iron Refinery), 158
Finns, 9, 67
Fire, 13, 14, 119
Fire, Great, of London, 9
Fire rooms, 26, 35
Fire wood, 213
Fireplace, 10, 18, 22, 24
Fireplace, The, Center of the Home, 18–37
Fishermen, 228
Fishermen, French, 212
Fishing, 125, 158, 211–216, 223, 224, 226, 230
Flail, 292
Flanders, 43
Flax, 26, 97, 292, 293
Flax Spinning Wheel, 293
Flax wicks, 23
Fleet, Dutch, 261
Fletcher, Governor Benjamin, 182, 185, 222
Flint Glass, 201, 207
Floors, 116
Flour, 182
Flowers, 47, 210, 294
Flowers as dyes, 294
Folding Bed, 34, 35
Food, 1, 22, 44, 56, 86, 114, 120–21, 273
Forage, 280–83
Forbes, Brig.-Gen. John, 119
Fords, 246
Forge, 158
Forks, 169, 190
Forks of the Delaware (Bethlehem), 87, 96, 262
Fort, 113, 117–18
Fort Bedford, 118, 119
Fort Cumberland, 118, 123
Fort Duquesne, 118, 119, 205, 306
Fort Ligonier, 118
Fort Pitt, 119
Foster, John, 132

344

INDEX

Four-poster Bed, 36
Fox, George, 63
Foxcroft, John, Jt. P.M.G., 269, 271, 272
Fractur, 80
France, 63, 226
Frankfort, Germany, 63
Franklin, Benjamin, 70, 81, 104, 187, 197, 205, 299, 300, 320, 322; (quoted), 24, 268, 270, 329; Joint Postmaster General, 268–72
Fraunces' Tavern, New York, 253, 254, 305
Frederick, Md., 123
Freedom, 273
Freedom of the Press, The, 186, 241, 302
French, The, 275
French Scientists, 322
Fresh River, 39
Friends Meetings, 58, 59
Frigate, British or Warship, 235
Frigate, Naval, 220
Fruit, 279
Fulling Mill, 82, 295–95
Furnaces, 158, 161
Furniture, 24, 32, 34, 44, 147–57
Furniture Style Modifications, 151
Fur Trade, 38, 39, 114, 122, 125, 193, 199, 215

Gage, General Thomas, 226
Galleons, Spanish, 221
Gambrel, Dutch, 44; New England, 44; Roofs, 44
Garnish (Plates or Porringers), 174
Gates, 165–67
Gates, Sir Thomas, 14
General Pickering, The (Ship), 224
General Washington, The (Ship), 238
Gentleman and Cabinet-Makers Guide, The, 149
George I, King of England, 65
Georgia, 5, 38, 129, 312
Georgian Mansions, 125–46
German Sects, 64, 69, 74
Germans, 52
Germantown, Pa., 64, 69, 93, 98, 136
Ghiselin, Cesar, 186
Glass (Composition), 199
Glass-Makers Street, New York, 199
Gloucester, Mass., 228
Gloucester Fisherman, The (Statue), 228
Gnadenhutten, 104, 109
Goats, 280
Goddard, John, 148
God's Acre, 93
Gold, 194, 312
Golden Eagle, The (Ship), 224
Goldenrod, 294
Good Order Established in Pennsylvania and New Jersey (Book), 282
Gosnold, Bartholomew, 212
Gottrecht, Father Friedsam, 78
Government, Nature of, 304

Governor's Palace, Williamsburg, Va., 139, 305
Governor, Royal, of Mass., 221
Graeme Park, Horsham, Pa., 136, 141, 143
Grammar Schools, 317
Grapes, 279
Grass, Common, 280
Gristmill, 82, 97, 292
Guilder, of Holland, 193

Hagerstown, Md., 123
Halfpenny, William, 130, 149
Hallways, 128, 142
Hamilton, Alexander, 314
Hamilton, Andrew (Dep. P.M.G.), 263, 264
Hamilton, Andrew (the Lawyer), 185, 241, 301; (quoted), 301–2
Hamilton, John, 264
Hamor, Ralph (quoted), 14
Hancock House, Thomas, and John, 140, 142
Hancock, John, 140, 314
Handles of Tools, 297
Hanging as Punishment, 178
Hannah, The (Ship), 225
Happy Union, The (Ship), 233
Harraden, Captain Jonathan, 224
Harrow, 297
Hartford, Conn., 39, 148, 246, 250, 277
Harvard College, Cambridge, Mass., 319
Hatchet, 245
Hats, 37
Hawthorne, Nathaniel, 221
Hayward, John, 261
Health, Science of, 322
Heidelberg, Electorate of, 201
Hell Gate, 47
Hempstead Plains, L. I., 331
Hendrickse, Ahasuerus, 182
Henricus, City of, Va., 15
Henry IV (The Play), 217
Hepplewhite, George and Andrew, 149–54, 155
Herb garden, 323
Herbs, 278; Medicinal, 102
Herdsmen, 284
Heredity, 225, 235
Hickory, 294
Higginson, Rev. Francis (quoted), 15
Highways, 245
Hinges, 166
Historical Society of Pennsylvania, 81
Hoes, 297
Holland, 36, 44, 47
Holley, Alexander Lyman, 165
Hollingsworth, Richard, 214
Hollow Ware, 174
Home Remedies, 323
Home Sweet Home (Song), 12
Homespun, 26
Hope-Chest, 26
Horn-book, 318

INDEX

Horse–Races, 304, 331–32
Horses, 39, 122, 127, 215, 250, 280, 283, 284, 286, 287, 288, 290–91, 292
Horseshoes, 101
Hospital, 104
Hotels, 100, 251
Hotspur, 217
House, first at Bethlehem, 89
House of Burgesses, The, 254, 267, 304
Houses, 1, 2, 3, 44, 127
Howard, Deacon, 252
Huber, Elizabeth, 205
Huber, Jacob, 205
Hudson, Henry, 38, 39, 44
Hudson River, 162, 164, 250, 333
Huguenots, 63, 68
Hull, John, Mint-Master, 160, 179, 187, 195, 314
Humphreys, Joshua, 238
Hunter, William, Jt. P.M.G., 268–69
Hunting Horses, 331
Hus, Jan, 88
Hussey, Christopher, 217
Hutchinson, Governor Thomas, 132–33, 271

Ice, 68
Iceland, 212
Immigrants, 65
Implements, Farm, 296
Indentured Whites, 148, 295, 323
Independence Hall, Philadelphia, 137, 140, 187
Indians, 5, 17, 67, 68, 94, 95, 112, 113, 114, 122, 159, 177, 194, 199, 241, 246, 275, 276, 280, 292, 295, 323
Indian Corn: See Maize
Indigo, 294
Industry, 101, 158
Influenza, 328
Information, 299
Ink, Printers', 82
Inkstands, 174, 186, 187
Inns, 251, 256
Inoculation, 329
Invention, Agricultural, 296
Ipswich, Mass., 258, 283
Ireland, 278
Iris, 294
Iron, 82
Iron industry, 327
Iron master, 205, 206
Iron ore, 158, 159, 160, 162, 164
Iron ware, 26, 122, 164, 297
Iron works, 3

Jail, 178
James I, King of England, 323
James II, King of England, 221, 262
Jamestown, Va., 5, 9, 14, 15, 16, 48, 199, 296, 322
Jansen, Catharine, 200
Jefferson, Thomas, 130, 309, 322
Jenks, Joseph, 160

Jersey, East, 48, 138, 162, 199, 263, 280
Jersey, West, 48, 199, 263, 280
Johnson, Edward (quoted), 15
Joiners, 28, 95, 148
Josselyn, English Traveler, 279
Jumel Mansion, New York, 135
Juniata River, 110, 118
Junta, Franklin's, 187
Justin Morgan (horse), 291

Kaufman's Creek, 69
Kaufman Farm, Pleasantville, Pa., 73
Keith, Governor William, 65, 136
Kenton, Simon, 114
Kettles, 20, 26
Kidd, Captain William, 221–23
Kieft, Willem, Director-General, 43
Killingly, Conn., 251
Killingworth, Conn., 275
Kimball, Fiske, 54, 132
King Street, Philadelphia, 233
King's College, New York, 319
King's Evil, 324
King's Highways, The, 246
King's Mountain, Battle of, 108
King's Throne, 30
Kitchen, 10, 18, 19, 24, 25
Klemm, John Gottlob, 95
Kloster at Ephrata, The, 74–86
Knight, Madam Sarah Kemble, 247, 249, 253, 265
Knives, 122, 169, 190
Knowlton, William Peter, 95

Lake Saltonstall, Connecticut, 161
Lakeville, Conn., 162
Lamps, 24
Lancaster, Pa., 209
Lancaster County, Pennsylvania, 64, 74, 106
Land Roads, 241
Land, Waterfront, 229, 233, 234
Landis Store, Berks County, Pa., 67
Lanterns, 24
Latches, 166, 176
Lathe-work, 26
Laryngitis, 326
Lead, 172
Leaders, Public, 274
Lean-to, 11, 18, 25, 26, 35, 128
Lebanon, Conn., 243
Lee House, Jeremiah, Marblehead, Mass., 144, 146
Leech, Hestor, 233
Leeks, 278
Lehigh River, 102, 109
Leighton, David, 326
Leisler, Jacob, 182
L'Enfant, Major, 57
Le Roux, Bartholomew, 182, 183, 185, 226
Le Roux, Charles, 185, 186, 226
Letitia Street House, 54, 57, 137
Letter-Carrier, 261

346

INDEX

Letters, Miscarriage of, 256
Letters Written from New England, 1686 (Book), 325
Levering, Bishop J. F. (quoted), 90, footnote
Lexington, Battle of, 227
Lexington, Mass., 180
Lightbody James, 236
Lighting, 23
Lightning Rods, 321
Lime Rock Forge, 162, 164
Linen, 26, 82, 292, 293
Linsey-woolsey, 292
Lititz, Pa., 67
Little Strength, The (Ship), 95
Live Stock, 39, 280, 283
Log Cabins, 9, 67, 115
Log Houses, 89, 99
Logan, James, 55, 111–12, 232, 233, 234
London Company, 9, 10
London, England, 221
London Merchant, The (Ship), 234
Long Island, N. Y., 11, 39, 211, 331
Long Island Sound, 225, 266
Longfellow, Henry W., House, 135, 136
Loom, 26, 82, 293
Louis XIV, King of France, 183
Lovelace, Governor Francis, 259, 261, 267, 269; (quoted), 259–60
Lucas, Eliza, 294
Lug-pole, 20
Lumber, 6, 9, 115, 125, 158, 213, 215, 226, 244, 250
Lutheran Church, 64, 69
Lynch, Head, P.M.G., 268

Madagascar, 197, 223
Madeira Islands, 214
Madeira Wine, 140
Mahogany, 149, 154
Maine, 5, 15, 211, 237, 265
Maize, 114, 275, 276
Manhattan, 38, 47
Manheim, Pa., 64, 203, 207
Manufacturing, 97
Map, Nicholas Scull's, of Delaware River, 234
Map of Philadelphia, 229
Maple wood, 169
Marblehead, Mass., 144, 213, 266
Mares, Flanders, 288
Mariner's Jewel, The (Book), 236
Market Street. Philadelphia, 233
Marketing, 158
Mary II, Queen of England, 320
Maryland, 4, 114, 148, 193, 239, 312
Maryland Gazette, The, Annapolis, 302
Masonry, 71, 132
Massachusetts, 2, 3, 4, 161, 162, 196, 212, 238, 256, 261, 263, 271–72, 314, 316
Massachusetts Bay, The Governor and Company of, 213, 325
Massachusetts Bay Colony, 3, 13, 14, 48, 65, 159, 178, 194, 195, 213, 286, 297, 324

Massachusetts Historical Society, 133
Mather, Rev. Dr. Cotton, 329; (quoted). 221
May, Cornelis Jacobsen, 38
Mayflower, The (Ship), 8, 28, 214
McAdam, John Loudon, 124
Meat Diet, 330
Medford, Mass., 132
Medicine, 322, 326
Melyn, Cornelis, 43
Mennonites, 69
Mercantile Policy or Theory, 215, 238
Mercer Henry Chapman, 167; (quoted), 168
Merchantman, 220, 223
Merion, Pa., 59
Merion Meeting House, 60
Messenger, 291
Metropolitan Museum of Art, 130
Meyer, Dr. Adolf, 102
Middle Colonies, 274, 280, 297
Middletown, Conn., 140
Military Training, 304
Miller, 291
Miller, Peter, 74, 84
Mining Engineering, 164
Ministry, 318
Mint, 177–78
Mint of Mass., Bay Colony, 195
Mints, 314
Minuet, 330
Minuit, Director-General Pieter, 42, 43
Mitchell, Dr. John, 329
Mitchell, Dr. S. Weir (quoted), 61
Moccasins, 120
Modern Builder's Assistant, The (Book), 130, 149
Mohawk Valley, New York, 63
Molasses, 216
Molds, Pewter, 174
Money, 191, 192–8
Monongahela River, 114
Monopoly, Postal, 262
Montagu, Lady Mary Wortley, 328
Montauk, L. I., 139
Montpelier, Prince George County, Md., 139
Moravians, 64, 87–109, 166
Moravian Church, 69, 89
Moravian Seminary and College for Women, The, 99
More, Doctor, 277
Morgan, Daniel, 106, 114
Morgan, Dr. John, 326
Morris, Robert, 314
Morris, Roger, House, New York, 135
Mortality, 322
Mortar, 15, 17, 116
Mount Airy, Va., 136, 139
Mount Pleasant, Philadelphia, 136, 137, 139
Mount Vernon, Va., 138, 305, 310
Music, 82–6, 89–90, 93–6
Music, composition, 84

347

INDEX

Musket, Smooth-bone, 104
Muskmelons, 278

Nails, 12, 101, 166–8
Nancy, The (Ship), 203
Nantucket, 217–9, 223
Narragansett Country, 178, 179, 288, 295
Narragansett Pacer, 288–90, 331
Narragansett Planters, 332
National Union, 299
Navy, American, 225, 238
Navy, British, 9, 10, 223, 232
Nazareth, Pa., 94, 96, 97, 106
Neale, Thomas, 262–3
Negroes, 216, 295, 323, 329
Neissen, Augustine, 92
Netherlands, The, 38, 44, 181
New Amsterdam, 181, 199, 213, 259
New Bedford, Mass., 219
New Brunswick, N. J., 95
Newbury, Vt., 252
New Castle, Province of Pa., 262
New England, 9, 10, 11, 15, 18, 19, 28,
  34, 36, 38, 44, 89, 128, 129, 132, 148,
  158, 216, 217, 228, 230 265 274, 278,
  297, 325, 333
New England Primer, 318
New England Shilling and Sixpence, 196
New Hampshire, 215, 239, 265
New Hampshire Gazette, The, Ports-
  mouth, 304
New Haven, Conn., 161, 246, 266, 283
New Jersey, 162
New London, Conn., 219, 266
New Market Race Course, 331
New Netherland, 38, 42, 43, 47, 258, 261,
  278, 293
New York, 4, 17, 28, 36, 44, 47, 95, 133,
  162, 175, 181, 182, 188, 193, 209, 226,
  239, 247, 263, 265, 312, 333
New York Gazette, The, 301, 302
New York, a Deputy Posmaster-General
  at, 264
Newbury, Mass., 266
Newfoundland Banks, 211, 214, 223, 228
Newport, Captain Christopher, 6
Newport, R. I., 148, 178, 321
Newspapers, 299, 300
Newspapers in the Mail, 269–70
Nicolls, Colonel Richard, 41
Nieuw Amsterdam, 38, 39, 44
Nieuw Nederlandt, 38, 42, 43, 47, 258,
  261, 278, 293
Noggins, 169
Non-Importation Agreement, 254
Nordic Race, 110
Norris, Richard (quoted), 229
Northampton County, Pa., 106
North America, 275
North Carolina, 312
North Carolina Gazette, The, New Berne,
  304
North, Lord, 223
North River, 38

Nova Scotia, 215, 262
Norwalk, Conn., 249
Nurses, 102

Oak, Red, 294
Oak Tree Coinage, 195–96
Oats, 97, 276
Oceanic Warfare, 180
Ohio River, 113
Oil for lamps, 24
Oil mill, 82
Old South Meeting House, Boston, 305
Oldtown, Md., 123
Oley Conference, 1742, 69
Oley Valley, Pa., 69, 72
Onclebaugh, Garrett, 184
Onions, 278
Opening of the Meadows, 283
Oratorio Societies, 93
Orchard, 82, 96
Orchestra, Symphony, 96
Organ, Pipe, 95
Opportunity, 273
Outbuildings, 138–40
Oven, 22
Oven wood, 22
Owen, Dr. Griffith, 328
Owned in England, Ships, 237
Ownership of Ships, 215, 216
Oxen, 250, 271, 283, 284, 286, 288, 290,
  297, 311
Oxford, Robert Harley, Earl of, 56
Oyster-shells, 15, 160

Pacers, 288, 290, 335
Pacific Ocean, 217
Packer's Path or Trail, 113, 122–4
Pack-saddles, 114, 122
Pack-train, 122
Paine, Ralph D., 221
Palatines, 52, 75, 105, 204
Palisade, 10
Palladio, Andrea, 128, 135
Panelling, 144, 146
Paper Mill, 81, 82
Paper Money, 177, 196–7
Parks, William, 300
Parsley, 278
Parsnips, 278
Pastorius, Francis Daniel, 63, 64
Pastures, 280
Patch, 105
Path, 246
Payne, John Howard, 12
Payne, William, 12
Peaches, 279, 280
Peas, 276
Peel, 22
Pegs, wooden, 12
Peltry, 122, 158
Pembroke Table, 155
Penmanship, 78, 79
Penn, Admiral William, 232

INDEX

Penn, William, 16, 48, 50, 51, 52, 53, 54, 55, 56, 57, 58, 60, 63, 67, 96, 111, 186, 197, 206, 229, 230, 232, 234, 262, 279, 288, 321, 328
Penn, William, Jr., 232, 234, 236
Penn's Sons, William, 236
Penn Family, 57
Penn, Letitia, 54
Penn's Quaker City, 48–62
Pennsbury, 55, 56, 60
Pennsylvania, 3, 4, 17, 50, 51, 52, 106, 132, 136, 138, 197, 230, 232, 238, 262, 263, 265, 312
Pennsylvania-Germans, 52, 63, 64, 65, 66, 71, 73, 106, 110, 111, 147, 278
Pennsylvania-German Farms, 52
Pennsylvania-German 5-plate Stove, 205
Pennsylvania State House, Philadelphia, 137
Penrose, Bartholomew of Bristol, Eng., 232, 235
Penrose, Bartholomew, 229–35
Penrose, Thomas (grandson of B. P. of Phila.), 232, 235
Penrose, Thomas (son of B. P. of Phila.), 235
Penrose, Thomas (uncle of B. P. of Phila.), 235
Penrose, Charles (gt. gr. son of B. P. of Phila.), 235
Penrose Shipyards, 234–5
Pent Roads, 243
Pequot Path, 246
Periwinkle, 194
Perkiomen Valley, 69
Perth Amboy, N. J., 266, 267
Peruvian Bark, 325
Petitions for Roads, 243
Pewter, 26, 121, 169–75, 176
Pewter, Composition of, 172
Pewterer's Company in London, 173
Pharmacy, 326
Philadelphia, Pa., 15, 47, 48, 53, 57, 58, 59, 61, 63, 64, 65, 69, 72, 124, 141, 148, 175, 181, 186, 187, 200, 209, 212, 226, 229–40, 241, 263, 265, 269, 291, 301, 306, 321, 330, 333
Philadelphia College, Phila., 319, 321
Philadelphia Courthouse, 136
Phips, Sir William, 221, 222
Physician, 102
Piazza, 133–4
"Pieces of Eight," 195
Pilgrims, 3, 28, 212, 297
Pilgrims (quoted), 8
Pinckney, Charles Cotesworth, 294
Pinckney, Chief Justice of S. C., 294
Pine Trees, 10
Pine Tree Coinage, 160, 195–6
Pine Masts, 213
Pirates, 180, 216, 220, 222, 237, 320
Piscataqua River, 213, 286
Piscataway (Post Office), 263
Pitchforks, 297

Pittsburgh, Pa., 119, 124, 164
Plantagenet Times, 18
Plantations, 96
Plantation Post (in Virginia), 258
"Plantation-built" Ships, 215, 237
Platters, 174
Plows, 297
Plowshares, 297
Plymouth, 3, 5, 8, 14, 16, 28, 32, 148, 194, 296
Porcelain, 175
Porch, 44, 133
Pork, 284
Porringers, 174
Portico, 135
Portraits, 37
Portsmouth, N. H., 213, 263, 266
Portugal, 214, 215
Portuguese Coinage, 195
Post or Post Office, 255
Postmasters, 267, 299, 300
Postmaster-General, 264–72, 300
Post-Riders, 267, 270, 271
Post Road, 259
Post Routes, 300
Potash, 122
Potatoes (White), 114, 121, 278
Pot-hooks, 20
Potomac River, 305
Pott, Dr. John, 325
Potts, Isaac, House, Valley Forge, Pa., 137
Pound Sterling of England, 193
Powell, Samuel, 92, 93, 100
Powers, Rev. Grant, 252
Powers, Rev. Peter, 252
Presbyterians, 52, 112
Printing Press, 81, 300
Preston, Conn., 243
Privateers, 180, 216, 219–20, 222, 224, 226, 227, 237
Privateer, British, 224, 225
Privateer, French, 234
Privateers, Tory, 225
Privateers, French, 234
Privy Council, 272
Prospectus, Penn's, 50, 51
Providence, R. I., 224, 246
Provincetown, Mass., 219
Protestants, 63, 69
Province of New York (See New York), 41
Province of Pennsylvania, Assembly of, 186
Public Affairs, 304
Public Buildings, 1
Public Occurrences both Foreign and Domestic (newspaper), 302
Public Schools, 317
Public Utility, 109
Pumpkins, 276
Puritans, 36, 37, 65, 89
Pynchon, John, 277

349

INDEX

Quakers, 52, 53, 57, 58, 59, 61, 62, 64, 69, 110, 111, 148, 230, 233, 237, 295
Quebec, Canada, 108, 205
Queen's College, New Brunswick, N. J., 319
Quero, The (ship), 227
Quincy, Josiah, 249
Quincy, Mass., 25
Quinine, 325
Quinsy, 326

Radnor, Pa., 61
Railroads, 225
Raleigh, Sir Walter, 181
Raleigh Tavern, Williamsburg, 253–54, 305
Rall, John, 245
Randolph, Edward, 262
Ranger, The (ship), 226
Rapaelje, Jan Joris, 39
Rapaelje, Sarah, 39
Rappahannock River, Virginia, 329
Raystown, Pa., 118
Reading, Pa., 69, 102
Reconversion of Coin and Silver, 177–79, 182, 189, 191
Recreation, 273
Reeded Column, 154, 155
Reel, 26
Reformed Church, 64
Revere, Paul, Jr., 180, 226
Revere, Paul, Sr., 179, 226
Revolutionary War, 10, 61, 104, 124, 147, 149, 164, 170, 175, 191, 195, 202, 209, 223, 227, 228, 237, 238, 239, 251, 252, 254, 288, 290, 294, 296, 297, 331, 333
Rhine, The River, 52, 63, 66, 71
Rhode Island, 15, 193, 238, 263, 265, 295, 331
Rhode Island College, Providence, 319
Rhode Island Gazette, The, Newport, 302
Rice, 193, 312
Richland, Pa., 210
Richmond, Va., 158
Riding, Horseback, 288
Riding Paths (horseback), 251
Rifles, 26, 105–8, 113, 114, 116, 117
Right Whale, 217
Rights of Way, 245
Ring in Nose (swine), 283
Rittenhouse, David, 322
River of the Mountains, 38
Rivers, 246
Road-Building, 251
Roadmakers, 119
Roads, 127, 241–54, 273
Roads, Plantation, 251
Roanoke Island, 158
Roasting Kitchen, 22, 23, 24
Roofs, 10, 12, 25, 44, 72, 73, 116, 176
Roofs, Tile, 72, 73
Roses, 71
Rosewell, Va., 142
Rotation of Crops, 275

Rotterdam, Holland, 63, 201, 203
Roxbury, Conn., 163
Royal Americans, 119
Royal Government, 314
Royal Governor of Virginia, 332
Royal Governors, 255, 256, 262, 263, 301, 304, 332
Royal Society, The, 321
Royal Treasury, 263, 271
Royall House, Medford, Mass., 132
Rubble, 132, 133
Rum, 215, 216
Rush, Dr. Benjamin, 329
Rush Lights, 23
Rye, 97, 276

Sad Ware, 173
Saddle Horses, 290
St. David's Church, Radnor, Pa., 61
St. Paul's Chapel, New York City, 245, 249
St. Stephen's Church, Bristol, England. 232
Salem, Mass., 5, 9, 15, 199, 211, 213, 215, 220, 221, 224, 225–28, 237, 266
Salisbury Iron Mines, 162–64, 250
Salt, 122, 123, 191, 215
Salt-Box House, 11, 128
Salt-Box House, The (book), 11
Saltcellars, 174, 190, 191
Salts, Individual, 191
Sanderson, Robert, 179, 187
Sanitation, 323
Saratoga, Battle of, 106
Saugus, Mass., 3, 159
Saugus Iron Works, 196
Saugus River, 160
Savery, William, 148
Sawmill, 82
Saybrook, Conn., 266
Scarlet Fever, 328
Schools, 98, 316, 317, 320
Schools, Boarding, 98
Schuyler, Margaret, 144
Schuyler, Philip, Mansion, Albany, 142
Schuylkill River, 15, 47, 64
Schwenkfelders, 69
Science, 321
Scotch House at Saugus, Mass., 3
Scotch-Irish, 52, 53, 106, 274, 279
Scrofula, 324
Scull, Nicholas, 234
Sculpture, 132, 133
Scythe Blades, 297
Sea-Captain, 228
Seminary for Young Ladies, 99
Senseman, Joachim, 92
Sesquicentennial Celebration, 1932, 54
Settle, 24, 26, 156
Settlers' Trails, 245
Seventh Day Baptists, 74
Sewall, Judge Samuel, 188
Shallop, 212, 213
Sharpshooter, 105, 106

INDEX

Sheep, 39, 280, 293
Shelters, 1, 2, 5, 13, 17
Shelters and First Houses, 1–17
Shelton, Daniel, 11
Shelton, Jane de Forest, 11
Sheraton, Thomas, 149, 154, 156
Shipbuilding, 125, 126, 212, 215, 216, 229–40
Ships, 211–28, 229–40
Shipwright, 212, 213, 221, 228
Shipyard, 229–36
Sickles, 297
Side-board, 30
Siderite, 163
Silver, 164, 170, 175, 194, 221, 312, 314
Silver "Bank," The, 177
Silver, Plated, 170
Silver Mines, 177
Silversmiths, 176–91
Silverware, 55, 176–91, 314
Silverware (William Penn's), 55
Sinclair, Sir John, 310
Singing, 82–86
Singstunden, 93
Sir Roger de Coverley, 330
Sitting Room, 25
Skippack Valley, 69
Slate House, The, 54
Slave Trade, 216, 237
Slaves, 148, 215, 295, 323
Smallpox, 328
Smeedes, Jan, 199
Smith, Captain John, 6, 7, 9, 14, 48, 280
Smith, Captain John (quoted), 6, 280
Smith, Richard, 164
Smithfield Ham, 330, 332
Smout, Edward, 233
Smuggling, 216
Solgard, Captain Peter, 185
Sons of Liberty, 272
Sophia, The (ship), 215
South, The, 38, 138, 148, 274, 286, 291, 323
South America, 180, 325
South Carolina, 4, 193, 294, 312
South Carolina Gazette, The, Charleston, 302
South Kingston, R. I., 295
South River, 39
Spain, 214, 215, 235, 325
Spanish Coinage, 195
Spanish Colonies, 194
Spanish Possessions, 180
Spanish Milled Dollar, 195
Speedwell, The (ship), 220
Sperm Oil, 217
Sperm Whale, 217
Spermaceti, 217
Spermaceti Candles, 23
Spinach, 278
Spindle, 294
Spinet, The First, 95
Spinning Wheels, 26
Spit, 20, 22, 23

Spoons, 174, 190
Spotswood, Governor Alexander, 267;
    Alexander, P.M.G., 268
Springfield, Mass., 277
Spring Rooms, 67, 68
Springs, 97, 108, 115
Stage-Coaches, 246, 250, 252
Stairway, Second, 142
Stairways, 142–46, 149
Stallion, Spanish, 331
Stallions, 288, 331
Stamford, Conn., 249
Stamp Act, 140, 271
Standing Salt, 191
Standing Table, 26
Standish, Captain Miles, 32
Staten Island, New York, 43
Steaming, 20
Stedman, Charles and Alexander, 206
Stiegel, Baron, 10-Plate Wood-Stove, 205
Stiegel, Heinrich Wilhelm, 64, 203–10
Stiegel, Henry William, 205–10
Stills, 280
Stoep (or Stoop), 44, 133
Stone (building), 17, 132
Stone Cabins, 67, 68, 69, 72, 73
Stone Houses, 72
Stonington, Conn., 244, 266
Stools, 24, 26
Stoves, 205
Strachey, William (quoted), 322
Stratford, Conn., 11
Streets, Town, 245, 251, 273
Stuart, Gilbert, 187
Studley, Thomas (quoted), 7
Stuyvesant, Director-General Pieter, 41, 43
Sun Inn, Bethlehem, 101–2
Surgery, 322, 326
Susquehanna River, 53, 63, 64, 110
Swedes, 9, 64, 67, 100, 279
Sweet Potatoes, 278
Swiss, 63, 105
Swift, Dean Jonathan, 56
Swine, 39, 121, 280, 283, 284
Syng, Philip, Jr., 186, 226
Syng, Philip, Sr., 186, 226

Table, Banquet or Dining-Room, 155
Table, Gate-Leg, 26
Table, Tea, 155
Table-Chair, 156
Tables, 25, 26, 154–56
Tables, Drop-Leaf, 155
Tableware, 169, 190
Taking up Land, 115
Talbot, Silas, 224
Tamerlane (horse), 288
Tankards, 174
Tanneberger, David, 95
Tannery, 82
Tapering Legs, 155, 156
Tavern over ye Water, The, 100, 102
Taxation without Representation, 26;

INDEX

Tea, 122
Thanksgiving Day, 292
Thatch, 10, 12
Theatres, 304
Thetford, Vt., 252
Threshing, 97
Threshing Floor, 291
Ticonderoga, 166
Tile Floors, 73
Tile Roofs, 72
Tiles, 73
Timothy, 280
Tin, 172
Tinker, 172
Tobacco, 125, 193, 215, 312, 313, 314, 323
Tobacco, Shipping, 311
Todkill, Anas (quoted), 7
Tomahawk Right, 115
Tools, Farm, 296
Tools, Pennsylvania German, 66
Tools, Silversmiths', 188
Touches, 173
Town Roads, Public, 243 ; Private, 243
Towns, 251
Trading, 97, 101, 177, 193, 213, 216, 230
Trading Posts, 38, 39, 40
Trails, Indian, 241, 245
Trails and Roads, 241–54
Trammels, 20
Transportation, 211, 230
Trays, 174, 189–90
Trenchers, 26, 169
Trent, William, 232
Trenton, N. J., 232
Triangular Trade, 216
Trombone Choirs, 93, 95
Trundle Bed, 35
Truth is not libel, 186
Try-Works, 217
Tuberculosis, 328
Tuckahoe, Va., 143
Tulips, 47, 71
Tulpehocken Valley, 69
Turkey, 329
Turkheim, Upper Alsace, 69
Turnips, 278
Turn-Spit, 20, 22
Tyler, Moses Coit, 318

Ui (Dutch diphthong), 47
Ulcers, 324
Ulster, 52, 111–12
Undertakers, Companie of, for the Iron
Works, The, 159
Union of the Colonies, 299
Union of England and Scotland, 233
Unitas Fratrum, 89
United States Government, 314
Unity, Intercolonial, 255
Universities, 316, 318–320
University of Edinburgh, 326
University of Pennsylvania, 187, 321
Upholstery, 156

Upland, Pa., 64
Utensils, Cooking, 21

Valley Forge, Pa., 104, 137
Van Brugh, Carol, 182, 223
Van Cortlandt Mansion, New York, 133,
140, 141
Vanderburg, Cornelius, 182
Vases, 174, 189–90
Vassall, John (house), 135, 136, 142
Vegetables (truck garden), 120, 277
Vehicles, Wheeled, 251, 286, 296
Vermont, 162
Vertical Tendency, 136–38
View of the United States of America, A
(book), 239
Vine Street, Philadelphia, 229
Vines, 12
Virginia, 2, 3, 4, 9, 14, 36, 106, 114, 128,
136, 137, 138, 139, 141, 148, 158, 159,
193, 215, 220, 233, 234, 253, 258, 263,
267, 274, 278, 280, 286, 288, 291, 304,
309, 312, 313, 320, 325, 333
Virginia Gazette, The, 253, 300, 302
Virginia Horses, 332
Virginia Reel, 331

Wagon, Conestoga, 220
Wagon, Four-Wheeled, 297
Wainscoting, 144
Waite, John, 179
Waldy, Henry of Tekonay, 262
Wales, 52
Walker, Francis A., 192
Wallabout Bay, 39
Walloons, 38
Wampum, 194, 199
Warehouses, Public, 312
Warville, Brissot de, 249
Washington, D. C., 57
Washington, George, 104, 106, 119, 136,
138, 175, 225, 254, 305, 309, 326
Washington, George (quoted), 309–10
Water (see also Springs and Spring
Rooms), 124
Water power, 292
Water Supply, 109, 109
Watermelons, 278
Water-travel, 255, 269
Watson, Dr. Lambert, 325
Weather Vane, 93, 166
Weavers, 43
Weaving, 26, 82, 293
Weekly Journal, The, of New York, 301,
302
Welcome, The (ship), 58, 229, 232, 328
Welsh Barony, 57–61
Wendover, John (or Windower), 183
West, The, 113, 274, 290
West, an Englishman, 264
West, William, 229
West Indies, 194, 205, 214, 215, 216, 220,
221, 226, 235, 278, 288, 294

352

INDEX

West Indies, a Deputy Postmaster-General at, 264
West Point, 164
West Springfield, Mass., 291
Westmoreland, The (ship), 238
Westover, Va., 128, 136, 139, 141, 144, 166
Whale Fishing, 216–19
Whale fisheries, 223
Whalebone, 217
Whale-Right, 23, 217
Whale-Sperm, 217
Wharf, 229
Wharf, Tobacco, 311
Wheat, 97, 276, 277, 312
Widespread Plan, 138–40
Wigwams, English, 5, 6, 12; Indian, 5, 12
Wild Rye, 280
William III, King of England, 223, 262, 320
William and Mary, The College of (Williamsburg, Va.), 319, 320
William and Mary Period of Furniture, 151
Williams, Roger, 15
Williamsburg, Va., 269, 300, 304, 305, 306, 332, 333
Willow Tree Coinage, 195–96
Windmill, 292
Window Glass, 199, 201
Windsor, Conn., 246
Wine, 280
Winslow, Edward, 32
Winslow, Kenelm, 28, 32
Winthrop, Governor John (Jr.), 159–61, 258, 259, 321
Winthrop, Governor John (Sr.), 14, 48, 160, 213, 214, 324
Winthrop, Governor John, Sr. (quoted), 160

Winthrop, John, of Harvard, 321
Wistar, Caspar, 199–201, 210
Wistar, Richard, 201–3, 209, 210
Wistarberg, 202, 206
Womelsdorf, Pa., 68, 206
Wonder Working Providence, 15
Wood (building material), 132
Wood Sloop, 213
Woodshed, 291
Woodenware, 26, 121, 169, 176
Wool, 26, 43, 193, 292
Woollen, 82, 292, 293
Woollen Spinning Wheel, 294
Woolman, John, 54, 59, 60
Woolman, John, *Journal* (quoted) 59
Wrought Iron, 158, 162, 165–68
"Wyck" in Germantown, 200
Hugh Wynne (novel), 61
Wynne, Jonathan, 58
Wynne, Dr. Thomas, 58, 59, 72
Wynnestay 58, 59, 60, 72
Wythe, George, 314

Yale College, New Haven, Conn., 319
Yellow Fever, 328, 329, 330
Yokes, 283, 297
York, Duke of, 41, 262
York's, Duke of, Laws, 283
York, Pa., 209
Young, Arthur, 310
Ysselstein, 100

Zellaire, Henri, 68
Zeller, Heinrich, 68
Zeller, Fort, 68
Zenger, John Peter, 185, 241, 301
Zinzendorf, Count Nikolaus Ludwig, 69, 71, 87, 88, 93, 96
Zion Lutheran Church, Manheim, Pa., 210

A-63-31

353